Worlds Apart

Swanee Hunt

Worlds Apart

BOSNIAN LESSONS FOR GLOBAL SECURITY

DUKE UNIVERSITY PRESS   DURHAM AND LONDON   2011

© 2011 Duke University Press
All rights reserved
Printed in the United States of America
on acid-free paper ∞
Designed by C. H. Westmoreland
Typeset in Charis
by Tseng Information Systems, Inc.
Library of Congress Cataloging-in-Publication
Data appear on the
last printed page of this book.

To my partners

CHARLES ANSBACHER:
"Of course you can."

AND

VALERIE GILLEN:
"Of course we can."

AND

MIRSAD JACEVIC:
"Of course you must."

Contents

Many readers, including me, make a habit of flipping to the end of a book before plowing into the beginning. Some will find that practice particularly helpful with this volume. The policy analysis at the end answers the "So what?" that haunts every author hoping to impinge on the precious time of her audience.

Instead of leaving it up to you to cheat, I might have interspersed in the text allusions to those lessons. But pointing to my conclusions throughout the book would have been at the expense of a different goal: letting you arrive at your own understanding even as your awareness meanders or is yanked from one setting into another. My bias is that insight gained through such a personal process is richer and more lasting.

Thus the vignettes that follow are described as I understood them at the time I experienced them. No one was ready then to apply what we were learning to conflicts in Rwanda, or to ponder a future application to violence brewing elsewhere.

That said, if you open to the last section first, don't feel guilty. Otherwise, move through the experiences as I did, and let the realization come to you that despite moments of courage and beauty, there was something very, very wrong with the way this war and this peace were waged. And what was wrong, we need to—and can—make right.

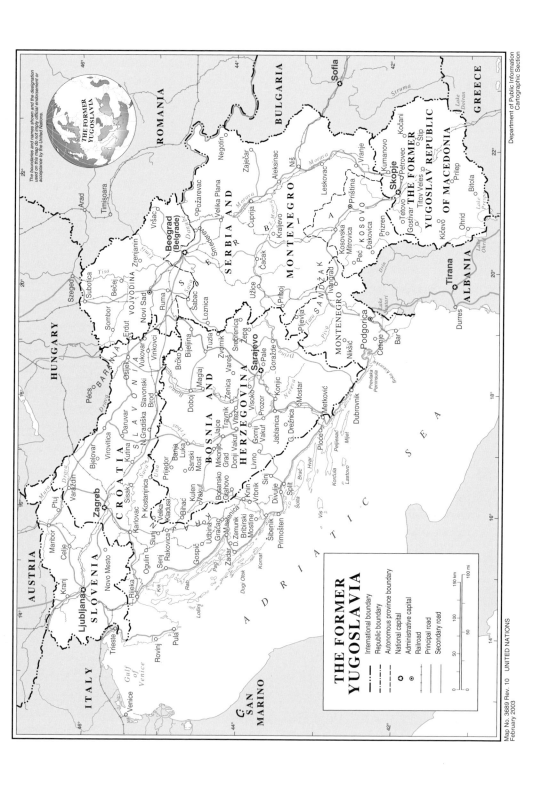

THE FORMER
YUGOSLAVIA

International boundary
Republic boundary
Autonomous province boundary
National capital
Administrative capital
Railroad
Principal road
Secondary road

50   100   150 km
50   100 mi

Map No. 3689 Rev. 10   UNITED NATIONS
February 2003

Department of Public Information
Cartographic Section

The boundaries and names shown and the designation
used on this map do not imply official endorsement or
acceptance by the United Nations.

THE FORMER
YUGOSLAVIA

Prologue

This book is about Bosnia—and beyond. Its lessons reach to Egypt, Iraq, Korea, Congo . . . any place we, as an "international community," try to stabilize a chaotic world. It is a story of grand intentions and missed opportunities, heroes and clowns, and a well-meaning foreign policy establishment deaf to the voices of everyday people. The former Yugoslavia is the setting but only the backdrop for this study in contrasts that play out whenever outsiders try to be helpful without including all the stakeholders in the decision making.

There have been oh-so-many words written about Bosnia[1]—mostly from two radically different perspectives. This volume is constructed from those disparate vantage points. One is from inside the conflict—life experiences chronicled in journalists' accounts, coffeehouse conversations, and love letters. The other perspective is from outside—the words and actions of government officials, military leaders, and other international actors who were often an ocean away from the conflict.

First, inside: In the heat of the war, people on the ground, particularly humanitarian responders, journalists (Yugoslav and international), and human rights workers, tried to awaken the world's conscience with vivid portraits: a child's wide-eyed hope, a soldier's callous remark, a mother in tears. The accounts were chilling, as their sleuthing revealed rape campaigns, concentration camps, and mass graves, opening the way for an international war crimes tribunal.

Then outside: Throughout the war, policymakers acted from their limited perspective. Then, after the conflict ended, as if to document their achievements, they hit the lecture circuit, describing ultimate victory over false starts, apathy, and deceit. They described tremendous difficulty as outsiders attempting to broker peace not only among Balkan parties, but also across multiple organizations of the international community.

For four years, I had the privilege—and frustration—of witnessing the Bosnian conflict from both perspectives. I was a confidante and admirer of many who lived through the war. But I was also a government official, making and observing decisions based on assumptions strikingly incongruent with what was happening on the ground.

Trying to write from either vantage point is fraught with difficulty. Descriptions of violence are hard to hear, yet they bear recounting. The fact that we cringe, that it sickens us, is not the point. History is history. This book only touches on the horror, but for some, even that bit of telling will seem gratuitous.

Also, although I will recount what I saw and heard within Bosnia, the experiences cannot be captured on pages of any book. Each Bosnian encounter was a gift—a lesson about courage in the crucible, love undefeated by hatred, cynicism, and cycles of hope. In my hundreds of hours with Bosnians, their memories came alive with mirth or lamentation. Descriptions of the wartime present or past were rendered with hands wringing in laps; visions of the future were unfurled with arms sweeping through the air. Most of our greetings and partings involved embraces and gifts. My Bosnian "sources" reminisced about life in bucolic Yugoslavia as we drove for hours past dynamited homes and fields untilled because of land mines. They divulged their dreams leaning over small tables in cafés, talking over loud pop music, until burly men in camouflage, toting automatic weapons, burst through the door to bark that curfew was about to start. In short, these were not sterile interviews, but glimpses into lives invisible to most policymakers.

Public policymaking can be impenetrably complex, and that was certainly true during the Bosnian war. Domestic US politics were on President Clinton's mind as military leaders advised him that Bosnia could be another Vietnam. Russian domestic politics were also in the mix. US State Department officials warned that action against Serb (Orthodox) aggressors could fuel Russian (Orthodox) nationalists, who were challenging moderate President Yeltsin.

Policymakers on both sides of the ocean were weighing broader geopolitical concerns. If NATO, which was created to stop a Soviet invasion of Western Europe, sent troops into what some called a civil war in Yugoslavia, where would the alliance's mandate end? Intervention might set a dangerous precedent of disregard for state sovereignty.

Foreign policy experts warned that ethnic splintering in Bosnia could spread down the entire Balkan peninsula, intensifying antagonisms between Greece and Turkey until they erupted, dealing a mortal blow to NATO. And given the ignominious 1993 US pullout from Somalia and the

UN's subsequent refusal to stop the genocide in Rwanda, the idea of an external stabilizing force for the world seemed to many a pipe dream.

Reflecting on what I'd seen on the ground and read in official accounts, I realized that these two perspectives derived from rarely overlapping realities. The gulf between those influenced by policies and those making the policies contributed to misguided efforts, wasted resources, and hardship as the war stretched on and then as the peace process slowly, ever so slowly, took hold.

Why was I able to see both sides? I was not in Bosnia continuously, but the arc of my ongoing involvement was much longer than that of most in the international community. Thus, I could discern patterns over time more easily than those who had to rotate in and out, sometimes only for a few months each time.

It also helped that my Bosnian work was always an "add on," lived in snippets, tucked between diplomatic and other responsibilities. I juxtaposed Balkan experiences with events outside the region. Twenty-four hours after listening to pleas of homeless refugees from Srebrenica, I might be reading stories to my children in a king-size bed with a down comforter. Thus every war-related experience was isolated, and it was only as I gathered them together, like so many pieces of a puzzle, that I realized they did not fit. Later I could arrange my experiences under broad themes. But even within those themes, "inside" and "outside" were related but detached. Unbridged, they could only coexist.

The problem was more than personal—it was systemic. Even in Vienna, the birthplace of diplomacy, the connection was broken between policymakers and people trying to survive in the nearby war zone. Officials had work to do. We were busy trying to save the situation. We couldn't afford to spend time chatting with citizens. Or so we thought. The conceptual link between national security and engagement with people affected by our policies was not in the tool kit of the US foreign policy establishment. That commonsense case had not been convincingly made.

There certainly were some policymakers who bored through cultural and institutional barriers. One couple, in particular, used religion as their bridge to connect with Bosnians. Soon after the Dayton peace agreement was signed, Claude Ganz, a successful California businessman in his mid-sixties, and his wife, Lynn, a media professional, invited me into their temporary home in Sarajevo. At the request of President Clinton, Claude and Lynn were giving eighteen months of their lives to help. They had invited to dinner the three prime ministers from different parties (part of the impossibly ponderous formula established in the agreement). Such a cordial occasion was rare, given that these three men represented political parties that had condoned hundreds of thousands of acts of violence against each other's community. Since at the peace talks the warring parties had been unable to agree on a straightforward system of democratic elections, the country's leadership was designed to rotate awkwardly among three members of the presidency. As we sat on the sofa, the Serb and Bosniak (Bosnian Muslim) leaders joked that they would take thirty-minute turns to sit on my right, while the Croat remained at my left.

After we came to the dinner table, Claude led a prayer before lifting a loaf of bread and breaking it. He described himself as a survivor of a World War II concentration camp, then spoke of the meaning of *tzedakah*, usually translated as "charity," but derived from the Hebrew word meaning "justice" or "righteousness." Our host understood the connection between seeking justice and finding healing. After probes about obstacles to establishing a central bank, railroad lines, and telephone connections, Claude posed the real question: "Will this country heal in our lifetime?"

There was a reason the central bank's creation had been stymied, the railroad had not been rebuilt, and telephone connections between former enemy territories were still not reliable. We all knew that the problem was not funding, but political will. And given the injuries of the war, that political will would not be available without some modicum of personal reconciliation.

And so Claude's invitation to remember tzedakah had political significance. One prime minister broke the silence: "Seven to ten years for the hatred to heal; and fifteen years to rebuild." Another added: "Five close members of my family were killed in the war. Still [he turned to the others] I don't hate these two men."

It was an honor to represent the United States and President Clinton as US ambassador to Austria from 1993 to 1997. But before arriving, I decided that if all I accomplished was to be a very good ambassador, my tenure would be a failure. I saw this appointment as an opportunity and obligation to use my platform to address the greatest needs around us. After sixteen years of working in inner-city Denver, I was accustomed to intractable problems like poverty, failing public schools, and teen pregnancy. Although the US-Austrian relationship was relatively unstressed, just next door to my new post, the Balkans were burning. Tens of thousands were dying each year while the UN, the United States, and Europe argued about how to respond. Geographically and politically, I was in a position to help.

I had plenty of assistance, including Foreign Service experts of remarkable vision. But unlike them, often asked to serve several masters

Austrian Foreign Minister Alois Mock was my first mentor in his passionate support for intervention in Bosnia.

Even a Bosnian refugee child can appreciate the simple game of "Here is the church, here is the steeple . . ."

and forced to consider the career implications of every decision, I was one of the 30 percent of ambassadors chosen directly by the president. As a political appointee, I could plot my own course. I felt my greatest responsibility lay in two directions: toward Bill and Hillary Clinton (whom I greatly admired) and toward the people in my reach who needed aid.

The proper extent of that reach was debatable from the State Department's viewpoint. There were repeated protests from midlevel officials that I shouldn't be concerning myself with affairs outside Austria. At our introductory discussion in the fall of 1993, however, the sage Austrian Foreign Minister Alois Mock pled for US intervention to stop the bloodshed occurring just south of Austria's border. (It was two years before we did intervene, under the auspices of NATO.) Ultimately, my work in the Balkans was what Austrian officials and citizens alike most told me they appreciated.

Why were the Austrians so interested in the former Yugoslavia? Much more than the capital of a country, Vienna had the self-consciousness of a regional hub. World War I had left Austria hydrocephalic: the defeat of the Hapsburgs had left the newly created country with an imperial capital, but no empire. Nonetheless, the Viennese remembered with crystal clarity that their territory from 1878 to 1918 had included Slovenia, Croatia, and Bosnia, which later became three of the six republics of Yugoslavia. It was, after all, on the streets of Bosnia's capital, Sarajevo, that Archduke Franz Ferdinand, the Austrian emperor's heir apparent, was assassinated by a Bosnian Serb nationalist in 1914, sparking what was supposed to be the war to end all wars.

Eight decades later, I wore a bulletproof vest as I briskly walked those same streets. Sarajevo, host of the 1984 winter Olympics and symbol of multicultural integration, was under siege. In more than twenty trips into the Balkan chaos, I encountered distraught presidents and prime ministers, traumatized children, effusively affectionate patients, war criminals, and community leaders. Extraordinarily caring members of my staff[2] joined me for experiences that were inspiring and exhausting. I spent time; I spent money; I spent energy. But I did not leave spent.

Acknowledgments

How could my name be on a book with so many helpers? I promise I played a significant role throughout the sixteen years of work that produced this manuscript, along with (in alphabetical order): Julia Appel, my student and then assistant, who helped with early editing and insisted (successfully) that I reorganize the whole darn book; Emily Ansbacher, who created scores of brightly colored files; Denis Basic, who did extensive research and offered a mountain of advice about the war that tore apart his homeland; Ariane Bradley, who helped me distribute my Bosnian stories among three books and a major article; Tom Butler—ah, Tom Butler, Harvard professor with a heavy red pencil and excellent advice; Maria Carroll, reader and early organizer along with Ariane, strewing pages across every table and couch surface, then the floor; Debbie Cavin, State Department colleague and scarily smart advisor for the last chapter of lessons; Valerie Gillen, my sidekick, who offered firsthand recollections, early edits, and—yes, again—organizational advice; Mirsad Jacevic, dependable, long-time friend; Erin Loughney, photo and fun consultant; Lara Nettelfield, detailed fact checker; Robert Niebuhr, another fact checker and a Yugoslav military expert; Chris Vaudo, dependable "man on the street" reader; Caitlin Wagner, photo archivist, who pored over my scrapbooks and then dug through boxes of unorganized snapshots; and Roxane Wilber, everything and then everything else. What a team.

All photos are mine, unless otherwise noted.

Context

Early in the war, Vice President Gore recommended that I read something he said had helped clarify his thinking: Robert Kaplan's newly published *Balkan Ghosts*. "Whatever has happened in Beirut or elsewhere happened first, long ago, in the Balkans," Kaplan wrote, in a dangerously broad historical sweep.[1]

Forgetting that peaceful coexistence has marked most of the region's history, commentators often portray southeastern Europe as a tinderbox. But Bosnians do not have a long history of intolerance; in fact, they have generally taken pride in their "multiethnic" society. (Since most Bosnians are descended from the same Slavic tribes that invaded the Balkans in the sixth and seventh centuries, it would be more accurate, although cumbersome, to speak not of "ethnic" but rather of "ethnoreligious" groups. Religion is what really distinguishes the factions.)

Many outsiders persisted in describing the conflict of the 1990s as a "religious war," although Bosnians were not given to regular attendance at church or mosque, practicing their religion mostly on holy days. At religious feasts, organizers were careful not to serve food prohibited by another faith. Calls to prayer from Sarajevo's mosques mingled with pealing bells from Catholic cathedrals and Orthodox churches that stood within a few blocks of each other.

Repressed during fifty years of communist rule, religion was revived yet abused during the breakup of Yugoslavia. First, religion was used in the Balkans, as it has been throughout the world, to cloak a political power grab. Then, after the war, Balkan religious leaders had a politicized base on which to build their contemporary religious communities. Many Bosnians who had never identified with any particular faith felt compelled to do so. However tragic the motivation, they now claimed a religious identity. Churches and mosques were built or rebuilt everywhere.

Bosnia's religious history was of particular interest to me, since I'd spent eight years in theological training. The country became Christian under Roman rule, but ensuing foreign invasions eradicated that early influence. After the failure of Dominican missionaries sent from Rome, the Franciscan order put down roots in 1340. Close to the common people, Franciscans were the main disseminators of Christianity during the Middle Ages. In time, sixteen Franciscan monasteries were established in Bosnia. But the Franciscans were not without blame. It was one of their priests—later defrocked—who headed the World War II Croatian death camp at Jasenovac, where hundreds of thousands of Serbs and Jews died. In 1994, Pope John Paul II installed a cardinal in Sarajevo, but Vinko Puljić's voice was often drowned out by fiery priests supporting hard-line nationalists who advocated the annexation of Herzegovina (the southern part of the country) to Catholic Croatia. Their hate speech was a great embarrassment to other Catholic priests, including Franciscans, in Bosnia.

Across the region, the Orthodox Church was identified with nation-states: hence, faith groups called themselves Greek Orthodox, Russian Orthodox, or Serbian Orthodox. The Great Schism of 1054 left Serbs divided between the Catholic Church and Orthodox Church; but by the early thirteenth century, Serbian principalities had been united under Orthodoxy. By the fifteenth century, the Serb Orthodox Church was at the height of its power and prestige. One hundred years after Serbia fell to Ottoman rule, the Serbian patriarchate was restored by the Turkish Sultan Suleiman the Magnificent, whose grand vizier was, remarkably, a Serb. As one would expect from a faith so identified with the state, in the 1990s, Orthodox leaders backed the Serb nationalists, refusing to speak out against their aggression. Throughout the war, the Orthodox Church insisted that it was caring for the victims of aggression.

Islam arrived in Bosnia with the Ottoman conquest of 1463. Favorable tax laws, more than religious zeal, encouraged many Bosnians to convert. Islamic life was increasingly liberalized from the late 1800s, without the prohibitions against alcohol and images of living things rigorously observed. Secularization was slow and steady, as Bosniaks left home to attend universities in Vienna and Budapest, especially during Austrian rule. Muslim women worked in Sarajevo factories in the 1920s; and the *reis ul-ulema*,[2] the highest Muslim religious leader, insisted that veiling was not a religious duty but a custom.[3] Given this history, anxious talk in the 1990s about "an Islamic state in Europe" was perplexing to most Bosnians.

Jews played an important historical role in Bosnia as well. Most Euro-

pean Jews were Ashkenazi, part of a medieval diaspora. But Bosnia's
Jewish community descended from some of the two hundred thousand
Jews driven out of Spain by Ferdinand and Isabella in 1492. These Sephardic Jews were welcomed by the Ottomans: remarkably for Europe,
the Jews' civil, legal, and social positions were left unregulated by
the state, and they were free to build synagogues and schools. During
Austro-Hungarian rule, they enjoyed equal rights. Many spoke Ladino,
a form of medieval Spanish; some claimed to have passed down ancient
keys to Spanish homes, in the hope that one day they might return.
Although ten thousand Bosnian Jews were killed by the Nazis, notably,
nearly all who fled returned after World War II. In the 1990s, Bosnian
Jews were known for feeding the vulnerable of all faiths and organizing
convoys for the elderly and children to leave.

Given Bosnians' history, religion was an extremely weak explanation
for war. Furthermore, a large portion of contemporary Bosnians simply
didn't identify themselves as belonging to one ethnicity or another. They
were simply Yugoslavs. Some 40 percent of marriages in Bosnian cities
were ethnically mixed. Without differences of skin color or language,
and with religious affiliation observed mostly in rites practiced just a
few days a year, "ethnic differences" were limited to alphabet (Serbs
mostly use Cyrillic, while Bosniaks and Croats mostly use Latin letters)
and names. Even those with Bosniak names often had a Serb or Croat
mother, and vice versa. Ultimately, though, ethnicity was only one of a
host of identities incorporated in the lives of Yugoslavs, along with class,
party membership, and home region.

Not a religious or even an ethnic war, the Balkan conflict instead
emerged from events and conditions set in motion at the end of World
War II. Yugoslavia suffered devastating losses during the war—more
than one million dead[4]—most caused by struggles between the competing Ustaše, Chetniks, and partisans (respectively, Croatian nationalists,
Serb nationalists, and anti-Nazi communist sympathizers). At the end
of the war, the charismatic partisan resistance commander, Josip Broz
(known as Marshall Tito), assumed leadership of what would become
the Socialist Federal Republic of Yugoslavia (SFRY), composed of six republics (Bosnia-Herzegovina, Croatia, Macedonia, Montenegro, Serbia,
and Slovenia) and two semi-autonomous areas (Kosovo and Vojvodina).[5]
Tito became Yugoslavia's "president for life."

Tito split with Stalin in 1948, and Yugoslavia became a leader among
the nonaligned countries, which remained neutral in the cold war. While
Tito's policies did result in a staggering number of deaths—estimates are
250,000 during his first year—Yugoslavia became the least repressive of
the many socialist regimes in Eurasia. Yugoslavs enjoyed considerable

freedom; they could work and travel abroad. Still, in the strong-arm manner of communist leadership across Eastern Europe, Tito cemented his control by silencing dissent and suppressing differences within the country. Tens of thousands of political prisoners, professed nationalists, and sympathizers with the Soviet system were sent to Goli Otok ("naked island"), a prison on a small island in the Adriatic Sea.[6]

Conventional wisdom holds that conditions leading to the Yugoslav wars of secession developed as a result of Tito's death in 1980, since he had kept a lid on ethnic differences. This analysis is only partially correct. True, his death catalyzed the conflict; however, the cause was not an eruption of ethnic strife that had been repressed during his rule. Instead, the region's exploding nationalism seemed to be the reaction of a country in political and economic crisis.

To reward Tito for refusing to be a Soviet puppet, the United States had poured financial aid into Yugoslavia, creating an unsustainably high standard of living.[7] When communism imploded, starting with Gorbachev's assumption of power in the Soviet Union in 1985, America no longer needed to encourage an independent regime in Eastern Europe. US support and other foreign loans to the region decreased dramatically, and the Yugoslav economy suffered. Factories everywhere were running at a loss, real wages were plummeting, and costs were soaring—up to 250 percent in 1988. From this point forward, Yugoslavia experienced a protracted period of inflation and hyperinflation without historical parallel. Eventually, a 500,000,000,000 (five hundred billion) dinar note, the highest denomination note ever, would barely pay for a cup of coffee. Meanwhile, the federal government owed the largest part of its debt—twenty billion dollars—to the West in hard currency.[8]

The economic crisis was compounded by a dysfunctionally complex political landscape. Tito had left the country without a stable plan for succession and with a collective presidency (representatives of the six republics plus the two autonomous regions rotated into the position annually). It was a weak structure later exploited by the unscrupulous. In the late 1980s, when a schism developed between reform-minded elites and old-guard factions, a wily opportunist, Slobodan Milošević, crept into the political void. The discontented populace was ripe for his decisive, if heartless, leadership. Thus the story of the Bosnian war is the story of an evil genius—one who seized a moment of uncertainty in a nascent democracy, disoriented by a political vacuum and the grueling economic transition to a free-market economy that was no longer supported by American largesse.

Representing conservative forces within the Communist Party, Milošević began to fuel ethnic conflict to marginalize the party members who were pushing for democratization.[9] His decade-long propaganda campaign was reminiscent of the Nazis' push for power in Germany in the 1930s, likewise launched through state-controlled media. Newspapers, radio, and television extolled the superiority of Serbs and emphasized the Muslim threat, creating a climate of fear for everyone—for those who had nothing to lose as well as those who had everything to lose. With hate-mongering speeches and vicious media attacks, Milošević fanned the embers of war.[10]

In a nation without clear political direction, the armed forces had taken on increased importance. The army that Tito had built, with ample support from the United States, found itself fighting for Milošević's corrupt political regime.[11] Milošević purged the ethnically mixed Yugoslav People's Army (JNA), leaving its leaders almost exclusively Serbs.

Alarmed by the pro-Serb propaganda and Milošević's encroachment, the Republic of Slovenia declared independence from Yugoslavia in December 1990, after a referendum garnered 88 percent support for that move; the Republic of Croatia soon followed. In response, the JNA moved to dismantle republic-based forces in favor of a centrally directed system of defense. Slovenia resisted, refusing to disarm and instead setting up an underground alternative command structure. Those measures were successful in rebuffing Serb attempts to take over the republic's defenses.

Having failed to consolidate the forces, Serbia launched a military offensive against Slovenia. But the lack of Serbian residents in Slovenia led to a two-pronged problem: Milošević had to rely on the JNA alone, and soldiers in that army did not have the same motivations for fighting that they eventually would find where there were Serb cousins to "liberate." In the face of these constraints, the Serbian aggression lasted only a few days before collapsing.

Turning their sights on likelier successes, the JNA next targeted Croatia by encouraging resident Serb insurgencies. Serbs in the JNA united with Serbs in local paramilitaries to launch an offensive of rape, murder, demolition, and terror until they claimed a third of the new Republic of Croatia. Tens of thousands of Catholic Croats fled their homes, streaming into Zagreb, the capital, or into nearby countries like Austria for refuge.

In January 1992, Croatia and the rump Yugoslavia (dominated by Serbia) established a cease-fire.[12] Shortly thereafter, Bosnians voted overwhelmingly for independence in a referendum that the Bosnian Serb minority largely boycotted. Bosnia's president, Alija Izetbegović, a former lawyer imprisoned in 1983 for allegedly advocating a Muslim insurrection, was reluctant to acknowledge that a peaceful solution to the crisis was impossible. But in April, a Sarajevo peace rally ended in six deaths when Serb snipers opened fire on the one hundred thousand marchers. War had come to Bosnia.

The ensuing siege of Sarajevo was brutal. The high-rise housing and office buildings were without electricity or running water for months at a time; without the use of their elevators, residents hauled water in whatever containers they could find, up endless flights of stairs. Shelling was relentless. The civilian death toll climbed every day.

A UN arms embargo, designed to keep the region from becoming more violent, only froze the military imbalance in favor of the Serbs,[13] leaving Bosnia, the poorest of the six republics, with only a badly equipped, rag-tag semblance of an army. During this period, Belgrade created the Bosnian Serb Army to do its bidding, providing paramilitary forces, regular soldiers, guns, and tanks. Working in parallel with these paramilitary gangs, which included psychopaths pulled out of prison, the army followed a strategy of war crimes that drove millions of non-Serbs from their homes.[14] The appearance of a separate Serb military force inside Bosnia would mislead some policymakers into thinking that the Bosnian conflict was a civil war of parallel parties. In reality, it was an aggression waged on a newly independent state that had gained membership in the United Nations in May 1992.

Meanwhile, the homeland defeat of Franjo Tuđman, the Croatian president and a former general, by the Serbs created pressure for him to be victorious elsewhere. He turned to neighboring Bosnia. In his plan for a land grab, Tuđman found an unlikely role model in his enemy, Milošević, whose proxy aggression was paying off as Bosnian Serb forces pushed non-Serbs off their farms in eastern Bosnia. While publicly denying complicity, Tuđman struck a private deal with his erstwhile nemesis to divide Bosnia between their two states. The western portion would be annexed by Croatia, the eastern half by Serbia.

Using the same ethnically targeted approach as the Serb nationalists, Tuđman encouraged and supported Bosnian Croat extremists as they expelled non-Croats out of areas near Croatia. He turned the Croatian army loose on the Bosniaks, who were now being attacked from two directions in a genocidal squeeze. Thus embattled, Bosnia began at last to create a real army.

It was almost inconceivable that such human devastation was taking place almost within a stone's throw of Venice and Vienna, even though those cities had been engaged in a savage conflict a mere half-century earlier. But many factors conspired to create psychological distance between the carnage in Yugoslavia and Western Europe's polished elegance.

For one thing, Milošević had been successful, preaching the power of ancient hatreds. Over time, the political environment became psychotic: misperceptions metastasized and delusions flourished. Outsiders were reluctant to intervene, innocently or willfully imagining that ethnicity was the primary sorting mechanism of the society.

Another factor was history, which had done its own sorting. The early years of the conflict saw the international community split along World War II lines: Germans and Austrians supported Croats; French, Russians, and the British supported Serbs. Islamic countries, understandably, supported Bosniaks. At a more abstract level, US support for victims of Serb ultranationalism had historical roots in the American melting-pot experience and commitment to diversity (if not equality) as a national value. And at a gut level, Americans knew bullying when they saw it. They knew the good guys from the bad guys, even if most policymakers didn't.

Within the foreign policy establishment, discussions revealed yet more paralyzing divisions: Pentagon resistance ruled out deployment of US ground troops in the Balkans, although some in Washington advocated the use of air power against the Serbs. But several European allies were concerned that bombing might endanger their own troops on the ground, committed as UN forces to protect deliveries of humanitarian aid. The Russians still clung to their support of the Serbs, in part because they were cousins in the Orthodox faith, and in part because the splintering of Yugoslavia might encourage secessionists like those in Chechnya.

This ongoing policy debate stifled the voices of the Bosniaks and others for whom the consequences of inaction were catastrophic. By the end of the war, nearly eleven thousand people would die in Sarajevo and more than one hundred thousand in Bosnia overall,[15] which had a prewar population of less than four million. The demographic breakdown of the injured and dead reveals the terrifying objective of Milošević's plan. Although Bosniaks were only 40 percent of the population, they accounted for 88 percent of civilian casualties.

Today, Bosnia is in the late stages of multiple transitions: from war to peace, relatively liberal totalitarianism to troubled democracy, controlled economy to free market, international ward to self-reliant society. Still, as Bosnians move forward, they face a wall of stereotypes. The world at large seems to have given up on lasting peace in the Balkans, which reinforces Milošević's false claims that people in the region bear intractable and ancient hatreds.

A decade after the guns were silenced, perhaps enough time has now elapsed to allow those of us who had influence to make an honest appraisal of what happened. For four years we tried and failed to stop the killing. The best we can do now is learn from the past.

The war ended in several steps. In 1994, I helped usher in the Washington Agreement to end fighting between Croat forces and the Bosnian army and to create a joint military and a political federation. A year later, the Dayton Peace Agreement[16] brought the overall war to a halt. But, ironically, that pact realized the warmongers' goals by dividing the

Vice President Gore read widely about the Balkans—from Rebecca West's 1941 classic, Black Lamb and Grey Falcon, through modern reports— seeking more than a surface-level understanding. Though I admired his thoroughness, I did not agree with his assessment that conflict in the region was inevitable.

Staring at an apartment building on the front line in Dobrinja, it was easy to imagine families crouching in the hallways behind their homes, terrified for months—even years—by the intermittent shower of shells and bullets.

Like segments of an Alexander Calder mobile, crushed cars were piled up as barricades against the shelling of Sarajevo. Symbols of prosperity converted into a defense against barbarism.

Briefing President Clinton, along with Secretary of State Christopher and Communications Director Dee Dee Myers. The exchange was, as usual, rapid-fire, with no time for social graces. Just bullet points: Waldheim, no; Bosnia, yes.

country into two entities along new, ethno-religious lines: the Bosniak-Croat Federation and Republika Srpska. Bosnia has since been laboring to gradually dismantle Dayton, so that it can become a stable democracy like its neighbors in the European Union.

This volume is not an indictment of those in the international community whose policies allowed years of hardship and who ultimately crafted a flawed peace agreement. We were balancing competing values, guessing what might come of one choice or another, trying to anticipate consequences. In hindsight, wretched mistakes were made by well-intentioned people who were distracted, lost their nerve, and misjudged actors and events. We did not do the good that was in our power to do.

Those were dark times, and we were all groping. If there had been a lighted path, we would have found it. Sitting at our big desks as we made decisions that affected every level of Bosnians' lives, those of us in the policymaking community had no inkling of the extent to which we were worlds apart.

I.
War

Sarajevo's Olympic soccer field, once the site of throngs cheering for elite athletes, now hosted silent and crude markers for the dead.

Officialdom

1. INSIDE: "Esteemed Mr. Carrington"

On 3 July 1992, a plane landed in Sarajevo, carrying the diplomat Lord Carrington. He had a string of illustrious titles: former British defense secretary and foreign secretary, former secretary general of NATO. That summer day he was representing the European Community.

Only six hundred feet from the ramshackle airport, where a disabled Russian transport plane lay nose down, lived Nurdžihana Đozić. Her apartment was on a front line, under constant attack from Bosnian Serb forces. A journalist, born in eastern Bosnia, Đozić had worked in Belgrade for years before moving to the now-blighted neighborhood of Dobrinja, on the edge of Sarajevo. Ironically, her apartment had been built as part of the Olympic Village—a symbol of multicultural dexterity and discipline. She and her neighbors had been crouched in their cellar since the beginning of the fighting three months earlier.

Đozić gave me a copy of the letter she had drafted to the visiting British dignitary. She'd braved heavy shelling and snipers to run across the street to a fabric store, now a makeshift press center. There she read her letter into a microphone for radio broadcast:

Esteemed Mr. Carrington,
We, the citizens of what is probably the largest concentration camp in the world, beg you to keep in mind that 30,000 inhabitants of this neighborhood have awaited your arrival. We are Muslims, Serbs, Croats, and other nationalities. Those who think we were attacked because we are not Serbs are deluded. Deranged Serbs attacked Serbs here, deceiving their own nation with their moronic ambitions.

Impatiently, in cellars and shelters, we turned on long-distance transistors to hear the results of your peace talks, to find out whether we will soon be able to take a step into the street without fear that we have stepped into death. Our hopes were in vain.

Can you imagine what it's like to live almost ninety days in a cellar, with manic artillery volleys overhead, demolishing and burning indiscriminately? Can you imagine what it's like to live without electricity, water, food, air? Without dignity? Can you imagine what it's like to give birth, become ill, and die in the same cellar?

When the artillery rounds abated for a short time during your stay in Sarajevo, we hurried to the nearest parks, shielding ourselves from snipers. Making coffins from pieces of furniture, we quickly buried, with as much dignity as possible, the newest civilian victims. Tears of pain and anger flowed down the faces of mourning mothers, children, and the elderly. Tormented and degraded by hunger and exhaustion, we were powerless to silence the nests of machine guns, much less the shells and tanks. Meanwhile you, Mr. Carrington, were negotiating with our killer, with Radovan Karadžić. After all we'd endured, that news wounded us even more.

Finally, Sir, we don't know "the warring sides," nor "the three sides who have been called by you to the negotiating table. There are those who kill us (and they will never kill us all) and those who at least endeavor to protect us. Given this, Mr. Carrington, if you come to Sarajevo again—and we sincerely hope that you will—pass by at least a few of these destroyed buildings, and see the innocent blood on the streets. Do that as a small gesture from a wise, worldly diplomat, but also to instruct your conscience.

No one has the right to take away an entire season from us. No one has the right to do that: not politicians, not the Yugoslav People's Army, not mercenaries, not domestic traitors and criminals. Nor do you have the right simply to observe without understanding what is really happening.

Respectfully, and with the conviction that we will try, with help, to find an escape from the dark, damp cellars, where we have been driven, right before your very eyes,

The Inhabitants of the Sarajevo
Suburb of Dobrinja

2. OUTSIDE: A Convenient Euphemism

International journalists were in a hole, reporting on events too tragic to be believed and policymakers too unfocused to respond. After all, the busy officials had a host of other problems on their minds, such as European unification, money laundering, NATO expansion, and genetically modified foods.

It was easy to forget, looking out over the broad landscape, that each marker represented someone's son, husband, father, brother—a lifetime of hope and of promise. Use the wood as fuel to keep the living warm, or as a marker for the dead? A terrible choice.

Many reporters hoped that "if the audience perceived events as real, they would have to act."[1] To avoid that pressure, some international officials de facto colluded with the aggressors by barring reporters from scenes of the worst atrocities. The officials claimed that journalists would further destabilize a chaotic situation; but in truth, damning accounts might have forced officials to admit that death camps existed.

In fact, the US Department of State narrowly avoided just such a predicament. John Fox, an Eastern European specialist on the policy planning staff, granted that "the US government had in its possession credible and verified reports of the existence of . . . Serbian run camps in Bosnia and elsewhere, as of June, certainly July, 1992, well ahead of the media revelations."[2] But it was only after an August 2 exposé of the camps by the investigative reporter for *Newsday* Roy Gutman that a State Department spokesman acknowledged the camps' existence.

The next day, Assistant Secretary of State Thomas Niles retracted the confirmation in a statement to Congress: "We don't have, thus far, substantiated information that would confirm the existence of these camps." Representative Tom Lantos (D-CA) decried the secretary's "diplomatic double talk." According to John Fox, who was painfully aware of the contradiction, "I was told that we couldn't afford to continue to confirm the existence of these camps." Those instructions, he claimed, came from the very top—Secretary of State Lawrence Eagleburger, who had been ambassador to Yugoslavia. But Warren Zimmerman, another former ambassador to Yugoslavia, agreed that there was a deliberate effort to "downplay the importance of these camps . . . [because of] the desire not to create a situation where we would have to respond."[3]

The concealment effort involved more than Foggy Bottom, as the State Department is known. Occasionally the public was given poorly informed oversimplifications, such as President Clinton's remark that "until those folks get tired of killing each other over there, bad things will continue to happen."[4] Granted, the president was in a bind—wanting to avoid US military intervention, but needing to appear decisive. He also had to be aware that the Russians would construe US military involvement as a threat to their security. The last thing Clinton needed was for that important relationship to be damaged.

On the other hand, concerned members of Congress reminded the White House that leaders of rogue states were watching the new administration. If the Senate Foreign Relations Committee or the National Security Council ignored the extermination of Bosniaks, their inaction might be interpreted as a sign that the United States would not confront other threats, such as the development of biological weapons in Iraq or the training of terrorists in Sudan.

And the United Nations? The UN war crimes panel in early 1992 delayed looking into allegations of genocide. Instead of full research and disclosure, empty resolutions and ultimatums abounded. Resolution 713. Resolution 815. Resolution 819. Resolution 824. Resolution 836. Resolution 844. Resolution 908. Resolution 913. In the first eighteen months of the war, the UN Security Council passed forty-seven resolutions and the president of the council issued forty-two statements related to the war.[5] Meanwhile, as the Serb police chief in the northwestern city of Banja Luka confirmed, droves of civilians were being deported in railway cattle cars.[6] That image evoked Jewish deportations from the same city during World War II, the very crime in which Kurt Waldheim—who went on to be UN secretary general and president of Austria—was eventually held complicit.

In fact, Austria was the first member state to beseech the UN to establish "safe areas" inside Bosnia—enclaves in which Bosniaks could find protection. But objectors worried that UN troops would be required to protect the areas. Some said the term implied that other places would not be safe, thus inviting Serb attacks there. Lord Owen of Britain and Cyrus Vance of the United States, respected co-chairs of the International Conference on the Former Yugoslavia, expressed reservations, with Owen noting that the safe areas were "flawed in concept" and would encourage "ethnic cleansing."[7]

"Ethnic cleansing" is a code for murder or expulsion because of lineage. Those two words, having entered the English language in the 1990s as the translation of a phrase often used by Yugoslav media, were becoming commonplace in sanitized discussions about the war. But this Orwellian word twist was nothing new. As early as the 1930s, Soviets had referred to the "cleansing of borders" when forcing Poles from their homes. Nazis, too, used the expression. An area from which the entire Jewish population had been expelled was said to be "cleansed of Jews." During World War II, the idea entered Yugoslav military doctrine. An Ustaše commander referred to "the prearranged, well-calculated plan for cleansing our Croatia of unwanted elements." On another side, a Chetnik urged his compatriots to "cleanse [the territory] before anybody notices and with strong battalions occupy the key places . . . freed of non-Serb elements."[8]

Although the notion of ethnic cleansing was known to be a distortion of an evil reality, the term still took root as the war progressed, spreading tendrils into the international media. An attentive reader objected to the *New York Times*: "We should not invite into our language terms which obscure political realities. . . . For the Nazis, to murder became to 'grant a mercy death,' genocide was 'the final solution.' But none of us is free of the danger of self- (and other) deception through language corruption. . . . Soldiers ruthlessly killing innocent civilians or brutally expelling them from their communities out of ethnic hatred is not 'cleansing.'"[9]

Officials in the international community no doubt wished they could grapple with the trouble that had appeared on their watch. But ultimately, overlooking or euphemizing the grotesque cruelty in the southeast corner of Europe was a moral sacrifice most seemed willing to make. Many took time for no more than a paternalistic shake of the head over Balkan troublemakers.

3. INSIDE: Angels and Animals

Sitting at my kitchen table, Drago Štambuk leaned forward, his chin propped on his palm. He was anxious to give me his perspective on the war—through a Croatian lens, but still nationalist. A medical doctor and published poet, Štambuk had grown up on the Dalmatian coast. He was close to President Tuđman and had served as Croatia's ambassador to India and Egypt. During the war, he was posted as ambassador to Britain.

"I was galvanized when I saw the bloodshed and destruction," Štambuk told me. "So I telephoned the British Foreign Office and said, 'I'm very worried about what's going to happen in Yugoslavia. May I speak with somebody?' The person said, 'I can meet you for lunch in a pub.' So we met, and I told him, 'I believe in preventive medicine. Can you do something politically and diplomatically—you meaning the British government, or the West altogether—to prevent this war? Because it's going to be terrible.' He listened but made no comment. That's how the meeting ended."

Štambuk told me he tried to make politicians and journalists comprehend what was happening:

> Why couldn't they have listened to people like me who understood the country and knew what would follow? The signals were all there. You just needed to read them and draw the conclusion. And it was a terrible conclusion.
>
> When Tito created Yugoslavia, he insisted on equality among ethnic groups. He would kick one on the head and another in the eye. So, regarding ethnicity, we were all more or less equal. But when he died, this equality wasn't good enough for the Serbs.

According to the former ambassador, Milošević and his cronies had actively fomented the strife. The Academy of Arts and Sciences, an influential group of Serb intellectuals, published an inflammatory memorandum in Belgrade in 1986.[10] "It was clear what would happen," Štambuk said. "From ideas, to words, to deeds. Milošević stirred up normal people around the country. Then Serbs in all the republics started taking over institutions. They manipulated the law to put the whole budget of Yugoslavia into the Serbian kitty. Serbia was trying to take over the country from the inside. It was like marriage rape."

A key moment in Milošević's political power grab, Štambuk explained, was an incendiary 1989 speech "to a million people gathered in Kosovo, calling on all Serbs to unite. People in the other republics started focusing on their own people, like the Croats in Croatia. Elections with nationalist parties were organized. The Serbs in Belgrade looked at the other republics and claimed, 'These are separatists!' That simply wasn't the case. Separatism was born in Belgrade."

"Before the war," he mused, "I never thought of myself as this or that ethnic group. And then all this started happening. . . . You begin to think, 'Where do I belong?' And it's natural to try to find your own group."

Once people are divided into groups, conflict grows in the gaps between them. He said, "It's so easy to react, to kill in revenge, to do the same things to the other side. But for me, just common humanity was most important." Štambuk looked away, sighed, then continued: "One of my friends said, 'I can forgive Serbs everything, except one thing. I cannot forgive them for making me fight.'"

Drago Štambuk was interviewed on TV in response to an April 1993 massacre of more than one hundred Bosniaks—mostly women, children, and elderly men—in the village of Ahmići. He recounted the experience to me:

> Even though Muslims and Croats had lived peacefully together, all the Muslim homes were destroyed, while the Croat section was untouched. Croat militia burned some of the victims alive.
>
> I was representing Croats in the UK. I saw the burned bodies of the Muslims on the television, and I was horrified. The announcer said "Croats did it." Then the interviewer leaned toward me and said, "Now Croats are like Serbs."
>
> Margaret Thatcher had told me, "Stay with what you want to say. You don't have to answer their questions." But I couldn't do it. I was so shattered. There I was, standing for people doing horrible things. And I said—it just came out—I said, "I'm ashamed to be here." That was the only human thing I could say. "I'm ashamed to be here." I repeated it twice, because one time wasn't enough.[11]

Not everyone supported Štambuk's frankness in the studio that night, he told me:

> A few Croats called and said "Why didn't you lie on television last night? Serbs always lie." I said, "I didn't, because then I'd be like them."
>
> I thought if I managed to convince people of the truth, that would be enough.

They'd be on the side of the victims. It was a huge disappointment when I realized that wasn't the case. In the real world, interests are more powerful than principles. That was a great awakening for me. There were always agendas I didn't know about. I had to play to politicians' interests. That was the terrible lesson, that politics is rooted in selfishness and greed. Sometimes politicians set a house on fire, then extinguish the fire to get credit, rather than preventing the fire in the first place.

"So the war was allowed to go on," the poet continued. "And when I met with refugees brought to England, their stories were terrible. What is it with human nature? How can people become so bestial? Is it only that they lose their sense of shame? Or is it that we are, inside, capable of wonderful, angelic deeds, but also heinous crimes? If you say that part of our nature is animalistic, I think you are not being kind to animals."

> The way the sea
> embraces the island
> gradually, steadily,
> so will we,
> children of God's providence,
> come to love ourselves again.[12]

4. OUTSIDE: Carter and Conscience

Former President Carter greeted me with a cherubic smile. I had met him just the night before, and he had spontaneously invited me to lunch the next day with a few friends at his suite in the Waldorf-Astoria, in New York.

An earnest aide, seemingly relieved that I had shown up, opened the door. We went right into the dining room and sat down at a formal table set for ten. On one side of the former president sat Mary Tyler Moore, the actress and activist. I was next to Jimmy and across from his lifelong partner, Rosalynn.

Most of the guests were related to Carter's world-renowned humanitarian center. Our conversation quickly turned political. Across the Atlantic, the soft underbelly of Europe was being ripped apart. For a year, reports of atrocities had been trickling out as Serb troops cut across multiethnic parts of Yugoslavia.

Bill Clinton, the new US president, was having a terrible time determining what to do about Bosnia. His forceful campaign rhetoric accusing President George H. W. Bush of impotence in the face of aggression had itself been rendered feeble. British Prime Minister Thatcher had urged Clinton's predecessor to take action, saying that "Serbia should be given

Rosalynn Carter was known to be one of Jimmy Carter's most trusted advisors, while he was president and afterward.

an ultimatum" to cease its nationalistic aggression or face "military re-taliation." Clinton, then governor of Arkansas, had insisted: "I would begin with air power against the Serbs, to try to restore the basic conditions of humanity."[13]

But a year later, Clinton in turn was being pummeled in the press. The *New York Times* columnist William Safire was particularly vocal: "No doubt the Bush acquiescence two years ago in the U.N. cutoff of arms to the Bosnian Muslims was a diplomatic blunder. But this year's false starts belong on Bill Clinton's doorstep. . . . Time is running out, Mr. Clinton. Avoid the U.N. trap. Send Europe the message: Bosnia alive or NATO dead."[14]

Clinton had recently consulted with Carter—not a common occur-rence, since the new president's aides seemed determined to keep as much distance as possible between him and his Democratic predecessor. Over lunch, Carter repeated what he had told Clinton: "Nothing I faced in my four years was this difficult."

Perhaps Jimmy Carter had watched the same C-SPAN coverage I had, with Lawrence Eagleburger, President Bush's secretary of state, offer-ing Congress a sophisticated critique of the Balkans that unfortunately echoed the line Serb nationalists had been promulgating for six years. Eagleburger should have known better. While US ambassador to Yugo-slavia and living in Belgrade, he had even labeled Milošević an "alleged war criminal" as early as 1992. Despite this concern, perhaps his view was skewed, since Yugoslavia's political leadership, like their powerful army, was dominated by Serbs. The oft-repeated justification for nonintervention was simple, easy for decision makers to understand—and stunningly wrong: ethnic and religious hatreds run deeper than we can imagine, and we'd best stay out of the quagmire.

"We shouldn't get involved in a religious war," concluded President Carter. "But Jimmy," Rosalynn countered, "We can't just turn away."

I sat pondering the discrepancy between this conversation and my tutoring by Balkan experts at the State Department. "Religious war" was not their explanation. They laid responsibility for the atrocities at the feet of politicians, not priests. But even more striking that afternoon with the Carters was the general feeling of helplessness, the sense that we could go round and round this topic for the rest of the day, for the rest of the week, and not get anywhere. No one had an answer.

Having said my goodbyes, I stepped into the elevator and stared absently at the wood-paneled walls. In the lobby, I walked briskly over intricate floor mosaics, my mind churning. Soon I would be assuming my post in Vienna, the self-proclaimed birthplace of diplomacy. If the problems of the war came my way, would I take them on? Might I even seek them out?

The urgency behind Rosalynn's words stuck in my mind. Then I shook myself. No more time to think about it. I was off to another meeting—ironically, with my predecessor in Vienna, Henry Grunwald, the former editor of *Time* whose family had fled the Nazis. There was so much to learn about diplomatic life. I hopped in a cab and sped across Manhattan.

5. INSIDE: "If I Left, Everyone Would Flee"

In a crowded Sarajevo coffeehouse, I found it odd to imagine that the charming, elderly man sitting across from me had been president of Yugoslavia. I was meeting with every leader I could, trying to understand the internal forces leading to the war, and Raif Dizdarević had kindly agreed to my request for an interview. Owing to Tito's impractical rotating presidency, Dizdarević had served only one year in office a decade earlier. He accepted some responsibility for the gradual disintegration of Yugoslavia, but he insisted that, if his advice had been heeded at the beginning of the war, he could have helped halt the slaughter.

Dizdarević told me it was the shelling of Sarajevo's children's hospital that prompted him to call Boutros Boutros-Ghali. The UN secretary general was meeting at that moment with the Security Council, discussing sanctions against Yugoslavia. "I explained that the Serbs and Milošević respect only force," Dizdarević said. "I knew Milošević well and had a lot of clashes with him. I think I had some effect on Boutros-Ghali, because he sounded very sad and hesitant. But he disappointed me greatly."

At sixteen, Dizdarević had joined Tito's partisans, along with his six brothers. He said he was an officer by the age of seventeen. The elderly man expressed pride in his Communist affiliation and didn't hold back his disdain for recent converts now filling political positions: "I've opposed fascism since I was a boy. That's why I'm a Communist. You don't change beliefs like you change a shirt."

The former politician reflected on the couple who were key players in the breakup of his country: Milošević and his ideologue wife, Mirjana Marković. Dizdarević was close to Marković's father, a long-time revolutionary: "When I was president and Milošević started rising and setting ablaze this nationalist fire, I was critical of his policies. Marković's father called me to tell me that I had his and his friends' support. From his sickbed, he said, 'Stop Slobodan Milošević. He is a very dangerous man. And unfortunately, Milošević and my daughter are a perfect pathological fit.'"

Dizdarević took that advice and, in an address to the nation on 9 October 1988, made clear just how dangerous he thought the couple was. He warned that unchecked nationalist agitation could lead to a state of emergency. But such admonitions, unsupported by action, did little to slow Milošević's progression to power.

Regarded as a failure by most Bosnians for not stopping the Serb hate-monger, Dizdarević gave me a poignant review of the collapse of the Yugoslav state and said: "After being in politics for half a century, it's easy to see how I should have done things differently, back when I had the chance. But what's important now is using wisdom from the past to affect the future." As we spoke, he named—and took responsibility for—three strategic errors that had allowed a revival of nationalism to destroy his country: "First, we failed to replace a worn-out system; we should have concentrated economic decision making among only a few key players. Second, we should have strengthened market economy policies to keep the republics connected. Third, we should have developed democracy, which is more humane and is the future; we had a framework, even in my generation, but we couldn't progress from our old ideas."

When the war broke out, Dizdarević was living as a retiree in Fojnica, his hometown thirty-one miles from Sarajevo. One day, when he was smudged with soot and oil from trying to fix his broken furnace, a UN Protection Force (UNPROFOR) vehicle pulled up. The soldiers asked if he could lead them to the former president of Yugoslavia, who was said to live around there: "I said I was he, but they didn't believe it. It took fifteen minutes to convince them."

Dizdarević's son, an engineer, had bought a house on Long Island, assuming his parents would live with him. "He had tried to persuade me I could be more useful to Bosnia from New York City," the former president told me. The UN soldiers asked why he stayed there, 550 yards from the front line: "I said this was my home, my father's house. If I left, everyone would flee."

As Serbian nationalists launched their attacks from the north and east, and Croat extremists began attacking from the west, Dizdarević sided with Bosnians trying to defend their state. Although he had refused rescue from the UNPROFOR troops, he tried to use his relationships with former UN colleagues to encourage international action, sending urgent messages to Ambassador Warren Zimmerman, Chancellor Helmut Kohl, and European Union (EU) commissioners.

One day, Dizdarević told me, a commander of the Bosnian army approached his house. Even though the officer wore tattered clothes, the former president was impressed by the wisdom of his military strategy. After the commander left, he went to his closet and pulled out various uniforms, including one from World War II. He added his hunting gear and money and had everything delivered to the commander.

The situation became increasingly dangerous, particularly since Dizdarević was a Bosniak. He received threats, and his phones were tapped. One magazine named him the key culprit of the war. "Can you imagine a former president armed in his own house?" he asked me. "I could often hear people walking around outside. The neighbors knocked on my door to tell me they were guarding me. I didn't know these people, but they did this dozens of times."

Dizdarević eventually decided to move into the capital to show solidarity with his fellow citizens. He would be recognized at any checkpoint, however, and Serbs, Croats, and Bosniaks all had reasons to dislike him. His solution came in early 1993, when a tunnel was dug under the airport. It was used for transporting the wounded to safety and bringing in military personnel and the meager supplies that were available for the more than three hundred thousand people in the city. One end of the tunnel was in Apartment 25 in Dobrinja, a unit with nothing to distinguish it from the rest of the shell-scarred neighborhood. The other end was a house next to a field that stretched to Mount Igman, long, flat, and tree-covered. The tunnel took four months to dig, with wheelbarrows used to remove dirt from five yards underground. It was laid with a track and supported with steel on the sides. As soon as it was usable, Dizdarević made his way through it into Sarajevo.

I wondered why, without appreciation or fortune, he had entered the besieged capital and stayed. The former president seemed desperately to want to compensate for his earlier failures. He sought involvement in high-level political discussions, beyond local UN military briefings. But among the new officials swept in during the 1990 elections, he represented the old regime. With a tinge of bitterness, he noted that no Bosnian—or American—diplomat, politician, or other leader ever asked him for advice.

6. OUTSIDE: None of Our Business

She was vintage diplomacy. Each time I met Pamela Harriman, I was taken with the exquisite competence and care with which she presented herself. In recent years, she had earned a reputation as a woman of substance, participating in policy conferences and leading delegations to Russia and China.[15] Given a decades-long familiarity with France that started during her studies at the Sorbonne, she was perfect for her post as US ambassador in Paris—a prime example of a political appointee bringing into the diplomatic circle the skills, contacts, and instincts that enriched the US foreign policy machine. Her energy and drive matched those of someone decades younger, but it was her charm and finesse that made her welcomed by the famously testy French, who dubbed her "the iron lady in the silk suit."[16]

During her confirmation hearing, Senator Jesse Helms had touched on the war in Bosnia, asking Harriman about France's concern that its soldiers on the ground would be harmed if the United States took military action against Serbia. She handled the question deftly, noting the delicacy of the subject and assuring the senator that she would support any position her country took.

At a meeting of American diplomats, I asked Ambassador Harriman what she thought about the war in the Balkans. After all, she had a trove of connections to draw on. Her first husband, Randolph Churchill, had parachuted into Bosnia when he served as British liaison officer to Marshal Tito's partisans. Later she became acquainted with Tito through her third husband, Averell Harriman—a railroad tycoon who became governor of New York, ambassador to the Soviet Union and ambassador to Great Britain, and was at the heart of cold war politics. In fact, the Harrimans attended Tito's funeral in 1980.

Considering my question, she recalled that Governor Harriman had conjectured that Yugoslavia would fall apart when Tito died. After a long pause, she ventured: "Maybe we should just stay out—like we did in the beginning—and let them kill each other off. After all, there have been conflicts there for centuries. Eventually one side wins."

I was dismayed by her response. The onslaught in Bosnia was barbaric to an extent almost incomprehensible in sophisticated, modern Europe.

Ambassador Pamela Harriman was my mentor and friend, but we were in different places when it came to intervention in Bosnia.

Only deliberate spinning could paint the conflict as anything but a violent land grab by both Croat and Serb forces. Clearly, Milošević had been successful in exporting his message of ethnic incompatibility to those in the international community looking for a reason not to get involved.

Newspapers' graphic reports of atrocities were interspersed with political pundits' warnings that there would be no end to the fighting in this "civil war." Still, I hadn't expected Ambassador Harriman to unwittingly echo the Serb party line, especially given her background. For one thing, she knew that England had gone to war half a dozen times in the past two centuries. She even told me several times how, as a young bride, she played cards late at night in a bomb shelter with her father-in-law, Winston Churchill. The prime minister, of course, had ardently opposed the strategy of appeasing rather than opposing Hitler. He had declared Chamberlain's 1938 Munich agreement "a total and unmitigated defeat"[17] and had defined an appeaser as "one who feeds a crocodile hoping it will eat him last."

I wondered how Pamela, for all her personal tenacity, could give up on US intervention in the Bosnian conflict. Did she not connect this situation with Britain's hope that America would enter World War II? Was one situation our business, but the other not?

I wished we could have the same empathy for Bosnians that we had had for the British. But perhaps that was asking too much, given that most Americans would not even be able to find Yugoslavia on a map of Europe.

Haris Silajdžić didn't suffer fools with easy grace. He often responded derisively to ill-informed questions. A refined intellectual, the Bosnian prime minister spoke beautiful Arabic and flawless English. He was a playwright and recited poetry to his friends as easily as others complained about the weather. The journalist Roger Cohen described him as "a brilliant, whimsical man, with a Hamlet-like tendency to speak in riddles."[18]

As Silajdžić's gaze reflected the flames in my fireplace, alliteration carried him into another realm: "Rusting and resting. While my helicopter flew over the Bosnian landscape, I looked down and saw trees rusting and resting . . ."

Silajdžić had come to our residence in Vienna around 10:00 p.m.—after a clandestine arms transaction, I suspected. I was in the living room on the phone with my husband, who was away conducting. The butler opened the door for the prime minister, who walked into the room and kissed me on the forehead. (Knowing Silajdžić's romantic tendencies, I arranged for the butler to come into the room every fifteen minutes.)

We talked about the intolerability of what had become all too real: the wave of war crimes now taking thousands of lives at a time. Recent atrocities had nearly driven him to madness, he said, and he was working to the point of exhaustion. Although he asked for a sandwich, it sat in front of him untouched until midnight. Then, just before leaving, he wolfed it down as if he were starved. "Winter is coming," he said. "I shall come back, for another dinner by your fire. It's clear that you and I were meant to meet. We will be together, even if not in this world. We are two stars in the heavens, and the crossing of our trajectories was ordained. Goodnight, Baby."

Fifty-year-old Haris was more than a moody, sultry ladies' man. Foreign minister and subsequently prime minister and president, he was the Bosnian leader who most consistently held out for diversity within one unified state. That put him at odds with the politicians ripping open the Yugoslav heartland, and his principles set him apart from State Department officials willing to capitulate by partitioning Bosnia.

Nobody could doubt his credentials. With a Muslim religious leader as a father, and an Islamic scholar in his own right, Silajdžić spoke with authority for devout Bosniaks. Nonetheless, he was quite secular and had a hard time with conservative Muslims. In fact, his academic career included positions in the United States. After teaching Arabic at the University of Pristina and holding a professorship in the faculty of philosophy at the University of Sarajevo, he became a professor at Cornell Uni-

Haris Silajdžić's party, The Party for Bosnia-Herzegovina,
was abbreviated "ZA" ("FOR" in Serbo-Croatian).

versity. He gave guest lectures at Harvard and think tanks such as the
Carnegie Foundation and the Woodrow Wilson Center. Given this com-
bination of Islamic understanding and personal moderation, Silajdžić
was well positioned to be an intermediary with the West.

Drawn to stars and media, the minister was a man meant for the stage,
not only as a playwright, but as an actor as well. One day, when I entered
his office, he had red daisies waiting for me. "Who bought these, you or
your secretary?" I asked.

"I did," he lied.

"I've heard you're in a funk, so I came to see for myself."

"Not true," he protested. "It's just an act I've developed over the past
five years—for special effects."

8. OUTSIDE: Unintended Consequences

Humanitarian relief in Bosnia was not as it appeared. We constantly
had to ask ourselves if our actions, however we intended them, were
more destructive than helpful. The question of the ultimate utility of aid
efforts turned up in conversations throughout the war.

A year into the war, as the situation in Bosnia was going from bad to
worse, an internal report commissioned by the State Department found

that 23 percent of air relief had been confiscated by Serbs. Instead of preventing genocide, the report said, the UN "may actually be facilitating its implementation." Could that be? Could food assistance abet genocide? Yes, it turned out, in at least three ways.

First, Serb troops demanded a portion of shipments as a sort of tax in exchange for letting the cargo past checkpoints they erected throughout Bosnia. Every load of food and other goods ended up supplying the aggressors.

Second, international aid workers on the ground were essentially hostages. Key policymakers warned that the UN employees' lives would be at risk if NATO forces stepped in to stop the killing. Thus, the very people who were trying to save lives by delivering humanitarian help became excuses for the delay in the international military response.

And third, some policymakers argued that NATO intervention could cause the delivery of humanitarian aid to be interrupted. Specifically, the Serbs might retaliate for air strikes on their heavy weapons by preventing UN trucks from delivering food to besieged towns. That leap of logic was laid out before me by a representative of the UN High Commissioner for Refugees in Zagreb. During an hour-long meeting in early 1994, he explained this deadly dilemma. But it made as much sense as a surgeon refusing to remove a cancer because the operation would inhibit the uptake of daily pain medication.

After laying out the policy, the official got up from his desk and closed the door. He came over to my chair and, leaning forward, whispered: "I'll tell you the truth, Ambassador. The UN ought to clear all of us relief workers out and bomb the Serbs. As it is, we're only fattening the victims for the kill."

9. INSIDE: The Bread Factory

"Go to the bread factory, Madame Ambassador. The people who work there are the true heroes of the war." I took the advice of Bosnian President Alija Izetbegović, a vibrant intellectual weathered by the war. Cautiously, I headed over to the Klas Bread Factory, a source of sustenance throughout the siege of Sarajevo.

In an armored Humvee from the embassy, we drove past commercial buildings with pieces of metal roofing now hanging like Spanish moss. When we pulled up to the bakery, six managers met me at the front door with considerable ceremony. All were men between the ages of forty and sixty, and they represented the ethnic diversity that made the city a beacon of multiculturalism: there were two Bosniaks, two Serbs, one Croat, and one from a mixed marriage. Their harmonious working relationship belied the warped paradigm of ethnic purity. In the office, I sipped coffee from a petite Middle Eastern cup and sampled cookies from the bakery, tasting the blend of East and West that made this place more like an American-style melting pot than other cities in Europe were.

For the tour, I donned a clean jacket and entered a world of powdery white. The building had little to distinguish it: the hundred-year-old mill house was a cavernous box with three small assembly lines. Outside were four large silos, surrounding a yard piled high with bags of flour supplied by the UN. The sacks doubled as barricades in doorways and windows. (Harkening back to World War II, one elderly manager compared that flour with the vitally important, powdered "Truman eggs.")

Within this industrial compound lay the story of Sarajevo. Nearly every pane of glass had been shattered by gunfire. Some were mended with tape; most had been replaced by thick plastic. Two of the silos gaped with wide holes. The mill tower had collapsed, and the walls behind the assembly lines were pocked by bullets. Still, hour after hour, year after year, the vapors of baking spiraled out of hooded smokestacks on the roof.

Here, four hundred women and two hundred men were risking their lives simply by reporting to work each day. Large numbers had been wounded, many losing limbs. Twenty had been killed. Snipers had picked off drivers as they made deliveries to more than 170 sites across the city. At one point, the shelling was so heavy that the workers were trapped in the bakery for a week.

This factory wasn't on the front lines. The targeting was strategic, an attempt by Serb troops to starve the citizens of Sarajevo, about half of whom were now refugees from the countryside. With the airport under siege and the roads blocked, the city's humanitarian supplies were sometimes cut off for months at a time. For over a year, there was no electricity, gas, or oil. The bakery used a sixty-two-year-old Sherman tank motor to run its generator.

No spare parts were available, so production was limited by equipment breakdowns. But in spite of the damage sustained by workers and machines, eight hundred thousand baked items and thousands of bags of pasta were produced daily. As I watched the noodles being poured into simple, clear, plastic bags, one of the managers remarked how psychologically essential even that packaging had become for Bosnians, a vestige of civilization during a time of barbarism.

In a society where the very infrastructure, not to mention the economy, had collapsed, the provision of six hundred jobs was a meaningful contribution. Granted, many of the employees were senior citizens and received only about two dollars a day—and a loaf of bread. But most

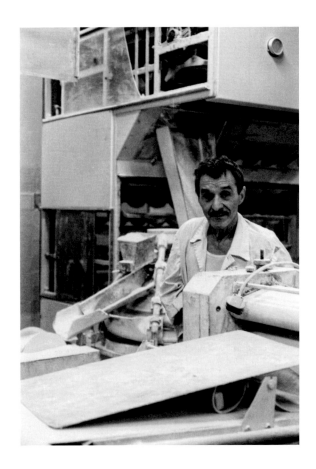

It was surreal or worse, my asking people who had survived a siege to pose for a picture next to their baked goods.

Bosnians had been working without wages for several years. Life had been simply a matter of surviving at the most basic level.

There was something familiar and reassuring about the warm, fragrant brown loaves. I reflected on how across cultures, bread has been a symbol for sustenance and nourishment—rich in both sensory pleasure and religious meaning for a city under siege. Twisted and twirled into small works of art, each loaf the factory produced was a symbol of unity.

10. OUTSIDE: Elegant Tables

Fancy dinners, accompanied by fine wines, rosettes of butter, and steaming rolls, were standard fare in Vienna, which was considered by State Department officials a "plum" posting, one of the most upscale in the world. I was growing accustomed to having political pabulum served up between courses of foie gras and cream of garlic soup.

Ursula Siler-Albring, the German ambassador to Austria, was a particularly forthright and open diplomat; I was glad my husband, Charles, had the pleasure of her company as I held forth to whatever bedecked dignitaries were at my side.

One evening, I dined in the splendor of the Italian ambassador's residence. By the time we had spread the napkins across our laps, the ambassador was lamenting (protected by a cloak of subjunctives) that if the Americans *would have* led a military intervention, the Europeans *would have* followed.

At another dinner, Prince Albert Rohan, a high official in Austria's Foreign Ministry, pressed for action. "If the West does not intervene in the Balkans, we'll be the laughingstock of the world," he warned. Rohan's view was typical of the conservative People's Party. It was a safe position to take, since Austria was precluded from sending combat troops onto foreign soil. But internal politics were nonetheless complicated. The Socialist Party, led by Chancellor (Prime Minister) Franz Vranitzky, insisted that the West should not get involved since the military endgame wasn't clear.

As it turned out, the question of whether or not to get involved in the war was a topic equally current in German circles. In Bonn only a few weeks later, I joined Ambassador Harriman for a visit to Richard Holbrooke, then US ambassador to Germany. As we sat at his table, an aide entered and handed him a secret cable, describing the bombing of a crowded Sarajevo market. Passing the telegram to Harriman and then to me, he remarked: "What irony. NATO may finally use military action, but only because of public outrage at what may have been a misfired, random mortar."

In fact, NATO did not act. And hundreds of dinner parties later, polite diplomats and earnest government officials across Europe were still hashing out the pros and cons of intervention. Stories of Balkan strife flowed as freely as champagne. With each, my colleagues and I nodded our heads appreciatively, not sure what else to do.

In January 1994, a dozen guests sat around the banquet table at our residence. I lifted my goblet to toast Ambassador Victor Jackovich, the first American ambassador to Bosnia, seated at the opposite end of the table. Since Sarajevo was so dangerous, the ambassador was living in Vienna, sharing our embassy offices.

With us was Daniel Spiegel, the compassionate US ambassador to the United Nations in Geneva, which includes the Office of the High Commissioner for Refugees. Dan, Vic, and I had gone earlier that day to Traiskirchen, a town near Vienna, where refugees were being housed in dormitories.

En route, I pulled out my briefing papers, neatly typed and ordered. They included transcripts of interviews with the refugees: a man forced to watch his eleven-year-old daughter being raped multiple times before he was struck down in front of her eyes. A son forced to perform sexual acts on his father. Eyeballs plucked from old women and stuffed down their throats. I did not finish reading.

At Traiskirchen, Vic moved among the families, speaking to them softly in their language. In my toast at dinner, I mentioned that at the camp, his demeanor seemed almost angelic. Perhaps I just needed to see some sign of grace in that hell. Blushing at the compliment, Vic diverted the conversation into the pros and cons of Austrian refugee policy.

In measured tones, he went on to describe the scene in Sarajevo. A reign of terror was being carried out by drunks on the hillside, he said, who were lobbing shells onto the city. They were bullies, acting with impunity. No one was even trying to stop them.

The bitter war was stretching into its second winter. "There's no end in sight," Ambassador Jackovich said. Life was difficult beyond description. A Sarajevan friend told Vic he had not eaten meat in two years. "Two years," Vic repeated, his voice trailing off.

The incongruity, however unintended, seemed almost contrived. As the guest of honor spoke, Christoph, our butler, waited patiently. With perfect posture, he balanced a large silver tray brimming with fare befitting an important diplomatic evening: filet mignon, surrounded by mounds of vegetables. What was not eaten that evening would not be wasted; we always collected our scraps for the handyman's dog.

SECTION 2 Victims or Agents?

11. INSIDE: The Unspeakable

A woman walked ninety miles across central Bosnia with her two small children, going well out of her way to skirt military roadblocks. She arrived exhausted and emaciated in Zenica, the fourth largest city in Bosnia, forty-eight miles north of Sarajevo. A staff member of Medica Zenica,[1] an aid organization serving hundreds of traumatized women, listened to her story.[2] Before their escape, the fatherless family had spent three months at an internment camp in Croat-controlled terri-tory, where they hung onto life with little to eat and abysmal sanitary conditions. The mother described her torment as she listened for hours on end to her children crying, locked up in the next room. In that camp, rape and other tortures were part of everyday life.

To the Medica worker hearing her story, the assignment of collecting statistics on this woman and the thousands of others so abused seemed a mockery of their experience. She'd asked me, "What do numbers mean, when one woman tells me she has been raped 150 times? And how many women have been killed and aren't here to tell us how many times they were assaulted?" Death frequently followed; too often the accounts could come only from witnesses rather than the victims themselves.

As war swept across the bucolic hills of Bosnia, stories of sadistic acts surfaced wherever a safe environment allowed the unburdening of memories.[3] Although men and boys were not immune to sexual humilia-tion and rape, most such acts were perpetrated against women—tens of thousands of them.

While the reports were numbingly abundant, every horror was unique. Each belonged to only one person. Still, the stories had a strong collective frame. In addition to isolated incidents of rape typical of war, Bosnian women of all ages were crowded into camps across the country: Keraterm, Omarska, Manjaca, Batkovici . . .

In the Trnopolje internment camp, women and girls were confined in a public hall; at nightfall, soldiers barged in and shone their flashlights onto faces in the crowd to pick out their victims. When three women were taken out each evening and failed to return, the entire remaining group—left waiting—understood what was happening. One camp commander added his own special twist: after raping the women, his soldiers slit their throats.

In rural communities, the raped girls could expect that their humiliation would be gossiped about, making them unmarriageable—part of a plan to slow the propagation of the "other" group.[4] In addition, ethnic identification was patrilineal. Attackers often taunted their victims, saying the women now would produce their rapists' offspring—as if their very bodies had been colonized. Thus sexual assault became an act of genocide.

For the women of Bosnia, the rapes were only one part of a long series of exhausting and terrifying experiences. Overwhelming trauma left some survivors mentally impaired. Still they had to reconstruct their lives, despite devastated homes, children with enormous needs, and elderly parents without healthcare. Having lost their men, women were left on their own to piece their lives back together.

Their stories reconnected me with my years in Denver, before I became an ambassador, particularly helping people who were hungry or abused. And so throughout the years of war, and in the peacetime that followed, I sought out moments away from my official entourage, to be in a simple space—in a school turned into a refugee camp, or the back room of a small NGO—with an individual woman, listening to whatever she wanted to talk about. My schedule, my passport, the presidential certificate on my wall all said I was "Ambassador." But I knew, and the woman beside me would have known, the limitations of a title.

Sitting close to this woman, my arm around her, I often felt more in touch with the world than I did in my diplomatic role. In the quiet, we exchanged a few words, perhaps pictures of our children. As we talked about her experience, and then about the life-threatening illness of my daughter, I was grateful for the humanizing moments she afforded me, away from the pomp and posturing of my role. Embracing her, I embraced myself, the evil we were forced to face, and the strength we mustered in spite of it.

Some women were emotionally distant, as if a thick scab had formed over their raw emotions. But to cover wounds is not to heal them. Perhaps time would be the ultimate cure. As each day passed, they would be able to integrate their experience into a stronger sense of self. The world would offer them acknowledgment and understanding, which they would transform into some sort of psychological reparation. Or would time simply allow the world to once again forget?

12. OUTSIDE: The Politics of Rape

Medica Zenica, empathizing with the survivors, complained bitterly that the International Red Cross and the office of the UN High Commissioner for Refugees (UNHCR) knew about the massive numbers of rapes but failed to sound the alarm.[5] The small NGO accused the Red Cross and UN of knowing about the camps as early as the summer of 1993. The truth was actually worse. In 1992, on 6 August and 10 and 11 November, the American TV news show *Nightline* carried stories on death camps, calling them Bosnia's "Hidden Horrors." *Nightline*'s 14 January 1993 show was titled "Rape as a Weapon of War."[6]

Infuriated by the lack of response, Medica drew a comparison to Hitler's time, "where the diplomatic policy being practiced by the League of Nations did not stop the dictator and slammed the doors in the Jewish refugees' faces, thus assisting the Nazis in their 'Final Solution.'"[7]

Indeed, the lack of official response was morally criminal, but the "international community" was too amorphous to accuse of the crime, and there was no framework for reckoning and no one to press charges. Ultimately, the cries of survivors and their advocates crescendoed into a roar that reached outside the war zone. A variety of NGOs sponsored research that described "systemic rape" as a tool of war in the Balkans. From the outside, it was natural to lump together the varied stories as systemic rape. Few wanted to think of the actual people — who these victims, these numbers, were. We could not bear to realize that every rape was as unique as the schoolgirl's aspirations or grandmother's memories it destroyed.

Dismayed by the silence of the policymakers, women in other countries began to speak on behalf of Bosnians, creating a growing sense of international solidarity. The rapes became a theme of the UN's Fourth World Conference on Women, held in Beijing in early 1995.

Still, many policymakers in America as well as Europe continued to ignore the evidence that officials on the ground reported to me: an elderly matron raped with villagers forced to look on; a father forced at knife point to rape his daughter; an AK-47 thrust into a woman's vagina, then fired; a young girl attacked by sixteen men in one night, the last purportedly a UN Protection Force soldier.

All the while, most Serb media vigorously denied the proof that was piling up: "The saga of the 'rape camps' in Bosnia provides the worst example to date of how a hysterical scare story can be accepted as good coin by the mainstream media. . . . What are the facts? No evidence has been produced to substantiate the claims of a 'systematic' campaign centered on 'rape camps.'" And, in a statement damning to the Red Cross and UN, the writer continued: "Neither the International Red Cross nor the UN High Commission for Refugees has come across any such camp in Bosnia. The only evidence is anecdotal."[8]

Predictably, Bosnian President Radovan Karadžić—a Serb and a psychiatrist—claimed the rape was "not organized, but done by psychopaths," and that "Muslim Mullahs" were behind the stories of mass rapes.[9]

Countering the detractors, some well-respected NGOs took up the cause. For instance, Human Rights Watch reported:

Women interviewed by Human Rights Watch described how they were gang-raped, taunted with ethnic slurs and cursed by rapists who stated their intention forcibly to impregnate women as a haunting reminder of the rape and intensification of the trauma it inflicts. In our view, the forcible impregnation of women, or the intention to so impregnate them, constitutes an abuse separate from the rape itself and should be denounced and investigated as such. Moreover, the rape of women in an organized fashion—whether in buildings where they are kept for the purpose of being raped or in camps where they are detained with family members—establishes that local commanders must know that their soldiers are raping women and do nothing to stop these abuses.[10]

But a different set of problems emerged as journalists, prosecutors, human rights activists, and therapists crowded into the survivors' psychological space with requests for interviews. One reporter told me she heard a colleague say, loudly: "I need a woman who's been raped and speaks English!" Surely the outsiders had no idea that they were re-injuring the wounded as they recorded testimony, asked research questions, made documentary films, and eventually brought survivors before US congressional committees or the International Criminal Tribunal for the Former Yugoslavia (ICTY) in The Hague.

Even academics, who had to follow strict protocols designed to protect the subjects of their research, added to the pain of the women with their analytical approach. Their questions, while coherent, were at a dramatically different level from the women's experience. "Did the description of genocidal rape against Bosniak women minimize the rapes of Serb women?" they queried. "Should the rapes of Bosniak men be considered in a different category? Were publicity efforts organized by outsiders—other than themselves—inappropriately capitalizing on the other's tragedy?"

As the attention grew, Bosnian women often felt misunderstood and misused. Yet it was difficult for them to know how to express their feelings, in part because they had competing impulses. Many felt an obligation to answer official inquiries. Some felt a strong drive to describe what they had experienced, as part of their healing. But many just wanted to get on with their lives and forget it all.

To be fair, some policymakers also felt conflicted as they probed into women's personal lives. But they had a job to do. The women had been violated, and justice needed to be meted out. That meant accounts to be written up. Depositions collected. Trials held. Testimony recorded. Verdicts announced. Punishment delivered.[11]

Whatever the good intentions, the observation bruised the observed. Survivors of rape and other atrocities hardly recognized their experiences in a catalogue of wartime accounts. That is because terror is essentially personal. Humiliation is an intimate moment, not easily shared. However accurately the outsider tries to record what has happened, violation is exclusive to the violated. Thus hearing their rape spoken of as an abstract social phenomenon further dehumanized the survivors, who had already endured so much.[12]

13. INSIDE: An Unlikely Soldier

Among those providing basic aid to the raped women taking refuge at Medica Zenica was a young woman named Selma. Sitting with me for hours in a smoky café, she shared her story of being shuttled between the roles of victim, agent, victim, agent.

A number of years had passed since her childhood in Africa as the daughter of a Yugoslav diplomat. There Selma developed her keen sensitivity to prejudice and discrimination. In 1990, she was in an adolescent slump. Her father had gone to serve in Lebanon, leaving his family behind in Zenica. In her own words, she "fell into bad company."

Sullen and angry, she sat watching TV, trying to understand the first eruptions of war in nearby Slovenia. Her six-year-old brother tried to comfort her: "Don't worry, Sis, I'll protect you." But when the news of mass rapes began, she didn't wait around to find out if he could. She lied about her age (she was seventeen) so she could join the Patriotic League, later part of the Bosnian army. Her mother watched as she packed her bag, asking: "Do you know what you're doing?" This was not the first time Selma had exercised her activist impulses. When she had organized students from her school in a protest march to Sarajevo, the demonstration had been stopped by police.

Frustrated again, she was going off for what would be a year and a half in the field, with the troops. Her military unit spent months on the front lines, including at Mt. Igman, the strategic front beyond the Sarajevo airport. Selma was the only woman among 120 men. At first the commanders tried to relegate her to making coffee, but she insisted she wasn't afraid to fight. She wore a jacket six sizes too big and shoes that swallowed her feet, but "I was the best logistics officer they had," she asserted in our conversation.

Selma wasn't immune to pain—physical or emotional. Soldiers gave her letters to deliver "if I don't come back." Friends died in her arms. Two, who were brothers, were killed on the same day. She told me she drove their bodies to a burial site, with prayer beads in her hand, hoping their coffins would not be opened at checkpoints and that her friends could lie in peace.

Because she spoke multiple languages, Selma was of particular value as a translator for arms deals and other undercover transactions. That also made her dangerous: she knew too much. "They wanted to get rid of me," she said, "because I was going really deep into things regarding money and weapons."

When she reached her psychological limit, Selma returned home and hung up her uniform. Her mother says she sat in a corner for months, consumed with anger. No longer able to reach out to others, she needed time to restore her spirit. Eventually, she used Medica Zenica to recover from the battlefield, staying with the organization from 1993 to 1996. When traumatized women needed food, she went to the Bosnian army to beg for provisions. When outside medical professionals arrived with over a million dollars sewn into the linings of their coats, she oversaw the distribution of the funds. She used a satellite phone to help survivors make connections with their families, and she found ways to deliver urgently needed medications.

As Selma and I talked for hours, she smoked incessantly, reflecting on her years of service and advocacy for the most vulnerable. She was simply trying to do what was right, she said; her effort had nothing to do with money. In fact, when she left the army, she didn't claim the pay she was due, thinking it would have made a mockery of her sacrifice, the betrayal of a principle.

Looking back, she had harsh words for the international community: "I always thought diplomacy was a nice, beautiful affair. You could meet friends from different cultures and smile all the time. But I learned that the international community is a battlefield. Human beings are just numbers in that world, just statistics. People say, 'fifty thousand dead.' They seem to forget that it's fifty thousand men, women, and children with names . . . with histories."

14. OUTSIDE: Happy Fourth of July

"The man on the roof with the machine gun is ours," Ambassador Jacko-vich whispered, as we stood on a stage in the backyard of the US embassy in Sarajevo. The hundreds in our audience had blended into an indistinguishable sea of faces. At his words, I looked up, until I spotted the ominous figure with dark glasses. "Glad to know it," I muttered back to Vic through a stage smile.

For months I'd requested permission to go to Bosnia, but my friend Dick Moose, undersecretary of state for administration, had refused. The last thing he needed was the kidnapping or death of an ambassador to complicate an already impossible situation.

With frustration, I could only watch from the safety of Vienna as opportunities for intervention were squandered. After a shell killed sixty-eight Sarajevans in the city's marketplace, NATO demanded that the Serbs' heavy guns ringing the city be withdrawn, but by only a matter of meters. For those listening at ground level, the ensuing international debate was farcical. A local journalist tried to put words to the lunacy:

> Where, actually, does the misunderstanding lie, if there is a misunderstanding at all? It is in the very assumption that moving the guns will change the minds of those who have been firing the guns at innocent civilians these two years. . . . As far as I am concerned, it is totally irrelevant to me after meeting a child whose leg was amputated. He went to bed Christmas Eve hoping that Santa Claus would bring his leg back.
>
> What do you think—did he get it? And what do you think it will be possible to talk about with that child one day, and with thousands of other Sarajevo kids whose hair turned gray before they even went to school, if they ever did get to school? It's all the same to me after talking to an 80-year-old grandmother who, amid the worst bombardment, walked through the middle of the main street and at the frantic warnings to hide because she could get killed, quietly but clearly answered, "That is why I am crossing the street like this, my son. But unfortunately, I won't get hit."[13]

Ambassador Jackovich understood the damage of dashed hopes. He also was tormented by the enforced distance between himself and the conflict he had been appointed to address. Eventually, despite the continued siege, Washington agreed to move his embassy onto Bosnian soil. Because there was a lull in the fighting, I had been able to talk Undersecretary Moose into letting me go to Sarajevo for the public dedication ceremony, selling the idea by saying I would convey remarks from President Clinton and Secretary of State Warren Christopher. Moose agreed on the condition that I fly in and out the same day.

Presidents, generals, and envoys waited here for cargo planes to take them out of Sarajevo.

It was not a simple journey, covering the 316 miles from Vienna to Sarajevo. I took a commercial flight north to Frankfurt, spent the night on the Rhein-Main US Air Force base, then flew south, strapped in with fifty thousand pounds of flour on a thirty-year-old military cargo plane.

As we descended, I moved into the cockpit, listening through a headset and peering through the clouds. The thick German accent of the air traffic controllers during takeoff had been replaced by Slavic. Voices from the cloud-hidden city seemed like spirits rising from war-torn valleys.

As we broke through the cloud cover, the first sign of life was children playing soccer beneath our flight path. But the innocence evaporated when we landed; I was told to run from the loading ramp of the plane to a wall of sandbags, then whisked into an American-made armored sedan. That first Sarajevo airport experience became the baseline against which I measured the city's progress over time. Our route was on the edge of the suburb of Dobrinja, where, a year earlier, two shells had exploded among players and spectators at another soccer match, killing at least eleven and wounding one hundred. Even a game of soccer could be deadly.

All around were vestiges of the two-year siege: buses turned on their sides as barricades, crumbling buildings, hand-painted signs on walls that warned "SNIPER DANGER"—and endless rows of window openings covered with plastic printed with the ubiquitous blue UNHCR seal. I could see sky through the rubble of someone's kitchen, while red geraniums bloomed defiantly on the window ledge. Our car sped along empty streets, pulling up to the new embassy, a relic of Tito's administration now being remodeled for US occupancy. The building was freshly painted, but there was nothing inside.

I joined Ambassador Jackovich as he greeted a mix of Bosnian political and military leaders, UN officials, NATO personnel, international media, and Bosnian friends of the embassy. We were a crowd of three hundred, gathered on a sunny lawn to share a moment of hope.

When the beleaguered Bosnian president, Alija Izetbegović, arrived, we walked onto the stage. Standing behind the flag-draped podium, less than five hundred yards from Serb bunkers surrounding the city, I stared into the crowd, wondering what mix of thoughts and emotions they were sending our way.

It was my time to speak. I had asked the office of the secretary of state for a statement to read. What I received, just before I left Vienna, struck me as tepid, disrespectful of the enormous pain these people were living with. Instead of delivering those words, I assured myself that I was the president's representative (albeit to Austria), so I should feel confident speaking on his behalf. Better to ask forgiveness than permission.

Through me that day, President Clinton described to the crowd how another nation, founded across the Atlantic, had struggled to build a peaceful, multiethnic society. Our country, too—however imperfectly— was built on principles of tolerance and the celebration, rather than fear, of differences. That is why we would stand behind the people of Bosnia in the face of ideologues who denied those values, I said, well aware that I was pushing the administration with that declaration.

The crowd applauded enthusiastically. No one mentioned that as we were lauding these lofty ideals, a meeting of international officials was taking place in Geneva, with the agenda of awarding the Serb aggressors 49 percent of the country, as well as part of Sarajevo.[14] Since at the time the Serbs held 70 percent, the agreement might have seemed like a diplomatic success, until one remembered that prior to the onslaught the country had been basically multiethnic. Ceding any portion to Serb purists would be a reward for assailants whose crimes were antithetical to this celebration.

Even in the middle of a war, Ambassador Jackovich had managed to

I can't imagine who took this picture from the roof of the embassy as I brought the words — or at least sentiments — of President Clinton to the crowd in the yard of the new US embassy in Sarajevo, with President Izetbegović and Ambassador Jackovich on the stage.

Literally on the side, next to the stage in the embassy yard, the women who had become my teachers posed to remember this day when their voices were heard by a visiting diplomat.

arrange for hamburgers and hot dogs, a flag-bearing color guard, and a five-piece military band. I watched as the Stars and Stripes was slowly raised above the embassy for the first time, with loudspeakers broadcasting a tinny rendition of the American national anthem. The flag hung limp as it crawled up the pole. Then suddenly it caught a breeze and unfurled dramatically as the anthem recalled "the home of the brave."

15. INSIDE: Women on the Side

Waiting for me at the opening ceremony of the US embassy in Sarajevo were six women of different professions, all of whom spoke English. We gathered around a table on the patio—the only furniture at the embassy. The women had agreed to give me their critique of the current political situation, as well as their experience of the carnage.

The meeting had been conceived months earlier, when Ambassador Jackovich asked me to co-sign a strongly worded cable to the secretary of state supporting a robust program to encourage democracy in Croatia, Serbia, and Bosnia. Any way I could convey to Washington the potential at the grass-roots level would be welcome, Vic told me. He had even come to talk with a group of Balkan women who had made their way across the battle lines, against all odds, to Vienna to meet with me. They weren't complaining, helpless, or hopeless. Instead, they focused on restoring their country, using their knowledge of hardship to forge connections with others in need. Such women leaders could help stabilize the Balkans, and Vic agreed that their voices had been missing at negotiating tables and in strategic discussions to end the war. He would arrange a meeting in Sarajevo.

That was the preamble to our patio meeting at the embassy, where a distinguished journalist described her feelings when she received emergency food packets from the UN. This was a woman who had frequently traveled, who had dined in fine restaurants. She was at the same time grateful for and indignant over the desiccated supplies: "They didn't understand us at all. They thought we were primitive." MREs (Meals Ready to Eat) were a bitter signal to her that war had become an ongoing reality. "I wanted to slam it in their faces," she said.

A hospital administrator told how she had brought nervous, tightly strung paramilitary soldiers into her kitchen, sat down with them over some coffee, and assured them everything would be okay: "Women spend their whole lives negotiating. I knew how to calm down the soldiers, because we mothers know how to help our children and husbands talk."

A third woman had not seen her eighty-five-year-old father in two years. He lived only a twenty-minute walk from her doorstep, but on the other side of Serb lines. She was a physician and had been his caregiver. Now she couldn't reach him, and she had no word of how he was faring in the acute deprivation of war—or if he was even alive.

Although markedly different in nearly every other way, each woman insisted that this was not an ethnic or religious war. They described to me events and relationships that, they insisted, disproved the notion that their country was doomed to divide. Instead of embracing dogma, they described to me how they had helped neighbors of every persuasion celebrate holy days. Suddenly, everything had changed. Others weren't "Croats," "Serbs," and "Bosniaks," but demonized "Ustaše," "Chetniks," and "Mujahideen." True, ethnic grievances of years past had to be acknowledged, but such historical factors were not deterministic, the women asserted. Instead, the attacks were acts of bullies and had to be met with fierce resistance, not an ethnically based solution.

As I listened, I tried to make the speakers' descriptions of brutality fit their appearances. Although I cringed at the thought of evaluating these professional women by their attire, I couldn't help but notice that they were dressed more stylishly than I was in their fashionable summer skirts, high heels, and pearls. But to them this was a statement—a refusal to despair. "Every day," one whispered, "I get up and take my bath from a cup of water . . . and put on my makeup."

16. OUTSIDE: Contact Sport

At center stage in the policy arena was a mechanism dubbed the Contact Group. Nowhere was the dysfunction of the international community more evident. Several concerned nations created the team in April 1994, aiming for an efficient solution to the conflict. Representatives of the United States, Britain, Russia, Germany, and France met periodically, airing their differences as they strained to come up with a plan. There was even discord regarding the makeup of the group. Italy was angered at being excluded, especially since it was the nearest neighbor to Yugoslavia. Still, all three fighting parties had high expectations for the Contact Group.

Assistant Secretary of State Richard Holbrooke's deputy, Ambassador Robert Frasure, represented the United States at the meetings. When the Contact Group convened in Vienna, he invited me to accompany him. As we walked in the door, he whispered: "The parts are already determined. Everyone knows everyone else's lines. This is just Kabuki theater."

Bosnian Vice President Ejup Ganić was appearing before the group that day. The United States, Bob told me, would make a point of not seeming very supportive of him, so as not to alienate other Contact Group members. The Russians, he said, would insist that no force be used against the Serbs. The French would back that view. The British would add that "there are no white hats"—no good guys—in this conflict. The Germans, prohibited from having troops on foreign soil, would push for others' troops on foreign soil against the Serbs. The Americans would listen, then support the German position, although insisting on multilateral action through the UN.

The play was performed exactly as Ambassador Frasure had predicted.

The Contact Group was the source of the 4 July 1994 Geneva peace plan to give 49 percent of the country to Serbs.[15] The plan included disincentives to either side if it rejected the proposal, but it was no secret that the objectors would be the Serbs. The disincentives included stricter sanctions, a serious enforcement of heavy weapon "total exclusion zones" around safe havens and Sarajevo, and the lifting of the arms embargo on the side that accepted the package. The UN expressed concerns about the notion, saying that it might pull out the protection forces because they would be seen as supporting one side in the conflict. Never mind that the supported side, unlike the other, would be in compliance with the peace plan.

The Serbs did reject the plan, and the fighting heated up again. Despite passionate telegrams to Washington from the US Embassy in Sarajevo pleading for action, no significant military assistance was forthcoming. In fact, to his domestic audience, President Clinton reaffirmed his promise that American ground troops would not be put in harm's way by being sent to Bosnia. Meanwhile, international actors continued to play their scripted parts as the killing continued.

Deadly Stereotypes

17. INSIDE: An Artificial War

Miloš Vasić was the editor of *Vreme* (Time), an independent weekly in Belgrade. In a *New Yorker* piece, he wrote:

> It's an artificial war, produced by TV. All it took was a few years of fierce, reckless, chauvinistic, intolerant, expansionist, war-mongering propaganda to create enough hate to start the fighting among people who had lived together peacefully.
>
> Imagine a United States with every TV station everywhere taking exactly the same editorial line—a line dictated by [former Ku Klux Klan leader] David Duke. You, too, would have war in five years. . . . First you create fear, then distrust, then panic. Then all you have to do is come every night and distribute submachine guns in every village and you are ready.[1]

Vreme's readers were not backward people, ready to believe the first propaganda thrown their way. Throughout Yugoslavia, including Bosnia, there were plenty of well-educated, urbane observers who could have told outside policymakers, had they been asked, that the war hysteria was the result of a carefully planned disinformation campaign.

Instead, for most Bosnians, hearing Milošević's theme being picked up and repeated by outsiders was infuriating. They knew the argument of inevitable divisions was patently wrong—an artificial construct promoted either by power-hungry nationalists or by foreigners who didn't know that they didn't know what they were talking about. The Bosnians marveled at onlookers' acceptance of Tuđman's and Milošević's propaganda and his solution: a population shuffle, with Bosnian Serbs joining an expanded Serbia, Bosnian Croats joining an expanded Croatia, and Bosniaks emigrating to Turkey or elsewhere.

Struggling to be heard above the din of war, some Sarajevo media tried to expose that wrongheadedness. Often their despair was couched in a sardonic tone: "It's important to preserve the smile, even an idiotic one," wrote Zlatko Diždarević. The editor of the lone surviving independent daily, *Oslobodjenje* (Liberation), he added a prescient warning that even if Karadžić were to pull his forces back until the world's attention turned away, "soon the idea of a division of Bosnia and Sarajevo as the only solution will come back in through the front door, [where] various war criminals will be sitting."[2]

To help the wider world recognize Sarajevans' anguish, the Bosnian editor begged his international colleagues to go outside of the Holiday Inn where they were holed up, and spend time with regular people. Fortunately, some did, like the *Boston Globe*'s Elizabeth Neuffer, who listened to one Bosnian family after another describe their lives before the war: "You could all but hear camera shutters clicking, preserving Bosnia . . . in someone's mind's eye. *Click.* See, we all got along, Muslim, Croat, and Serb. *Click.* Our town had a mosque, but it also had an Orthodox cathedral. . . . *Click.* . . . *Click.* . . . We were communists, but we experimented with capitalism. . . . Here are the photos of us all hosting international tourists at the 1984 Winter Olympics in Sarajevo. *Click.*"[3]

These journalists often risked death to inform the world. Covering atrocities took its toll. According to one, "we distanced ourselves psychologically from the action like people about to leave friends and family, to preserve our emotional equilibrium and our sense of integrity. . . . [W]e belonged neither in Bosnia nor in policy-making circles. By definition we were eavesdroppers and voyeurs."[4]

The task was especially difficult for American reporters. They knew their country was the best equipped (literally) to stop the war, yet most of their readers knew nothing and cared less about Yugoslavia. And even more were clueless about why there were "Serbs" living outside Serbia, and why "Croats" didn't mean just the people in Croatia.

18. OUTSIDE: Clashes

The Harvard professor Samuel Huntington seemed preoccupied with dividing lines. When he came to Vienna, the intellectual elite packed a gilded auditorium to hear the author discuss his article in *Foreign Affairs*,[5] precursor to his influential book, *The Clash of Civilizations*.[6] I greeted the professor warmly. He seemed pleased to have the American ambassador on stage as a respondent to his lecture.   ·

Huntington's thesis was that the fundamental conflict of our time would be between not ideologies but cultures. Pointing to the end of the cold war that pitted communism against "the free world," the professor asserted that in the absence of political and economic ideologies with which to identify, people increasingly would turn to culture as a more permanent self-definition. Such "civilization-consciousness" would increase as modernization drew groups into closer contact with each other. Ultimately, ancient animosities, real or apocryphal, would be rekindled.

The professor's recommendation to the West was to stay removed from states whose cultures were "incompatible" with our own. Trying to impose Western values on a non-Western state was a prescription for resentment. Better to stay detached. Huntington saw inevitable fault lines dividing the world, and one of those fault lines ran straight through the Balkans. For these reasons, he counseled against trying to preserve multicultural states.

Professor Huntington's thesis was well argued, but dangerous. I responded, when my turn came to speak, that we have choices in the lenses through which we view experience. In the same settings described by Huntington, we find rich examples of those who cross cultural lines. Whether through political task forces, academic study groups, or arts festivals, many if not most societies revel in their blend of traditions. To ignore collaboration among diverse cultures and look instead at the world through the lens of division becomes self-fulfilling. I ended my comments by noting that Huntington's argument, extended into the political realm, would provide justification for ethnic cleansing in the former Yugoslavia.

The professor had the last word at the podium, where he defended his fault line argument with vehemence. We parted company in the hallway behind the auditorium. He seemed not to hear my goodbye.

I later learned that Croatia's nationalist president, Franjo Tuđman, cited Huntington's *Clash of Civilizations* as justification for his attempt to seize half of Bosnia to create Greater Croatia. According to his ambassador to the United States, the strongman frequently mentioned to his political colleagues that it was his favorite book.

19. INSIDE: Crossing the Fault Line

From Bosnians, I heard scores of stories that contradicted Samuel Huntington's assertion, like the one told to me by a thin, middle-aged woman named Nafija. Her story was intertwined with that of Goražde, a town on the Drina River, nestled in a forested mountain area about sixty miles southeast of Sarajevo.

With its chemical manufacturing and machine production, Goražde's industry was more robust than that of the rest of the country. But driving to Nafija's battered town, I noticed that the surrounding landscape itself told an incoherent tale: a beautiful cliff overhanging a bombed-out lodge . . . spreading trees nearly hiding the charred ruin of a home . . . a brook running along the road—one of six springs that supplied water for the encircled town.

Starting in the sixteenth century, Goražde had been a significant trading center of the Ottoman Empire; four hundred years later, it was still at a crossroad. Of the town's prewar population of thirty-seven thousand, 30 percent was Serb, but once the war started, an ominous population shift took place. As Serb troops overran more and more of eastern Bosnia, non-Serbs fled their homes in the countryside, pouring into the UN safe havens of Srebrenica, Žepa, and Goražde. With the largely Bosniak influx, the town's population swelled to fifty thousand. Meanwhile, most Serb residents had obeyed orders from nationalists, abandoning their homes so that a wholesale massacre of the remaining inhabitants and refugees could be carried out.

Although the UN had guaranteed the safety of Goražde, and the British had warned that aggression would be met with "a substantial and decisive response,"[7] military support didn't follow the lofty words. France seemed willing to step in, but only with backup from US Apache helicopters, and Washington was flatly unwilling to provide the expensive aircraft.

"There were only four UNPROFOR personnel, and they stayed in the basements," said one refugee wryly.[8] Without opposition, the Serb army grew bold, continually shelling tens of thousands of civilians in the town. But instead of capitulating, Nafija's community resisted. Goražde was the only one of the three safe havens not to fall, ultimately, to the Serbs.

Encircled, Goražde became synonymous with human perseverance and ingenuity. Locals, left without electricity, constructed makeshift electric generators in the river. Wicks were fashioned from rags soaked in recycled motor oil. When humanitarian relief was cut off, some citizens traversed snowy mountain passes to get supplies. Still, provisions became alarmingly scarce, and the market adjusted accordingly. One *ox*, or about seventy dollars, could buy a box of cigarettes. Later, three hundred dollars would buy a pound of tobacco, which some enterprising citizens had planted. At thirty dollars a quart, cooking oil was prohibitively costly. Eventually, the town came to rely on supplies intermittently dropped by parachute.

Surgeons from around Bosnia arrived a year into the war. Shortly afterward, the siege was complete and they found themselves unable to leave. Day and night, they labored to save lives without medicines or supplies. "Those doctors did for this town what even God didn't do," a refugee remarked.[9]

The townspeople responded to the destruction with inventiveness and stubborn love. Nafija told me how she'd been walking down the sidewalk, hand in hand with her nine-year-old daughter, when a Serb shell hit a bank nearby. A piece of shrapnel penetrated the girl's stomach. An hour later she was dead.

The next day, a Serb woman came to Nafija looking for assistance. She was cold, and Nafija helped her locate firewood. Not long after, the Serb woman learned that her benefactor's daughter had been killed shortly before their appointment. She searched for days to find the mother who had put aside her grief to reach across Huntington's "fault lines" and come to another woman's aid.

"Why did you help me?" the Serb asked when she found Nafija.

"Because you're a human being who needed help," Nafija answered simply. Finding no words, the Serb woman walked out of the room.

"I don't hate the people who killed my daughter. They will answer to God," Nafija told me. "But when I helped that Serb woman"—she paused, and tears spilled down her cheeks—"I've never felt so good."

20. OUTSIDE: "The Truth about Goražde"

Even the most irrefutable testimony could be garbled as it echoed in the halls of power thousands of miles away. Despite ongoing Serb hostilities against Goražde, on 4 May 1994, the Task Force on Terrorism and Unconventional Warfare of the House Republican Research Committee delivered a devastatingly anti-Muslim report to the US Congress:

> While Bosnian Serb aggressiveness has undoubtedly played a large part in the Goražde tragedy, what is less known is the role played by the Bosnian government and military in instigating the conflict and in efforts to draw the West, particularly the United States, into the war generally. . . .
>
> At the outset the advantage went to the Bosnians who, backed by "Afghan"—mainly Arab—volunteers, were able to drive out the Christian population in what was described as an act of "ethnic-cleansing." . . . By exploiting UN relief efforts into the town, the Bosnian Muslims were able to infiltrate Goražde, taking advantage of the fact that the Serbs were compelled to withdraw in order to make way for humanitarian operations. . . .
>
> With Goražde now fully under attack, the Bosnian Government began an extensive propaganda campaign aimed at the West and at highlighting the plight of the town's civilian population. . . . The United States' Ambassador to

On a crumbling Goražde sidewalk, in rain boots and traditional bloomers, a quartet of war-weary but resilient women met me—a frieze of endurance. Their enclave was one of only three "safe havens" in Bosnia not to fall to Serbs.

the United Nations and the Chairman of the Joint Chiefs arrived in Sarajevo to declare their sympathy for the Muslim population. . . . From this point on the essence of Bosnia strategy became one of drawing down Serb military actions against Goražde in order to elicit western sympathy.[10]

Such reports, crassly accusing victims of inviting aggression toward their own people for the sake of sympathy, contributed to the policy paralysis that allowed the war to go on and on. Words like "Afghan" were sprinkled around, seemingly to strike fear in the hearts of policymakers and further reduce the impetus for intervention.

That was the confused and highly charged atmosphere in Washington as I sat in Assistant Secretary Holbrooke's office, trying to think how I could be more effective in advocating an end to the war. Would another call to the White House make a difference? More encouragement to the press? Should our embassy's political officer be pressuring the Austrians, sending a démarche—a demand—for collective action to his counterpart in the foreign ministry?

As Holbrooke and I talked, Bob Frasure, his frustrated deputy, entered the room. Ambassador Frasure wryly described *yet another* White House "principals' meeting," where, he said, *yet another* report of atrocities had elicited from our halls of power *yet another* soft "démarche-mallow."

Despite the mushy thinking that clogged the channels of international action, a crystal clear message was sent from Sarajevo by a group of Bosnian Serbs who refused to take up weapons under General Ratko Mladić, head of the Bosnian Serb Army. These "loyal Serbs" formed an association supporting a unified Bosnia, held conventions, and published proclamations imploring outsiders to confront the aggression threatening their homeland.

At an institutional level, the Bosnian government had taken care to maintain the diverse leadership typical of the prewar republic. Although ethnic divisions would become more pronounced as a result of the war, during and immediately after the war, I frequently met Serbs who were integrated into the Bosnian power structure.

One such man took on heroic stature to the besieged Sarajevans. Jovan Divjak, a general in the Yugoslav People's Army stationed in the capital, remained there to fight on the side of the Bosnian army. Although reviled by some Serbs as a traitor, he provided weapons and command leadership to the resistance; personally comforted the bereaved; and gave the international media a Serbian voice supporting multiethnic ideals. Word was that he even dug trenches.

Gray-haired, around sixty, with warm eyes and an embracing voice, Divjak welcomed me into his office after the war to describe how he had thrown in his lot with the city. He commented on the irony of how, surrounded by snipers and tanks, he had called out orders to Bosniak soldiers in his heavy Serb accent.

The general was born in 1937 in Serbia, where he and his divorced mother lived on the edge of poverty. As a boy, he won the hearts of waitresses, who hid pieces of meat in piles of vegetables on his plate so the cashier wouldn't charge him for the more expensive food.

Young Jovan developed a lifelong appreciation for education. When his mother couldn't afford to send him to college, he entered the military academy in Belgrade; although he lacked money to buy books, he could use the libraries. On top of academics, he excelled in sports and even served as secretary of the academy's League of Communists.

As one of the twelve best students in the academy, Divjak joined Tito's elite guards and went through officer training in the Yugoslav People's Army. He was sent to Paris to study French, where the fallout from a love affair led to his being punished with an assignment to the boondocks—Sarajevo. There he remained for eighteen years, teaching teenage cadets. Divjak was proud of the army, in which, he insists, there was no room for nationalism.

Jovan Divjak was serving as commander of territorial defense when the war started. (Significantly, he calls it "the aggression," rather than "civil war.") I asked why someone from Serbia would stay in Sarajevo during the siege. Those who left weren't loyal to Bosnia, the military man maintained. Those who stayed were standing up for the ideal of a state that would protect people of all cultures and faiths.

President Izetbegović had taken the "loyal Serb" to Washington in September 1992 to demonstrate the diversity of the Bosnian military. Divjak said he'd felt like a "Serb bear" on display at think tanks such as the Center for Strategic and International Studies. Washington's disconnection from the Balkan people was clear. To his amazement, when the commander showed foreign policy experts maps and gave reports of how Bosnians and Croats were cooperating, the policymakers showed him their own maps and insisted that the situation on the ground was quite different from what he knew firsthand.

Divjak was determined to be fair during the war, offering reproaches to all sides. In 1993 he wrote to Izetbegović, complaining about Bosnian paramilitary thugs who were throwing Croats and Serbs out of their homes. Nor did he withhold his criticism of the president for being sucked into war. Divjak disagreed with those who blamed Izetbegović for not building up a robust military defense at the first signs of conflict. Better years of enslavement than to lose 250,000 lives, he insisted. But in May 1995, he faulted Izetbegović for ordering an attempt to break the siege of Sarajevo. At that time, the Serbs had eighty to one hundred tanks and armed vehicles and one thousand artillery pieces, and the Bosnians had none. Divjak could only watch, frustrated and distraught, as four hundred lives were wasted in that failed effort.

On 2 June 1995, the general condemned Serb aggression in an interview with a Bosnian news reporter. He talked about Vojislav Šešelj, one of Serbia's most extreme nationalist political leaders, who had hijacked the airwaves. "By his own admission over Pale television," Divjak told the reporter, "Šešelj killed a Sarajevo citizen. It couldn't be more ironic that the victim was a Sarajevo Serb, who throughout the war worked in the city's main bakery for the common good. Meanwhile, the guy's two sons were in the Serb militias. . . . Just another example of the absurdity of the bloody Bosnian conflict."

More than just conveying his contempt for the ruthlessness of the Serb aggression, the interview put forward his analysis of the siege. "Sarajevo is always a target because our capital is a model for the solution of the whole problem of Bosnia and Herzegovina," he said. "The fate of the state depends on whether Sarajevo remains a multicultural city. Serbian extremists are aware of this, which is why their anger is so directly aimed at the city and its inhabitants."

In addition to being a fervent champion of progressive ideals, the general was a handsome romantic. He gathered roses from the front lines to bring a smile to the faces of women, young and old, who could not escape the city.

Although his heart was gentle, Divjak seemed to thrive on danger. In July 1993, he took American news broadcaster Dan Rather to the front lines, where two days earlier a Bosnian commander had been killed. After diving for cover during a live broadcast, Rather received a call that his insurance would be canceled if he stayed out with the general.

Life in the commander's own home was difficult: his wife was hospitalized for more than a year with clinical depression. Nonetheless, he recounted how he helped people whenever he could. When a shell killed three children, a soldier suggested that the general visit the bereaved family; being a Serb, he hesitated. Ultimately, he decided to go, and when he found the grieving family and friends in a cellar, the mother exclaimed, "Look! Our commander came." Sobbing, she told him how she'd held the children's dismembered bodies against her chest, brains slipping between her fingers. Two years later, he urged her and her husband to have another child, even though she was forty-four. Little Muhammed was born just after the war ended. The general showed me the boy's picture, hanging on his office wall.

Divjak took pride in his role as a go-between. He kept a record of the thousands he helped, such as the children for whom he found educational scholarships. Interestingly, he claimed to have no religious grounding. In fact, the general told me, instead of believing in a higher being, he was more comfortable with the notion that a magnetic field or other physical elements brought order to the universe.

That thought led to another—a visit by a woman in her forties, a hospital worker with four children, who said she'd been praying night and day for her family. She'd sent three of them to Slovenia when the war started, keeping only the youngest with her in Sarajevo. When she told him that her husband had been killed, Divjak let her use a satellite phone to call her children outside Bosnia. "Daddy's in the field, so he can't talk with you," she explained.

"Why don't you tell them he's dead?" the general prodded.

"I want to tell them face to face. Please help me go see them for a month," she begged.

Divjak used his connections with President Izetbegović to get her permission to leave with a state delegation six months later. He admitted that when she came to see him before departing, he grew impatient with her. "You see, ma'am, your god didn't help you," he said brusquely. She grew pale and then blushed.

"No, sir," she said, "God chose you to help me."[11]

Some people believed the Yugoslav conflict was preordained. When Chairman of the Joint Chiefs of Staff John Shalikashvili visited my office in Vienna, I pushed for American action to stop the war. "That's the Balkans," he replied. "They'll have to find their own solution."

"But what about NATO?" I insisted, remembering US Ambassador Robert Hunter's concern that "NATO may die on the hillsides surrounding Sarajevo," discredited for failing to respond to the crisis.

"Shali" was plain-spoken: "NATO is a blob that serves a function just by being there. It doesn't need to act." It seemed that he shared a reluctance to engage in military action. Rumor had it that he believed Communist military historians' inflated claims that Tito's partisans had held down twelve German divisions during World War II. (More sober estimates are that only two reservist divisions were held down; it was on the basis of exaggerated assertions that the general calculated it would take one hundred thousand troops to overpower the Serbs.)

Thus for commanders, sending in American troops seemed like an enormously risky proposition. Military leaders would have to be convinced, beyond a doubt, that national interest required our involvement. Otherwise, they saw their job as keeping their forces out of entanglements. If the conflict went awry, political backing for US involvement would vanish, they feared. In their minds, intervention was being pushed primarily by overly enthusiastic members of Congress and State Department operatives.

I was clearly in the latter group, which frequently put me at odds with military leaders for whom I otherwise had great respect. In two trips to Stuttgart, Germany, I received briefings from the four-star general in day-to-day command of the American armed services in Europe (EUCOM). Chuck Boyd was a thoughtful, articulate, and affable fellow, who had spent 2,488 days in North Vietnam as a prisoner of war. He was a true hero.

During one briefing, I sat with other ambassadors at large tables arranged in an open square. Several generals took turns standing before us. They reported on EUCOM's broad mission—across Europe, the Middle East, and Africa—then gave details regarding specific hot spots. For most of the briefing, I was a compliant student, absorbing terms, concepts, and details of operations I knew only from newspapers. But when the generals turned to the Balkans, I understood the subject at least as well as they did. That is when the trouble began.

When the generals repeatedly described Bosnian leaders as "the Muslims," I protested, noting that the five-person presidency included ethnic

Serbs and people from mixed marriages. In addition, I asked, why should Bosniaks be described in terms of religion when Serbs and Croats were not? I further reminded General Boyd that the Bosniaks had pledged to protect their multiethnic society, in contrast to the aggressors, who were routing non-Serbs from their homes in the name of "Greater Serbia." The other generals were clearly embarrassed that I was contradicting their commander.

Soon, an intelligence officer stood to describe the "Bosnian Muslim extremists"—a term that was misguided if the goal was insight, but right on the mark if the goal was nonintervention. I wrote a note to my defense attaché from Vienna, sitting on my left: "They're so wrong." The colonel wrote back: "Tell them." Once more, I spoke up, asking if anyone in the room had ever met the extremists they were describing. No one had. "Well, I have. And there's nothing extreme about them," I countered.

At the heart of the question of extremism was the reputation of President Izetbegović, whom I knew as a contemplative attorney approaching the end of his career. Izetbegović had been jailed by Tito's Communist authorities in the 1940s for belonging to the Young Muslims, who sought the right to religious expression and extolled the Islamic way of life in a unified Muslim community. Izetbegović was in jail from 1983 to 1988.

In fact, Orthodox and Catholic thinkers had also been incarcerated. Some believed Izetbegović's 1983 trial was an attempt by the Communists to be evenhanded in their religious oppression, for the notion that Izetbegović's *Islamic Declaration*—his 1970 book on the modernization of Islamic politics—was extremist required an extreme bias. The offending document never mentioned Bosnia, much less advocated the idea of Bosnia as an Islamic state, as the prosecution claimed.

At the beginning of the Bosnian war, the Belgrade Ministry for Foreign Affairs translated the treatise into English and distributed it to Western governments as proof that Izetbegović was an Islamic fundamentalist. However, careful readers noticed that the essential ideas of the declaration, which was not widely read in the Balkans, were that nationalism is divisive and Communism is inadequate. Instead, the author pointed to Islamic government as the most suitable for a society in which the majority is "practicing Muslims." But, he noted, few of Bosnia's Muslims were "practicing" during the secular Tito era in which he wrote. Thus Izetbegović did not advocate an Islamic government for Bosnia. He actually warned that in societies with a non-Muslim majority, like Bosnia, "the Islamic order [would be] reduced to mere power and [could] turn into tyranny."[12]

In other writings, Izetbegović described Christianity as a "near-union of supreme religion and supreme ethics."[13] He also extolled Anglo-Saxon philosophy and culture, and the social-democratic tradition—hardly the rantings of an Islamic extremist.

Granted, the future president proposed the revival of Islamic tradition in Bosnia, despite the discouragement of religion under Communism. But, he allowed, either Western democracy or an Islamic state with religious tolerance could be used to counter the excesses of modernity.

At the EUCOM briefing, such nuance did not prevail. Privately, General Boyd warned me I had been duped by "Muslim propaganda." "There are no good guys in this war," he cautioned.

"But I've had these people in my home," I insisted. "We've had dinner together many times. I know them."

"Well, you should have had more Serbs for dinner," he replied.

23. INSIDE: Family Friends

My family loved dinnertime with the Ganićs. We had a lot of similarities—our financial security, the age of our children, and our moderate religious faith (although the two fathers were essentially atheists).

Since the war started, Emina and her brother, Emir, had rarely seen their father: Ejup Ganić, a member of the federal presidency, had a price on his head. As refugees in Vienna, they were living incognito, using Fahrija's maiden name. She even warned her children not to speak Serbo-Croatian when they were in public, such as on a playground or waiting for a bus. Although a family of means back in the Balkans, they were now cloistered in a tiny apartment.

Dr. Ganić had spent nine years studying and teaching mechanical engineering in the United States, at MIT and in Chicago. I met him in the spring of 1994, when he managed to leave Sarajevo. When our paths crossed near a crowded airport baggage claim, my embassy political officer whispered, "That's Ganić." Weary as he must have been, he had the stride and comportment of a major player, someone who was helping his fledgling country maneuver through a treacherous time. Introducing myself, I asked casually where he would be staying. In perfect and polite English, he dodged the question.

Months later, I was visiting Ganić in the intensive care unit of a Viennese hospital. He'd been flown in after a serious automobile accident in central Bosnia. He would require multiple surgeries, with steel plates to repair a badly broken body.

Armed guards were just outside the door of his room. Ganić lay on the bed, his long, broad frame seeming remarkably delicate under the thin sheet. His skin was a yellow hue, and he was hooked up to needles and

*Fahrija, Ejup, and young Emir Ganić, chatting with Charles. If they were
dangerous extremists, we sure missed it.*

tubes; to lighten the moment, I joked that he looked like Frankenstein,
with stitches running like railroad tracks across his arm.

The hospital staff, having discovered that they were treating an un-
identified Balkan political figure, petitioned the chief administrator to
have him removed. They were concerned that they might be harboring
a war criminal, or that the hospital might become a target of violence. I
interceded with the physician in charge and won a few days' reprieve.

Keeping constant watch at his side was a worried Fahrija. She was a
medical doctor herself, trained in dermatology at Cook County Hospital
in Chicago. Given the stress on the family, I invited the Ganić children
to meet ours at the embassy residence. Fahrija accepted gratefully, since
she was spending days and nights at the hospital—not a happy environment for eleven-year-old Emir or sixteen-year-old Emina.

A couple of days later, sweet Emir walked through the door with a
bouquet of flowers for my daughter, Lillian. Then he joined our Teddy,
transfixed before a SimCity computer game. Communication was no
problem, since the Ganić children, raised in America, were more comfortable in English than any other language. But I knew from Fahrija that
the refugee experience had taken its toll. Emir was constantly anxious,
unable to sleep alone, and afraid of going anywhere on his own.

Emina, in contrast, was spirited and opinionated—and an intellectual
match for any parent. I thought to myself how, in her tight black skirt,

she was far more worldly than my daughter. As we got to know each other, she talked about crushes, shoes, and theater. But inside, she later confessed to me, she had the same insecurities and need to belong of any teenager. On the other hand, coming from a war zone with a father still at the heart of the conflict, she had a sense of specialness, even self-importance: "My God, our life is so much more complicated, and therefore more valuable," was how she described her adolescent feelings.

We continued to enjoy having Fahrija, Emir, and Emina around our dinner table. We were like family.

24. OUTSIDE: Extremists

Vice President Ejup Ganić spent months recovering from his accident. When his condition stabilized, he was moved to a military hospital on an army base with tight Austrian security. He must have known I was passing our conversations on to the State Department and White House. Assistant Secretary Holbrooke, in turn, sent me messages to convey regarding the diplomatic effort he was leading to stop the war. I was to reassure Ganić that America was resolute that eastern enclaves not be bargained away to the Serbs but stay in Bosniak hands.

While we from the State Department were working with Ganić, the Pentagon and CIA continued to dwell on the perceived threat of Muslim extremism. Many military and intelligence officers were convinced that the Bosnian army, which we wanted to strengthen, had been infiltrated by Mujahideen—mostly Arab fighters trained in states like Pakistan or Afghanistan to wage "holy war."

From his hospital bed, Ganić watched news broadcasts showing Iranian and Sudanese street mobs burning American flags to protest US inaction to stop the genocide of their fellow Muslims. This worried the politician, who was concerned about a negative impact on his cause. First, he said, outside demonstrations distracted from the Bosnian message of tolerance. Second, the demonstrations drew a link between a modern European country and conservative Islamic states. "If my daughter were imprisoned the rest of her life behind a veil, [he pointed to his forehead] I wouldn't stay in that country," he said. Despite my reports to Washington noting these conversations and the misunderstandings in the EUCOM briefing, I continued to hear US intelligence sources describe Ganić as a "Muslim extremist."

Ironically, it was the absence of help from the West that forced the Bosnian government to accept and even seek out aid from Iran.[14] Compelled to establish ties with anyone who would help, Bosnian officials made trips to Islamic states—trips subsequently cited as evidence that they were extremists. But the turn to the East was necessary since, in 1991, the UN arms embargo (Security Council Resolution 713) had forbidden aid to the military in the former Yugoslavia. Granted, that move was an attempt to reduce violence and increase security in the region. But because Serbia had already appropriated weapons and other resources from the heavily armed Yugoslav National Army and Territorial Defense Forces, the resolution froze the imbalance of power, giving the Serbs overwhelming advantage.

The Clinton administration therefore was caught in a policy tangle over arms aid to the Bosnians. The US public tended to support isolationism; and even among those inclined to intervene in the Balkans, there was a dispute about whether we could act alone or only as part of a multilateral effort. Clinton's sympathies were with the Bosnians, and he was not an isolationist. Still, the president was reluctant to break the UN embargo unilaterally, because he needed UN backing on other issues, such as sanctions against Iraq.

Congress added to the tangle as many representatives advocated unilateral action. This tug was led by conservative Republicans who loathed the UN, particularly Senator Jesse Helms, chairman of the Senate Foreign Relations Committee, who called Clinton weak for being constrained by the embargo. Yet those same representatives were incensed when the administration, as a compromising action, decided not to enforce the embargo, allowing both Croat and Bosniak forces to arm themselves through other countries' contributions. In 1994, US Ambassador Peter Galbraith tacitly conveyed to the Croatian government that we would look the other way as the Croats secretly acquired weapons. It was a passive means of supporting the arms flow, but not as damaging to the UN as open opposition to the embargo.

Despite being on record as supporting the lifting of the arms embargo, Republicans in the Senate Foreign Relations Committee convened to investigate Ambassador Galbraith and Assistant Secretary Holbrooke. Although Galbraith had been working in a complicated and highly stressful diplomatic setting, he was repaid by being raked over the congressional coals. It seemed there were clean guns, supplied by the US, and dirty guns, supplied by Islamic states.

All this Vice President Ganić understood. In our private conversations in 1995, he called the Islamic warriors who had entered the conflict "the kiss of death." "We know what to do with them," he assured me. "There are not so many. Maybe fifty or so. We can just round them all up and shoot them." I chose not to encourage him, even though the issue of Arabs among the Bosnian forces had by that time risen right to the top: I was asked about it in three separate conversations, with NATO Supreme Allied Commander George Joulwan, US Secretary of Defense William Perry, and President Clinton.

Eventually, it became clear that their concern was well founded. Islamic extremists had gained a foothold. They were not only supplying arms but also fighting alongside the poorly prepared Bosnians. Moreover, I was informed that they planned to assassinate a certain American working in Bosnia. The State Department strongly advised him to leave the region, but Ganić told me he depended on the man's expertise and vowed he would protect him with Bosnian troops. The American also insisted on continuing his work.

I decided to talk directly to the man to convince him the danger was real and too great for him to stay. After several tries, our Vienna office reached him by phone. The American said he would not leave the country unless I personally requested it.

"Do you have children?" I asked.

"Yes," he replied.

"How old?" I continued. Both were teenagers.

"Well, at least they're launched," I said, matter-of-factly. I did not suggest that he abandon his Bosnian work. At my next visit to the CIA, however, I examined the intelligence on the plot. I was more than convinced. When I returned to Vienna, I told the man not to stay in Bosnia unless he was sure that he would not crack under torture and was willing to lose his life. He left.

When I raised these matters with President Izetbegović during one-on-one meetings in Vienna and Sarajevo, he insisted that the brigade of 175 imported Muslim fighters had been disbanded and had turned in their arms. But, he said, some might have married Bosnian women and therefore could stay in the country . . . some might have been kidnapped as they tried to leave, so he could not find them . . . his troops might have refused to drive them out . . . besides, many of them were "dissidents" not welcome back in their home countries . . . furthermore, there were only seventeen Iranians in Bosnia plus their ambassador, who anyway had offered to send home the "educators and technical advisors," keeping only embassy personnel. . . .

The stakes were too high for such obfuscation. I had just learned of a shocking development in our investigation into the assassination plot: one of Izetbegović's chief political aides was implicated. When I informed the president, he asserted that no one in his government had been part of any plan to assassinate an American. But I had held in my hands evidence to the contrary. He wanted to see the proof. Considering what could be deciphered from the documents regarding our intelligence operation, I decided not to respond to his request.

I had one more meeting with Izetbegović in the home of Austria's President Thomas Klestil. I sat across the dinner table from Vienna's mayor, Helmut Zilk, who was maneuvering through the meal without two of his fingers—having nearly been killed by a letter bomb from a domestic terrorist infuriated by the mayor's support for Bosnian refugees. After the dinner, in a private talk with Izetbegović, I segued from Zilk's account of his tragedy: "You must intervene to keep Mujahideen out of Bosnia."

The president chose his words carefully. "Our government has the whole situation in control," he replied, staring into my eyes.

"Frankly, Mr. President," I countered, with dueling intensity, "I trust you're *not* in control, because we know what's going on." Indeed, NATO troops soon stumbled across what they described as an Iranian terrorist training camp tucked away in a hunting lodge and containing weapons, including children's toys wired to explode.[15] Their report touched off a firestorm in Washington.

Similarly, Republican Representative Benjamin Gilman would later assail President Clinton, saying that Iranians "even have a cultural center in Sarajevo."[16] (Of course, Republicans had voted to slash funding for American cultural programs abroad.) Several months later, walking down a street in Sarajevo, I came across a small storefront. The new Iranian center in Sarajevo was no grand building, with seductive Ottoman architectural intricacies and cavernous dens into which victims might be drawn. It was instead a small, nondescript space with three shelves of Korans—and no readers. It appeared that the congressman had wasted his ire.

For all the hoopla about the Islamic cultural center in Sarajevo, I found a "library" of eight books. And where was the American center? Not funded; not found.

Ultimately, we were left wondering whether our political and intelligence officers were underreporting or overreporting fundamentalist dangers. From our extensive antiterrorism work in Vienna, I was familiar with methods that extremists used to infiltrate a community and was thus alarmed by stories I was hearing: families offered stipends if fathers wore a beard; small-town children given candy, but only if their mothers covered their heads. I also started to count headscarves on the streets of Sarajevo. True, the numbers were increasing. But perhaps some were being worn by war-displaced farm wives who needed to keep hair off sweaty foreheads—the same villagers who were now refugees that purportedly made up 30 percent of the capital's population.

A perverse circle, indeed, if US nonintervention resulted in streets filled with women wearing headscarves, who were then used as evidence of extremism, which substantiated the unworthiness of the Bosniak cause, and became reason for nonintervention.

Fissures and Connections

25. INSIDE: Family Ties

During the war, families faced dreadful choices. When troops approached, when a house next door was blown up, when military barricades blocked the road, mothers and fathers had to make terrible trade-offs to save their children's lives.

The war ripped apart the fabric of families, leaving them frayed. There was a sense of helplessness for many parents and children—not only for mothers, but also fathers and sons, who traditionally were responsible for protecting their families. Sons weren't around to bury elderly parents or grandparents who collapsed along roadways during village purges. Husbands couldn't save their wives from being raped. Fathers couldn't stop grenades from exploding in schools where their children huddled in fear, cut off from home.

One Bosnian friend told me of Fadila, a university-educated professional, and her engineer husband. The couple and their two teenage sons lived with all the trappings of middle-class comfort: a television and VCR; an apartment in town and vacation place in the mountains. Hearing of advancing Serb forces, the engineer drove into the hills in a last-minute attempt to save what he could at their cabin. He didn't return that night. Soon, Fadila received word that he was dead. Witnesses told her that the killer said he didn't want to waste a bullet on her husband and so cracked his skull with the butt of a gun.

Distraught and terrified, Fadila fled with her two boys, boarding the next bus with only her purse—no documents, hardly any money. The bus took them to the coast of Croatia, where the threesome spilled into a pool of hundreds of thousands of refugees. There, Fadila faced a new threat: as soon as her boys turned seventeen, they would be inducted into the Croatian army and sent to the most perilous front lines. The widow was desperate to get her sons out of Croatia. With help from a friend abroad, she arranged for them to be sent as refugees to Germany. They were safe; but now she was alone.

Others had more excruciating escapes. A sickening story on the evening news told of a Bosnian father who, when his village was attacked, fled with his wife and several children into the night. As they crept through the underbrush to circumvent enemy checkpoints, the infant son began to cry. The mother did everything she could to silence the baby, without success. "Better one dies than all of us," the father finally muttered, as he put his hands around the baby's throat and strangled his child.

26. OUTSIDE: Federation

My lobbying efforts seemed to be falling on deaf ears. Analysts continued to discourage intervention. Adding to the other justifications, they mentioned the mind-boggling complexity of not only multiple armies but also paramilitary groups with little or no central command. Early in 1994, the State Department made a new attempt to manage the chaos. If Washington could unite the Bosniaks and Bosnian Croats (headquartered in the south, in Herzegovina), a three-way war would be consolidated into a Serb offensive and a Bosniak-Croat counteroffensive. But given the terrible losses inflicted on the Bosniaks by the Zagreb-backed Croats, getting the two groups to join forces, figuratively and literally, would be difficult at best.

After almost two years of war, in a dramatic shift of alliances, Croatian President Tuđman presented to Bosnian President Izetbegović a rough plan for a Bosniak-Croat Federation, which would cover approximately half of Bosnia. The proposal was premised on an undefined "confederation" of this federation with the Republic of Croatia. (When I apologetically asked a State Department official to explain the difference between "federation" and "confederation," he said, sardonically, "No one really knows what these words will actually mean, but if Tuđman wants a 'confederation' we'll give him a 'confederation.'")

The framework of a settlement was brokered by the United States, with a detailed agreement to be hammered out in Vienna. As the local ambassador, I would host the talks; Ambassador Chuck Redman, an accomplished career diplomat, would be the US negotiator.

The delegates arrived at the embassy, meeting in our large conference room under the gaze of a dozen international press cameras. Given the tensions between the Croats and Bosniaks, that was the only time the two negotiating teams would be together for days. Thereafter, the dozen or so Bosniaks met in the small "ambassador's dining room" just outside my office, while an equal number of Croats worked in our administrative meeting room. Ambassador Redman and his staff shuttled back and forth between the two.

Dozens of issues had to be navigated. One day an Austrian official asked about rumors that the Croats had backed out of their agreement regarding selection of the federation's prime minister. "No, we've already settled that," Ambassador Redman said.

"But," the questioner pressed, "I've heard they've changed their minds."

"I'm not giving them that option," Chuck retorted.

I looked in on each group regularly. The rooms were cramped, the men disheveled, the papers piled high. We waived our no-smoking rule rather than have progress impeded by nicotine cravings; but every time I opened a door, the tobacco stench was dense.

Several days into the process, late in the afternoon, I found a weary young man with bloodshot eyes, leaning over a computer. "Do you have a model that would be good for a constitution—with cantons?" he asked. Bemused, we found a prototype, compliments of the Swiss embassy.

The State Department had consulted former NATO commanders to determine how the two armies could unite under joint Bosniak-Croat command. Once this part of the agreement was settled, the United States would provide "education and training," to advance reforms for the post-Tito military and develop a unified command structure for the former adversaries—a Herculean assignment.

The Bosnian Croats were undoubtedly following orders from Zagreb. Tuđman's scheme to absorb the western half of Bosnia into Croatia was well known, but as the war stretched on, the Croatian strongman seemed to have given up on his dream of helping Milošević drive the Bosniaks out of the region. He was willing to settle for an undefined confederation with Croatia.

It was fascinating to observe discussions without definitions. For Tuđman, "confederation" seemed to mean that once the Bosnian Croats and Bosniaks united inside Bosnia, that territory could somehow become part of his Croat domain. For US policymakers, however, the proposed confederation could have been as limited as a unified economic entity. Given the wide discrepancy between these formulations, the US negotiation sponsors decided that the nature of the future relationship between the Bosniak-Croat Federation and Croatia was better left ambiguous. Tuđman could imagine whatever he wanted, so long as he came to the negotiating table.

However expedient, this was a slippery political slope—perhaps even encouraging ethnic cleansing. Creating a confederation defined by ethnic majorities granted de facto success to those who opposed integration. After all, union for Croats meant division for Bosnia. Thus the plan entrenched ideas that the international community was purporting to fight.

More insidiously, the confederation legitimized and branded ethnically "pure" regions of Bosnia, which in the future might more convincingly be annexed by Croatia and Serbia. Serbs were already calling the portion of Bosnia that they had overrun Republika Srpska, "the Serb Republic." If confederation were possible between the Croat-dominated area of Bosnia and the nation of Croatia, why could or should not the Serb-dominated region of Bosnia be free to confederate with Serbia? Notions of confederation could easily evolve into perceived US support for dividing Bosnia between the "Greater Croatia" and "Greater Serbia" conjured up by Tuđman and Milošević.

Following the Croatian leader's election in 1990, the two presidents met as many as forty-seven times throughout the war and were rumored to hold one another in high regard, even during the worst of the violence. Many of their communications concerned their desire to split Bosnia between them. At a restaurant meeting in 1995, Tuđman took out his pen, sketched Bosnia on a napkin, and then drew a line carving up the country.[1]

As outrageous as that action was, the question remained as to how Serbs could thrive within a Bosniak-Croat Federation. Were they simply to be consigned to a catch-all category of "others," meaning any non-Bosniaks and non-Croats? This was a slap in the face to the "loyal Serbs" like Jovan Divjak, who were already paying a price for staying. It was easy to imagine the psychological burden on, for instance, a Serb husband living with his Bosniak wife in the Bosniak-Croat Federation. She would be in the defined power group, while he would simply be "other." It seemed we outsiders were now codifying the language of the separatists parsing the country.

My office was spread with CIA-produced maps showing the eastern Serb-controlled mass of Bosnia in pink, the Croat-dominated sections in yellow, the shrinking Bosniak remnant in green. Bright colors of a patchwork quilt, with only a few apparent blemishes: patches of green on the right side of the map. Those were the rural enclaves of the UN-declared safe havens Goražde, Žepa, and Srebrenica, completely surrounded by pink. How to simplify the patchwork?

For days on end, the politicians had been holed up in their separate rooms, arguing among themselves over the best tactics to secure their gains, as their wordsmiths proposed terms and conditions that were

*After I sang "Simple Gifts," Bosnian Foreign Minister Irfan Ljubijankić,
on the far left, claimed the keyboard. The Balkan song fest he led was a far
cry from formal negotiation tactics. Ljubijankić died 28 May 1995,
when his helicopter was shot down by rebel Serbs near Bihac.*

then rejected by the other room. Everyone was exhausted; the negotiations were stuck. To help move the process along, I organized a dinner complete with harpist, small round tables, an encouraging toast,
fine food, our engaging six-year-old, a sing-along at the piano, and our
clumsy family dog.

The evening was successful; the negotiations would move forward.
But as he left our residence, one thin, wan negotiator said to me in a low
voice that he could only stare at his plate, thinking of his daughter back
in Sarajevo, hungry and trapped in that hellhole.

27. INSIDE: School Days

When her parents learned over the radio about the blockade around
Sarajevo that had been erected overnight, twelve-year-old Irma was ex-
cited. No school! Irma and her classmates didn't have to finish the spring
term. The teachers just gave them the same grades they'd made the first
half of the year and declared that school was out.

But come fall, the fighting hadn't stopped, so schools resumed classes. Parents weren't the only ones concerned about children. School administrators and teachers who might be willing to risk their own lives were at a loss about whether or not to hold classes. They left it to parents to decide, on a day-by-day basis, whether to send their children to school. Sometimes the shelling was so intense that Irma's family spent two to three weeks in the basement of their apartment building. When the worst seemed over, the parents ventured out to their jobs. But should they allow their only child also to go out, to school?

I met Irma through my interpreter Vjeko, her father, who was endlessly worried about her safety. Irma's mother, Azra, and Vjeko told me how they discussed their options: "Some parents never allowed their children to go. My friend let her daughter out just one day, and she was killed. But everything is in God's hands, we decided. If we didn't let her go, a shell could still hit the house." It was an agonizing decision. Irma's mother was always afraid her daughter wouldn't come back. But not letting her leave their apartment building would be like keeping her in prison, her parents decided. For the sake of her overall well-being, Irma needed to go to school.

"In September or October I started seventh grade," Irma told me. "I still have my diplomas. They were very simple, on two sheets of paper, with the Bosnian lily."

A year and a half into the fighting, it was time for Irma to move on to high school. Now she would have to go along main city streets, past sniper areas near the Presidency Building. Azra explained: "I had to go to work, because I was afraid I would lose my job as an architect. We worked from 9:00 to 2:00. Since there was no construction going on, we couldn't carry out new designs. So we tried to figure out how to save historical buildings that were burned out. But I had a friend, Zlata, with a small shop on the corner near the cathedral. I asked her, 'Please look after my Irma.' Sometimes my daughter stopped by the shop on her way home, and, if she could, Zlata gave her a small cake."

Irma piped up: "If we'd waited until we were certain that it was safe, we would never have gone to school." The shelling, she said, usually started about 5:00 a.m. and continued for two hours. During the lull that followed, children and adults hurried through the streets. The attacks often resumed in the afternoon, but there was no predictable pattern. Sometimes there was a reprieve until after 8:00 p.m. But the uncertainty was cruel when, after a period of quiet, the explosions suddenly picked up again.

Which route to take to school—the quickest or the safest? But then, no way was really safe.

Every day Irma met her friends at a halfway point: "We would go

Insightful and delicate Irma.

through some buildings, then sneak along side streets. They were narrower, so they were safer. We entered the school through the front door; the side door was the most dangerous because it faced the hill, where the snipers were."

School wasn't full-time, and classes were smaller since fewer children came. Many of the instructors, like Irma's French teacher, had left as refugees. But Irma noted with respect in her voice: "Even with the war, they didn't let up. They didn't change the standards. We had an old Latin professor. She tortured us. I remember how difficult the classes were more than I remember the war."

Textbooks grew old. Single sheets of paper that came as humanitarian aid replaced notebooks. "We did almost everything we did before," Irma said, "but we didn't have a gym, since it was being used by the army. And there was no one to give music lessons. But we sometimes had music in the streets, and often in the shelters."

Students like Irma tried to focus on their schoolwork, although for six months homework had to be done by candlelight. Sometimes Irma's parents put oil-soaked cotton in a coffee cup, lit it, and set it up high to light the whole room.

Hardships or none, Irma was still a teenager. "I was sure I knew best," she told me. "One day, after school, my friends and I climbed about twelve feet up on metal bars over the window to carve our names on the outside walls. I was sent to the principal. Another time, when I was

Graffiti, but not the work of hoodlums. Young people painted their names on this wall, which might still stand even if their lives were destroyed. A self-made grave marker to say yes—yes, they had been there.

in eighth grade, I went swimming with five or six boys and girls. It was during a cease-fire, when there was less shooting. We jumped into the river, near the destroyed library, with all our clothes on, as if we were at the seaside. I went home sopping wet. Looking back, it was a stupid thing to do, because of the snipers."

Two years into the war Irma was able to go to an after-school program run by an Austrian humanitarian group, SOS Kinderdorf: "For three hours each day we studied English, French, German, graphic design, and drawing. It was safe, there was something to do, and they gave us a sandwich." The children were asked to create "warning posters," and their work was even exhibited. Design became Irma's passion, which she pursued full force.

Every school community in Sarajevo had endless stories of how it tried to carry on with some semblance of normalcy in the midst of absurdity. As the principal of Irma's school led me through the building a year after the war ended, she described how she had wrestled with the dilemma of whether to hold classes. If a shell hit the school and the children were killed, she said, how could she live with herself? Ultimately she decided on a compromise. She wouldn't use the upper floor or the courtyard, which were more exposed to shelling. All the classes would be in the basement or on the ground floor.

Every level of education had its own bizarre—sometimes tragic—challenges. An accounting professor shared this story with me:

When the attacks started, I managed to make it into town. I wanted to get to my school, since I hadn't turned in my final marks. I was holding the grade ledger, thinking about one of my students who was having a hard time, and wondering how I might help him. Just then, a colleague came up and said, "Haven't you heard? The president just announced that all students should be given passing grades." I pointed to the bad marks of that student. "Lucky for him!" I chuckled. Another professor turned to me, crying. "He's dead."

Surrounded by extraordinary danger, faculty members also struggled with the mundane. A professor of architecture told me how she taught in a modern building with no electricity, the sounds of shells and bullets punctuating her lectures. Wanting to offer more than a furrowed brow, I asked if she might like me to somehow get some architectural journals to her. She looked at me patiently and replied, "That would be nice, but what we really need is pencils."

28. OUTSIDE: Forces and Counterforces

Seated on the stage of the White House Old Executive Office Building, Presidents Clinton, Izetbegović, and Tuđman looked pleased with themselves as they picked up their pens and signed the federation agreement. I was anything but pleased as I looked across the auditorium, filled with negotiators and other Balkan policymakers. Not one woman had been included in the deliberations. Somehow, I had colluded with a distorted power structure. More than forty women's groups had been trying to prevent the war, yet we organizers had failed to add chairs at the negotiating table for those who had most vociferously argued for the open society we said we were trying to foster. I wondered: If half the room had been women, would collaboration have been so difficult?

In other settings as well, divisions ran deep. Not since the Vietnam protests, I was assured by those who should know, had the State Department been so split. Early in the war, young diplomats assigned to the Balkans quit to protest the lack of action against Serb President Milošević and his Bosnian Serb cronies, President Karadžić and General Mladić.[2] The financier and philanthropist George Soros hired the administration's dissidents, employing them in a gadfly Balkan task force. There they could use their expertise to needle Secretary of State Warren Christopher, whose energy seemed consumed by the Middle East conflict. Morale was decidedly low in Foggy Bottom.

That policy fissure did not start with the Clinton administration. In 1992, Secretary of State James Baker had belatedly but successfully pressed President George H. W. Bush to order military action to stop Milošević. The order, however, was not executed—ironically, because of candidate Clinton's call for stronger action in Bosnia. As he dropped in the polls, Bush pulled Baker from the State Department to run his flagging reelection campaign. The new secretary of state, Lawrence Eagleburger, was more wary of becoming involved. Given his experience as US ambassador to Yugoslavia, his warnings to Congress carried great weight. With no leader left to push for action, Defense Secretary Dick Cheney's counsel against intervention prevailed, allowing the death and displacement of hundreds of thousands more Yugoslavs.

Elected in November 1992, President Clinton had faced a four-star challenge. First, given the independent candidate Ross Perot's campaign accusation that the Arkansas baby boomer had been a draft dodger, Clinton's suitability to be commander in chief was in doubt. Second, his appointment of Representative Les Aspin as the new defense secretary was rejected behind the scenes by Pentagon powers, so that Clinton was forced to replace him. Third, Chairman of the Joint Chiefs of Staff Colin Powell was intent on ending his own military career with a Gulf War victory, not a Balkan blot. Finally, at an otherwise long-since-forgotten town meeting, a questioner had won a commitment from Governor Clinton that, if elected president, he would support a policy of nondiscrimination against gays in the military—a move that caused enormous consternation at the conservative Pentagon. These four factors conspired to leave President Clinton weak vis-à-vis a military establishment that was determined not to enter the Balkan fray.

In the absence of decisive action from the White House, the State Department and Pentagon were at a standoff. The barbs were sometimes sharp, such as a reputed exchange between Ambassador to the UN Madeleine Albright and General Powell during which she asked in exasperation if his US military was anything more than an education program for inner-city youth. Several Pentagon officials verified to me that the general was resolved not to send troops to the Balkans.

Powell recommended to the president that only "overwhelming force" be considered. Some detractors conjectured that military leaders furthered their objective of avoiding entanglements by presenting worstcase scenarios that projected massive casualties. This was not a new approach; military strategists who had not wanted to become involved in the 1991 Gulf War also had projected huge American losses.

The result of their pessimistic estimates was that the White House deferred to the advice of Powell and like-minded advisors. The president summoned Richard Holbrooke back from Germany, where he had served only a year as ambassador. Named assistant secretary for European and Canadian affairs, Holbrooke was given a new charge: clean up the Balkan mess. He stepped into the role with energy, commitment, and clarity of purpose. The president, in a subsequent private meeting, asked me what I thought about the assignment. Afterward I told Dick what I had answered: "Holbrooke is brilliant and a bully—a good choice to go up against Milošević."

Unfortunately, the assistant secretary's confrontational personality, while often effective against war criminals, was remarkably counterproductive within the State Department. Secretary Christopher, a gentlemanly attorney, had a distinguished reputation as decorated statesman and civic leader. He had played a lead role not only in the normalization of relations with China but also in the release of US hostages in Iran. However, Christopher was reputedly as averse to conflict as Holbrooke was comfortable creating it. At least two other seasoned professionals told me they resigned after being recruited by the secretary to work on Bosnia because they couldn't—or wouldn't—work with Holbrooke. The secretary, they said, seemed unwilling to mitigate the internal discord.

Holbrooke, meanwhile, had a bigger-than-life problem stemming from his bigger-than-life personality. He complained to me that he was unable to get any face time with Clinton because, he had heard, the president did not want to be pressured. Thus, Holbrooke asked me to carry the message to the Oval Office that it was in the president's interest to move on the Balkans before the next election campaign heated up. Republican Senate Majority Leader Bob Dole, the challenger, had long been urging a stronger response to the violence. The slaughter of Bosnian innocents could provide a damaging campaign theme against the president.[3]

From all I had seen and read, I was convinced that Dick was right regarding the need for decisive action. To press the case, I met with several members of Congress, as well as their staffs. Sitting in their high-ceilinged offices, I stared at walls covered with pictures and paraphernalia from back home. Each time, I delivered compelling statistics, reports from the ground, and the urging of Europeans for US leadership. One member of the House Committee on International Relations looked at me, puzzled. "Madam Ambassador," he drawled, "I get lots of calls and letters from my constituents about highways and taxes. No one has ever contacted me about the Balkans."

Still searching for allies, I met with a top advisor in the White House. I insisted that the Serb military strength was being exaggerated. He listened graciously but countered my arguments: "If we intervene, there will be a blood bath, and the president will be responsible."

The advisor was right about the blood bath. But it happened because we did nothing.

29. INSIDE: Blood

For Irma and her family, life in Sarajevo had become surreal. On the same sidewalks where friends had strolled, chatting en route to the cinema or a museum, people now ran with pounding hearts. Each day was marked by moments of courage, such as when a doctor braved snipers to wash off a dead man in the street so that his children wouldn't see him covered with blood.

Such scenes shaped Sarajevo's children. Irma's mother, Azra, described to me the uncertainty in which they lived: "I thought the war would stop after two months. I never guessed it would be almost four years. We imagined negotiations would solve it—that when President Mitterand came from France to see what was going on, he would tell people. He was here when sixty people were killed while waiting for bread. But when he went back home, there was still no action."

During the shelling, her father's anxiety was easily transmitted to Irma, who before could not have imagined that she would spend her early adolescence—just as Anne Frank did—hidden in a shelter and fearful that each day might be her family's last. Irma told me:

> It was during the war that I really got to know my dad. When you're together every day with someone, you notice every little detail. He was so afraid; afraid for me, for my mom, for everybody. I know he was doing the right thing when he kept forcing me to go down into the basement for shelter, but he made me panic. When we heard an explosion, he'd cry out, "Oh God, it's a shell!" He just kept drumming it in.
>
> He didn't mean any harm. He just wanted us to survive. But my life was much more complicated because he was so upset all the time. I hated it. A kid can't understand the role of a parent in such a situation. I knew it was serious, but I couldn't really comprehend. For every child in Sarajevo it was the same: We had to be grown-ups in small bodies.

Irma celebrated her thirteenth birthday in a basement storage area, where some seventy people from the apartment building had taken shelter. Azra recalled how she decorated her daughter's cake with small candles she had on hand, never imagining that they would be needed months—let alone years—later, for light: "Given the shooting, it was impossible to go to a store, but I had enough staples in my cupboard from before the war. I used them all up, and then we had humanitarian aid. We stayed night and day in the basement for more than six months, but after that, I would go upstairs sometimes to our apartment to make bread or cook. My husband, Vjeko, would be so angry."

The apartment cellar was crowded. Vjeko's Aunt Mira and her twenty-one-year-old daughter, Jasna, escaped from the front-line suburb of Ilidža and moved in with Irma's family. But Serb troops apprehended Mira's husband, a film director. In prison, they burned his arm with cigarettes. Mira and Jasna cried every day. Then a Serb colleague, the husband's best friend, got him out of prison. "He just appeared at our front door," Irma told me.

To celebrate Christmas, the family decided to try to be with Jasna, who had moved to an apartment near the National Theater. The shelling that day was terrible, but they made the trip safely. Jasna was a designer, and she had made a lovely gift for each person. "But," Azra told me, "we all knew her heart was with her boyfriend, Igor, a Serb fighting in the Bosnian army. She had his picture out where she could see it all the time. And on her refrigerator she had a sign that read, 'Igor, I love you.' Our sweet family time that day was shattered when someone came to say that Igor had been killed by Croats. Everything was destroyed in just one moment. For a long time after that, Jasna couldn't do anything but cry."

In between her cousin's heartbreak and other tragedies, Irma told me she developed close friendships with five girls:

> The six of us had gone to primary school together. We lived on the same street. One was my best friend, my soul mate, from the time we were little. When there was less shooting, we'd sit outside together. In 1993, after we started getting used to the fact that the war wasn't going to end, we put together a dance troupe, practicing in the basement. We turned a bicycle upside down and spun the pedals. The turning wheels normally generated electricity for the headlight, but we took some wires and hooked up the bike to my father's cassette player.
>
> We were really into Madonna, so we worked up some dances to her songs. One of our best was "Vogue." Another was by Ace of Base, which we recorded from the radio. We'd find some poor victim to turn the pedals while we danced and danced.

Her mother added to the description: "The girls wanted to be pretty, so they made dresses. And they wanted to be older than they were, so they put on makeup. When they or other kids had a birthday, the dance troupe would entertain. We were the audience, smiling and laughing. To us adults, it was funny—and we certainly needed a laugh."

Irma joined in again:

> We were really good. Once we were invited to dance at an event organized by the Egyptian UN troops, who were part of the UN Protection Force. That was huge for us. There were lots and lots and lots of men in uniform. The whole

Egyptian battalion was there. We were up on a stage, in costumes we'd made—each of us with a different colored skirt. They gave us lunch and a little extra food.

Then, one of the girls was sleeping in her flat, when a bomb fell directly in her room. It was three o'clock in the morning. Her brother was sleeping there too. She was lucky; her wounds weren't big. But her brother lost his arm. I went over the next day. There was blood all over the place. Then it dawned on me: That's the blood of my friend. I just stood there, staring.

30. OUTSIDE: Trade-offs

As a policymaker, it was easy to lose perspective. That became clear when I arrived in Brussels in the spring of 1994 for a two-day gathering of fifty-two American ambassadors stationed in Europe. As Deputy Secretary of State Strobe Talbott stood before us, each envoy sat mulling over the conundrums he or she was facing. Talbott declared: "But there is clearly one issue that dominates all others in Europe . . ." At last we'll talk about US policy in the former Yugoslavia, I thought. ". . . and that is *Russia*."

As the discussion unfolded, the venerable US ambassador to Moscow, Tom Pickering, expressed his concern about recent damage to US-Russian relations. President Boris Yeltsin was having a hard enough time with his political rival Vladimir Zhirinovsky; he did not need the United States to hand his ultranationalist opponent an inflammatory issue like Bosnia around which to rally popular support. After all, the majority of Russians were Orthodox, and most of them rejected the charges against the Serbs, their theological kin.

After Talbott sat down, Steve Oxman—then assistant secretary of state for European and Canadian affairs—began to speak about Bosnia. Suddenly he was called away from the dais to the phone. He returned soon to tell us that thanks to the United States, a NATO air attack had been ordered against the Bosnian Serbs. "Did anybody tell the Russians?" shouted Pickering from the back of the room—a reminder that every decision involved a complex dance of interests and players.

Heartened by Oxman's news, I sat whispering with Robert Hunter and Stuart Eizenstat, ambassadors to NATO and the EU, sitting on each side of me. At last the administration was acting, we sighed with relief. A few minutes later, Oxman was again called away to the phone. He returned to say that the reports were not true.

That evening I curled up on Stu's couch, watching the midnight CNN report: unchallenged violence, as villagers in eastern Bosnia fled for their lives. Although rumors of air strikes had been reported for several days, Serbs were moving on the safe haven of Goražde.[4]

Old newspapers I had carried off the plane told the story. One read: "After months of wavering, Clinton finally takes a stand; air strikes on the Serbs to save Goražde." But two days later: "NATO fails to respond to UN requests for air strikes; Goražde falls to the Serbs." Although the aggressors were unable to hold the town, those conflicting headlines captured the political chaos.

Two days after the meeting of ambassadors, I accompanied Austrian Chancellor Franz Vranitzky on his visit to Washington. We each had a full schedule of appointments and speeches, some together and some apart. I darted between the State Department and White House, considering reports, observing attitudes, weighing in — searching for any opening, any willingness for action in the Balkans.

At the National Security Council's offices, a worried Europe specialist told me privately that the president was "waffling on Bosnia." Now, more than ever, I needed to reinforce the importance of US action. NATO's failure to defend Goražde meant that the United States was the last power standing between Serb troops and even greater catastrophe.

Only a few hours later, I would be with the president and the chancellor in the Oval Office to discuss US-Austrian relations. It was not my place to introduce the topic so appallingly absent from the ambassadors' gathering in Brussels — this was a formal meeting between two heads of government. If President Clinton did not bring it up, only one other person could. I would have no opportunity to speak with Chancellor Vranitzky when he arrived at the White House, since I would be inside, briefing the president on US-Austrian affairs immediately prior to the meeting. So I rushed across town to the National Press Club and intercepted the chancellor, who had just completed an address. Although he was concerned, I knew he did not feel as strongly as I did about US action in Bosnia. Still, in the hall as he left his speech, I urged in a low voice: "When you see President Clinton, tell him he must not wait any longer for a European invitation. The United States *must lead* on Bosnia."

An hour later, I entered the Oval Office to brief the president. He was clearly distracted, having just hung up from a forty-five-minute phone call with Yeltsin. The president recounted the conversation with frustration. Responding to the US proposal of intervention in the Balkans, the Russian leader had agreed throughout the conversation that Serb troops had to be stopped. Then at the end, just before hanging up, he added abruptly: "But no bombs."

I laid out the key US-Austrian issues to the president and others gathered around his desk — Secretary of State Christopher, Vice Presi-

US President Bill Clinton, just hammered by Russian President Boris Yeltsin, looks uncomfortable; after members of the press were escorted from the room, Austrian Chancellor Franz Vranitsky offered no respite, reminding Clinton repeatedly that America must lead the international community in Bosnia.

dent Gore, National Security Advisor Tony Lake, and others. Peering over his reading glasses, President Clinton flipped through talking points on index cards, which he then laid on his desk. Minutes later, I stood behind him as he welcomed Vranitzky and his entourage.

Secretary Christopher suggested I take my place in a chair outside the inner ring. But the president motioned for me to sit next to the secretary on the sofa. "So where should I sit?" I whispered to Christopher. "The Man said for you to sit here," he shrugged.

Clinton asked Vranitzky about the European scene. To my relief, the Austrian led with the need for US leadership on Bosnia, emphasizing the point twice more in the half-hour meeting. The two men exchanged views on several other matters, sitting in the center of the world's most photographed crescent of uncomfortable chairs and sofas. The chancellor, a former banker, was dressed in Europe's most conservative best. The president wore a bold tie with grinning children.

Visiting a maternity clinic near the outskirts of Sarajevo, I stood before the white-walled building with gaping holes. It had been shelled while mothers were inside bringing life into the world. How had newborn babies become military targets?

The picturesque hills surrounding the city now sheltered nests of snipers, who calculated the best positions from which to pick off civilians and terrorize the population. (One such location was the Jewish cemetery—considered the world's most renowned Sephardic burial grounds, founded in 1630.) Over time, a pattern emerged. Hospital doctors treating the wounded noted that on certain days children were targets; on other days it was mothers. Some days, the victims were shot below the knees; other days, in the head. To forestall boredom, it seemed, a sport was evolving.

Life and death were played out not only in the streets, but also in medical facilities. Although clinicians eschewed ethnic labels, insisting that they were "just doctors," many had to flee as sadistic paramilitaries approached. Even so, hundreds of doctors and nurses were killed by snipers and targeted shelling. Some made the conscience-wrenching decision to take up guns, concluding that ending life was necessary to save life.

In other cases, doctors answered pleas over shortwave radio, braving enemy interception and minefields and traversing mountain passes to reach isolated and desperate enclaves.[5] In such besieged towns, medical supplies ran out as the number of injuries from shrapnel, bullets, and land mines swelled. Amputations of shattered limbs were performed without anesthetics by dentists or psychiatrists who never dreamed of being surgeons. Metal saws and other crude instruments were disinfected with hydrogen peroxide pilfered from chemical, paper, or car-battery factories.

The chief of pediatrics at the main Sarajevo hospital was Esma Cemirlic-Zecevic—a tall, middle-aged woman with blond hair pinned back in a French twist. She asked if she could show me around. We walked past large plate-glass windows giving a wide view of the hills. Jagged holes were covered with plastic and tape. Every window in the hospital was a hazard. A giant blue bladder of water was in the hallway—protection from bullets, the doctor explained. After a child was shot lying in his bed, parents moved their own bunks in front of the large windows, so they could comfort their children while serving as human shields.

The few rooms with no windows, formerly used for radioactive treatment, were filled with still more children's beds. Cramped, with no light source, those rooms were the safest, physically. But with the doors closed, they were pitch-black; and a candle did little to lift the spirits of the children confined there hour after hour, day after day.

My guide told me she'd been shot by a sniper while visiting the apartment of her sick niece. The bullet ripped through her shoulder, lodging close to her heart. International colleagues pressed the UN to evacuate her. Eventually, UNICEF took charge. A UN armored vehicle transported the doctor to the Sarajevo airport. She was then flown to Boston, where her brother lived, for surgery. As soon as she recovered, Dr. Cemerlic-Zecevic decided to return to the besieged city and fulfill her obligations at the hospital. Because UN air transport was suspended due to heavy fighting, her return trip would have to be via the ground route. After several days of travel, she made her way down Mt. Igman and through the tunnel into the city. The next day, she reported for duty—to continue treating her patients as best she could, with care if not medication.

One evening, the hospital generator stopped. The doctor told me how she took seven premature infants from their incubators, wrapped them in blankets, and kept them with her as staff and patients waited in the basement throughout a night of heavy shelling. One by one, the infants stopped breathing. When morning came, all were dead.

The doctor walked up from the basement and started her day, treating children so sick or badly wounded that their parents had braved the streets to bring them to the hospital. When I asked, as carefully as I could, how she had managed to carry on that day, she said flatly, "They needed me."

SECTION 5 The End Approaches

32. OUTSIDE: Security and Cooperation

The gap between rough reality and polite policy statements was mad-
dening to President Izetbegović, who managed to escape his besieged
city to attend the Budapest summit of the Conference for Security and
Cooperation in Europe (CSCE) in December 1994. Created twenty years
earlier, that organization comprised almost all European countries, plus
Canada and the United States.[1] The founding pact outlined general principles of international behavior and addressed economic, environmental, and humanitarian issues.

Covering the December meeting, the *Christian Science Monitor* let
loose a torrent of scorn: "With its failure even to issue a statement critical of the latest outrages by the Bosnian Serbs, the [CSCE] meeting . . .
joined the United Nations, the European Union, and NATO as another
international organization unable to take any meaningful steps for peace
in the Balkans. . . . The CSCE fiddled as Bosnia burns."[2]

I sat behind President Clinton, watching world leaders around the
gigantic table take turns expounding. The fiddle score, it turned out,
was an affected and stale proclamation, "Toward a Genuine Partnership
in a New Era":

2. We believe in the central role of the CSCE in building a secure and stable
CSCE community, whole and free. . . .

3. . . . We are determined to give a new political impetus to the CSCE, thus
enabling it to play a cardinal role in meeting the challenges of the twenty-
first century.

4. . . . Since we last met . . . the roots of democracy have spread and struck
deeper.

5. The spread of freedoms has been accompanied by new conflicts and the revival of old ones. Warfare in the CSCE region to achieve hegemony and territorial expansion continues to occur. Human rights and fundamental freedoms are still flouted, intolerance persists and discrimination against minorities is practiced. The plagues of aggressive nationalism, racism, chauvinism, xenophobia, anti-Semitism and ethnic tension are still widespread. Along with social and economic instability, they are among the main sources of crisis, loss of life and human misery. . . . This situation requires our resolute action. . . .

7. . . . The CSCE's democratic values are fundamental to our goal of a community of nations with no divisions, old or new, in which the sovereign equality and the independence of all States are fully respected, there are no spheres of influence and the human rights and fundamental freedoms of all individuals, regardless of race, colour, sex, language, religion, social origin or of belonging to a minority, are vigorously protected.

8. The CSCE will be a primary instrument for early warning, conflict prevention and crisis management in the region. . . .

10. . . . We have established a "Code of Conduct on Politico-Military Aspects of Security." . . .

11. . . . We have directed it [the CSCE] to continue its work in accordance with its mandate and to develop a framework which will serve as a basis for an agenda. . . . We have also mandated it to address specific regional security problems, with special emphasis on longer-term stability in South-Eastern Europe.[3]

Because the delegations came with unique sets of aims and understandings, they were unable to agree on focused objectives and enforceable provisions. The code's tiered mandate to "develop a framework which will serve as a basis for an agenda" mired the project from the start. In another paragraph, the importance of "start[ing] discussion on a model of common and comprehensive security for our region" did little more to dredge the project out of futility. This was hardly the hoped-for call to action.

After words and words and words, it was President Izetbegović's turn to speak. The declaration had at least mentioned "special emphasis on longer-term stability in South-Eastern Europe." With passion, he addressed his peers. How could that distinguished group calmly discuss cooperating on security and human rights while 250 miles away his city was being shelled as they spoke?

President Clinton's lips were tight as he stared at the Bosnian, knowing full well the responsibility of the United States as lone superpower. But whatever empathy he felt for Izetbegović must have been complicated by his resolve to strengthen his critical relationship with President Yeltsin. After all, Clinton needed Yeltsin's cooperation to fulfill his vision of an enlarged NATO, including Poland, Hungary, and the Czech Republic.

Izetbegović's speech provoked a response from the Russian. Exercised over the prospect of NATO expansion, which was perceived by his constituency as a threat, Yeltsin could not afford to lose both battles—intervention in the Balkans and the expansion of NATO. His meaning was unmistakable: "Europe has not yet freed itself from the heritage of the Cold War [and] is in danger of plunging into a cold peace."

NATO expansion or Bosnian intervention? Should Clinton risk the first by taking a strong stand on the second? The *Chicago Tribune* laid out the conflicting agendas: "How will NATO, a UN chastened by its Bosnia experience, and the large but weak Conference on Security and Cooperation in Europe . . . divide the tasks of collective security . . . ?"[4]

The *New York Post* was less patient:

> NATO has more important worries at the moment than the incorporation of former Warsaw Pact nations into the alliance, most notably, the crisis in the Balkans. But Russian President Boris Yeltsin's outburst at the European security summit in Budapest . . . certainly shoved the issue to the front burner. Yeltsin's truculent speech . . . overshadowed issues of more immediate significance: the Balkan war and Ukraine's decision to embrace the principles of nuclear non-proliferation. . . . Frankly, we don't think a right-wing putsch in Moscow is just around the corner. And the "Don't destabilize Yeltsin" talk reminds us of nothing so much as the endless Cold War chatter about the need to strengthen the "doves" in the Kremlin, lest the "hawks" win the day. It was nonsense then; it remains so now.[5]

Yet what sounded to the world like nonsense was in fact dissonance as each talented player came to the stage with music for a different piece. No matter how well tuned the instruments and attentive the players, the effect was cacophony.

Still, whenever they could, political leaders sought moments of harmony. One such moment was the twentieth anniversary of the Helsinki Accords, which created a standard for human rights across Europe. For the commemoration, I joined a well-heeled crowd gathered in the stunning Zeremoniensaal of Vienna's Hofburg Palace. Many of the leaders spoke poignantly of the hopes those accords embodied and the limitations of implementing them, as witnessed in the Balkans.

Between speakers, a trio of young men played soulful music by Haydn. I sat in my velvet chair, wondering how to account for the nonchalance of fate. Those boys could just as easily have been members of the Sarajevo Philharmonic, dodging snipers as they ran down alleys to rehearsal. Or worse, they were the right age to scramble into a tank or perch in the

I unabashedly joined conversations to make the case for international involvement, this time with President Richard von Weisecker of Germany, President Thomas Klestil of Austria, and Chancellor Vranitsky.

mountains above Sarajevo, looking down the barrel of a big gun, firing missiles into kindergartens. Even as I was trying to listen to the speakers, I was distracted by the lunacy—the extreme outcomes of happenstance.

33. INSIDE: Sarajevo Cinderella

Amid the staccato of guns and shelling, the International Committee of the Red Cross (ICRC) was one of the first organizations to enter Bosnia. The committee had been involved in every major armed conflict since 1864—after a Swiss businessman convinced a group of nobles that enemy troops deserved parity in medical treatment. The 1949 Geneva Convention and additional international protocols of 1977 gave the ICRC a mandate to trace the missing. During the war, the committee delivered eighteen million messages in the former Yugoslavia to try to keep families and friends in touch.[6] Bosnians I spoke with told of hopes raised, then dashed as they searched for loved ones. Enabling communication, the ICRC also verified whether people were alive or dead.

A Bosnian journalist told me of three children who became her neighbors. In the chaos of war, a girl named Ljilja fled with her brother from Knin, the Serb headquarters within Croatia. After a harrowing journey—traveling, then hiding, then traveling on—the two were able to find their sister for what would be a short-lived respite.

The sister lived in a Sarajevo suburb. Once a quiet neighborhood, it was now a distressed front-line location. For a whole year, the children tried to contact their parents back in Croatia. They relied on the ICRC to get their messages through. One day, after getting word that their mother was alive in Knin, the elated children wrote her a letter. She ran to her neighbors with the note in her hand, crying, "My children are alive! They're alive!" But her joy was too much to bear. She collapsed on her neighbor's doorstep with a fatal heart attack.

From that point on, Ljilja lost her spirit and her strength. Despite the effort of her new neighbor to restore her hope, she seemed to be trying to meet death.

The journalist told me of one day when Ljilja and her brother went out for water. All Sarajevans had been struggling to find basic necessities. Once water stopped flowing in their homes, they had to search across the city for open pipes. People traveled for miles, some hauling empty canisters in wheelbarrows and baby carriages.[7]

But some water stations, where people waited in line for hours, had become sniper targets. That day, as Ljilja and her brother stood in line, she was killed by a shell aimed at the queue. Her brother came back wearily, the neighbor said, holding only her slipper.

34. OUTSIDE: Failure at Srebrenica

In an exhaustive report after the war, UN Secretary General Kofi Annan would admit to the member states: "Having served as Under-Secretary-General for Peacekeeping Operations during much of the period under review, I am fully cognizant of the mandate entrusted to the United Nations and only too painfully aware of the Organization's failures in implementing that mandate."[8]

The "period under review" was the massacre at Srebrenica, a mountain resort that became the site of Europe's worst atrocity since Hitler. The drama started in April 1992, when the hamlet fell to Serb paramilitaries who had overrun most of eastern Bosnia. Local Bosniaks led by Naser Orić retook the town three weeks later.

Orić, a former police officer and Milošević bodyguard, would later be convicted of war crimes committed during his offensives that followed the reclaiming of Srebrenica. His forces accumulated bloody victories throughout 1992, destroying scores of Serb villages. More than thirteen hundred Serbs were killed and many others tortured—sometimes burned alive in their torched homes.[9]

The Serbs launched a counteroffensive, driving Bosniaks from surrounding areas toward hoped-for refuge in the beleaguered town. On 11 March 1993, when UN Force Commander Philippe Morillon went to the small hill community, he was shocked by the suffering of more than sixty thousand people, many living in the streets or on rooftops.

During Morillon's visit, the Serbs halted their attacks. Worried that his departure would trigger more shelling, Bosniak women surrounded his vehicle to block his leaving. After hours of unsuccessful negotiation with the women, Morillon accepted that he was trapped.[10] To calm the situation, he stood on the balcony of the local post office and declared: "You are now under the protection of the United Nations . . . I will never abandon you."[11]

After Morillon's unauthorized proclamation on 16 April, the UN Security Council passed Resolution 819, designating Srebrenica a "safe area" for Bosniaks driven from their homes—to be protected by "all necessary means, including the use of force."

Two days later, Morillon brokered a misguided deal on behalf of the UN between Bosnian Serb General Ratko Mladić and Bosniak General Sefer Halilović. Mladić would halt Serb attacks on the town; in exchange, the Bosniaks would hand over their weapons to a small group of Canadian UN monitors.[12]

The only country that offered troops to protect the mass of refugees was the Netherlands. Before sending in six hundred lightly armed soldiers,[13] Dutch Prime Minister Ruud Lubbers was personally assured by President Clinton that "air support" for the troops would be provided if necessary.[14] Indeed, the presence of the unit originally was conceived as a "'tripwire' for the use of air power."[15]

The situation began to deteriorate immediately. Diego Arria, the head of a UN Security Council delegation to Srebrenica, named it "genocide in slow motion."[16] The Dutch soldiers had orders to retaliate only if they themselves were shot at—not actively to protect the citizens. As it turned out, they could not even protect themselves. Short of fuel, vehicles, and ammunition, they were no match for the heavy artillery of some fifteen hundred Serb troops.

For the rest of 1994 and into 1995, Serbs restricted the movement of the UN troops and disrupted their convoys containing basic supplies, including food and medicine. At one point, they held seventy Dutch soldiers hostage.

Relations between the Bosniaks and Dutch were also tense. The few Bosniaks desperately trying to defend their town and draw more international support stopped UN patrols and took a hundred peacekeepers hostage for four days in January 1995.[17]

The ground rules that allowed the subsequent massacre were set at a meeting on 4 June in the Bosnian-Serbian border town of Zvornik. There, French General Bernard Janvier, supreme UN military commander in the former Yugoslavia, met with Bosnian Serb General Mladić. It seemed an officer like Janvier respected a *génocidaire* more than he did the ragtag Bosniaks. Despite overwhelming evidence that the vast majority of human rights abuses were being committed by Serb military and paramilitary forces, Janvier characterized Mladić as "a professional soldier trying to defend his people."[18]

The two "professional soldiers" struck a deal. But because the UN leaders who determined the rules of engagement ultimately had neither the vision nor the will to use the promised air power at their disposal, once again Mladić had the upper hand. "We were the supplicants," an aide admitted. "Janvier proposed the meeting. Janvier proposed the deal."[19]

"The deal" comprised three promises. UN troops would be safe from Serb threats; the Serbs would not be targeted by airstrikes; and they would free hundreds of UN peacekeepers whom they had been holding hostage.

Although outranked, British General Rupert Smith spoke up against the agreement five days later at a meeting in the Croatian town of Split. But Janvier reportedly replied, "I insist that we will never have the possibility of combat, of imposing our will on the Serbs."[20] This was just the nod the Serbs needed to wipe out Bosniak enclaves in their eastern Bosnia campaign.

On 11 July 1995, Serb troops entered Potočari, a nearby village to which the Srebrenica refugees had been pushed. The next day, Mladić stood before the refugees and theatrically compared himself to Allah, assuring them that no harm would come to them. Later, the show would continue as he patted a young boy on the head and his men handed out chocolates to children.

In the middle of the afternoon, twenty-five thousand Bosniak women were ordered by Mladić to take their young and elderly relatives and climb into a fleet of buses and trucks for the fifty-mile drive to Tuzla, outside of Serb-controlled territory. The women were told the men and boys would follow on foot. It was a cruel ruse. Within a few hours, the slaughter began. Over the next several days, thousands of men and boys would have their throats slit or be lined up, shot, and piled into mass graves. Only a few escaped through the woods.

As the bloodshed continued, Special Representative of the UN Secretary General Yasushi Akashi met with his military commander, Janvier, and several other officers to discuss NATO airstrikes against the Serb forces. Akashi described to the group how, over the phone with Milošević, he had tried to distinguish between "close air support" and the prohibited "airstrike." The Serb leader had rejected the distinction, saying that such a strike would violate General Janvier's agreement with General Mladić.

Milošević knew that UN approval was required for NATO airstrikes in the "dual key" policy adopted by the internationals: if he could dissuade the UN, he could prevent NATO from acting.

As the meeting proceeded, instead of meaningful intervention, NATO planes tried to hit Serb armored vehicles with free-fall bombs. Hearing of those limited strikes, Janvier ordered the Dutch battalion to withdraw from its observation posts to safer positions, retracting even that thin line of defense.

Milošević called again, outraged at the pinprick strikes. He maintained that the Serb advance was in response to "terrorism" by Bosniaks. As officials discussed the next steps, the onslaught at Srebrenica gathered momentum.

The Dutch soldiers had been abandoned. Except for NATO's minimal response, their pleas for airstrikes were ignored. Clinton's promised US support did not come, and Prime Minister Lubbers faced the specter of a panicked Dutch unit fleeing its post in a light tank, plowing through a cluster of Bosniaks trying to block the flight of their protectors.

The chaos not only engulfed the terrified Bosniaks and peacekeepers—it also threatened international authorities fearful of being blamed for the debacle. One of the Dutch officers later alleged that his defense ministry deliberately ruined film he had taken, which showed nine bodies lying in a stream—evidence that the killing began while the Dutch were still present. That film, he said, also included images showing Dutch soldiers helping the Serb military separate the men and boys from the women.[21]

Meanwhile, as women and parts of their families streamed in from Srebrenica, representatives of the UN High Commissioner for Refugees set up tents on the Tuzla airport tarmac. Already traumatized, the women became frantic as hours and then days went by with no sign of their husbands, sons, brothers, and fathers. Bosnian Serbs insisted to the women that once the men had been screened for "potential war criminals," they could rejoin their families.

On 13 July in Sarajevo, Bosnian Foreign Minister Hasan Muratović informed US Ambassador John Menzies that more than a thousand men had been rounded up and were being held in a stadium near Srebrenica. The same day, an understated cable from Akashi noted: "We are beginning to detect a shortfall in the number of persons expected to arrive in Tuzla. There is no further information on the status of approximately 4,000 draft-age males."[22]

She has survived Srebrenica but, in a sense, lost her life.
COURTESY OF TARIK SAMARAH

In Belgrade, ninety miles east of Tuzla, UN diplomats were meeting with Milošević to negotiate safety for their failed peacekeepers. Milošević persisted in maintaining that he had no control over Bosnian Serb military actions, including Mladić's attack. That claim was spurious, as evidenced in a behind-the-scenes report on 17 July from Akashi to Kofi Annan:

> Carl Bildt [a European Union envoy], Mr. Thorwald Stoltenberg [of the standing Geneva peace conference] and myself met in Belgrade with President Milošević. I was accompanied by General Rupert Smith.
>
> Milošević, at the request of Bildt, facilitated the presence of General Mladić at the meeting. Mladić and Smith had a long, bilateral discussion. Despite their disagreement on several points, the meeting re-established dialogue between the two generals. Informal agreement was reached on a number of points. . . .
>
> In view of the highly sensitive nature of the presence of Mladić at the meeting, it was agreed by all participants that the fact should not be mentioned at all in public.[23]

Once Srebrenica fell, the UN soldiers were in the hands of Mladić. They had faced excruciating choices. The fearful Dutch battalion "transferred 30,000 liters of fuel to the Bosnian Serb Army in accordance with Mladić's demands."[24] That Dutch fuel was used to drive prisoners to their execution and to bulldoze their bodies into graves.

A photograph from those hours was wired around the world. It showed a grim-faced Dutch commander holding a glass as the victorious Serbs toasted each other.

The Dutch finally left their station in Potočari on 21 July. Estimates are that more than eight thousand unarmed Bosniak men and boys had been murdered.

The UN envoy for human rights, former Polish Prime Minister Tadeusz Mazowiecki, had advocated the creation of protected safe havens in eastern Bosnia. After the massacre he resigned, declaring that "one cannot speak about the protection of human rights with credibility when one is confronted with the lack of consistency and courage displayed by the international community and its leaders."[25]

35. INSIDE: Magbula's Parrot

After almost a year of living under siege in Potočari, Magbula had heard Commander Morillon's promise in 1993 to protect Srebrenica. When Morillon had first come to investigate, residents of her village had crowded into his office and approached him on the street: "Everyone was after him asking the same question: 'Are we safe? Are you going to protect us?'" Magbula told me that, reassured by Morillon's pledge of UN protection, "we were all happy, believing that all the other refugees would be able to go back to their homes. And some of our people who had fled would be able to return."

Magbula herself went to see Morillon, carrying her parrot: "He asked me why I was giving him a parrot. I said, 'I have no food for my parrot anymore, and I want to give him to you, because you're going to be in a better position to feed him.' And then they took a picture of me and General Morillon. But after the fall of Srebrenica everything in my house was destroyed, so I don't have that picture anymore."

In Potočari, Magbula and her husband had built a home and raised two children. One son was away at college in Tuzla, and one was still living at home when the war started. When the Dutch peacekeeping forces head-quartered themselves in Potočari, Magbula passed their buildings on her daily walks.

She watched over the next two years as Srebrenica swelled with tens of thousands of refugees. She and her neighbors tried to help the people who came from farms to seek safety in the town: "There was a time when I had fifteen children in front of my door asking for something to eat, and we were doing our best to help every one of them." But no matter how many she helped, the refugees kept coming.

One day, Magbula heard megaphones atop trucks that were circling Potočari. The Dutch troops were imploring residents to come to the UN compound. "I asked what was *really* going on," Magbula told me, "and they explained that it would be easier to protect us all there. They said it was for our own safety." People wanting to run away were told to report to the compound. From there, the troops said, they could leave.

The road running by her house was jammed with thousands of pan-icked refugees, carrying the few belongings they had been able to throw together. Serb soldiers who entered the town on 11 July were shouting, "*Hajde, hajde!*" (Let's go!). "Then the people began stopping by, asking for water," Magbula said. "Some asked for something to wear."

Despite the UN's insistence, Magbula stayed in her house: "Everyone kept asking me why—why I wasn't going. And I said, 'I just want to stay home.' I didn't have any reason to leave. I never harmed anyone."

Eventually, Magbula decided to go to the UN compound. But she stopped short at the fence, where a hole had been cut so the refugees could get in: "I really didn't want to go in, because I knew I wouldn't be able to get out." Instead, she went back to her house with her elderly mother-in-law. She picked some vegetables from her garden, which had sustained her through the war. The two women brought the food to people inside the compound, including her family members, who "kept telling us we weren't safe staying in our house. So, finally, we joined them."

Instead of a refuge, in the darkness of night the compound at Potočari became a scene from hell: random executions, rapes, wild rumors, and primal wailing. Wednesday morning, 12 July, Mladić came to the UN buildings for a carefully coordinated stunt, reassuring the refugees with water, bread, and words of calm.[26] "He told us that he wasn't going to harm anyone," Magbula remembered. "He said, 'You're all going to go wherever you want. Don't worry; you're all going to be able to leave.' He told us we couldn't take anything more than a few personal items. Not even a spoon or a blanket. So I took just a few clothes. And I brought my documents with me—I thought that was the most important thing—and some of the family gold." Soon, Magbula lost even that.

Serb buses pulled into the UN compound. Magbula continued:

> That's when they started separating men from women. And I kept telling them, "I want to go with my husband. Why don't you take me with him?" They kept reassuring me, "Don't worry. We only want to interview him." That was the last time I saw him.
>
> When they separated my husband and me, he was the one carrying our belongings, so everything went with him. As we were leaving, I asked the Serb soldiers, "Where are you taking us?" They kept saying, To a safe place. Don't worry."

One month later, David Rohde of the *Christian Science Monitor* became the first outsider to investigate the crime scene. He found a human femur surrounded by bits of tattered fabric jutting out from one of several rich brown mounds of earth. Rohde also found an abandoned building in which someone or something had apparently been dragged through piles of feces. Bullet holes pocked the walls, and dried bloodstains splattered the floor.[27]

The scene corroborated descriptions by several male escapees of being crammed shoulder to shoulder into rooms, unable to move or relieve themselves, and being rubbed in feces. They described men and boys becoming psychotic and others committing suicide rather than share the fate of those they saw being tortured.[28]

Meanwhile, in Tuzla, a steady stream of Serb buses spilled out tens of thousands of bodies—alive and dead—onto the airport tarmac. There the survivors of Srebrenica waited, their moans blending together in an eerie, low hum. Days passed, and accounts began to emerge: large groups of men and boys fleeing through the woods, only to be attacked with heavy artillery as well as automatic weapons; mass graves; and the bodies of loved ones left lying in the woods to be devoured by wild animals.

The UN set up tents and served food, but the women were single-minded. Desperate mothers and wives stared into the trees, waiting for familiar figures to appear. Few did.

One of the few escapees was an elderly Bosniak refugee, who said he'd been in a group of six hundred men corralled for execution. The men were trucked twenty at a time to a nearby field and machine-gunned. The old man was left for dead among the corpses but crawled out before the bodies were bulldozed into graves. Other than tales like these, the women knew nothing of the fate of their family members who had been left behind.

The frantic waiting evolved into a thick, enervating pall of depression. Many committed suicide. Death upon death. Eventually, faced with inescapable conclusions, some survivors began to give up hope; others would cling to it for years.

The gruesome killing spree of Srebrenica, unimaginable only three years earlier, turned out to be the turning point of the war.

36. OUTSIDE: The Accident

Following the massacre at Srebrenica, it took nerve for the negotiating team led by Assistant Secretary Richard Holbrooke to head to the Balkans. Since face-to-face communication among Balkan leaders was more likely to be explosive than productive, the US team was going to try shuttle diplomacy. From the start, the trip was exhausting. The team traveled between multiple cities in a single day. Transportation was often complicated and indirect. And leaders with whom they met were generally quarrelsome and uncooperative.

On 19 August, these challenges collided. The team needed to go to Sarajevo, the city they had visited least, but Milošević and the Bosnian Serbs surrounding the airport had refused to guarantee their safety if they flew in. Instead, Holbrooke and his traveling companions were forced to take a helicopter from Split to a field in the hills outside Sarajevo. From there they would wind down Mt. Igman in a Humvee and armored personnel carrier (APC), on what had become known as the most dangerous road in Europe. But that day, they were advised by the UN that the narrow, twisting, red-clay track seemed the safest way into the city, since all others passed through Bosnian Serb lines.

General Wesley Clark, director of strategic plans and policy for the Joint Chiefs of Staff and military advisor to the team, asked Holbrooke to discuss something with him in the armored Humvee. Following them would be the APC, carrying a security officer and several members of the team, including Joe Kruzel, an academic with a delightfully playful side, representing the Department of Defense; the endlessly energetic Bob Frasure, Holbrooke's deputy, whose witty cables were read throughout the State Department; and Nelson Drew, an Air Force colonel and devout Christian who had headed a White House crisis task force on Yugoslavia.

After a while, the group began the most dangerous part of the journey on the crude road. Even though French troops were rebuilding the wide path and patrolling it with tanks, this stretch high above the Sarajevo valley was exposed to Serb fire.

The APC was trying to keep up, but at some point Holbrooke and Clark realized there was a problem. They stopped the Humvee and ran back around the curve, where they found that their comrades' vehicle had rolled over the edge, crashing through the trees on the mountainside.

Hope of finding survivors was short-lived. In two explosions, live ammunition the APC had been carrying (against regulations) was set off. Frasure and Drew were killed at once, trapped in the burning APC. Kruzel survived the crash down the incline and was pulled from the vehicle moments before the explosions, but his head injuries were severe; he did not make it to the hospital.

Hearing of the accident, I called Chris Hill, director of the Office of South Central European Affairs at the State Department. "No more American diplomats are going to die on that goat path," he said with grief and anger. Then he added, with equal fervor, that he would pursue a peace settlement no matter what: "Not because the White House wants it, but because I want to tell Bob's girls and Katharina that he died for something."

On 23 August 1995, the chapel at Arlington Cemetery was packed. As the crowd waited, President Clinton was talking at length with the teenage daughters of the deceased. I thought of how many times I had seen him doting over his daughter, Chelsea. Perhaps this encounter was affecting him more intensely than most.

"Our sadness can help us remember those in Sarajevo," he said in the chapel. Indeed, that day President Clinton announced a newly reconstituted negotiating team, including Hill. Meanwhile, Thomas Lippman noted in the *Washington Post* that time for progress could quickly slip away: Britain and other nations with peacekeeping troops were threatening to pull out, and another cold winter without fuel was around the corner in a capital whose people had already burned stair railings, furniture, park trees, and even books for warmth.[29]

Secretary of State Christopher released a statement, saying he was "shocked and saddened by the tragic death" of Robert Frasure, the chief US negotiator and a twenty-one-year veteran of the Foreign Service.[30] In the following days, newspapers lauded Joseph Kruzel's Harvard graduate degrees, ran pictures of Nelson Drew's grief-stricken children, and showed Bob's daughters at Andrews Air Force Base, where a military cargo plane had delivered the flag-draped coffins. One girl, waiting for the subsequent ceremony to conclude, held hands with her mother. The other sat with her arms in her lap, her head bowed.

37. INSIDE: Boys Pretending

An armored van carried me to a modest building on a side street in the heart of Sarajevo. Budi Moj Prijatelj (be my friend) was a center that, as its informational material said, "helped children realize their dreams and cultivate the tradition of a tolerant and multicultural Sarajevo." That was a tall order, given all that these young ones had suffered, and during such a delicate developmental time in their lives.

I walked by the small playground and into the building. The shattered windows were held together with tape. As soon as I stepped into the hallway, a gaggle of children raced over. Chattering excitedly, they flocked around me, their much-anticipated guest.

After the initial confusion, I was escorted to a classroom on my left, where I sat down to watch a skit prepared by half a dozen boys. Their teacher told me that they would now dramatize one of the many fruitless peace talks among power brokers. How on earth, I wondered, could children know about such high-level politics? But clearly they understood that their young lives hung on those talks.

The budding actors came from all ethnic groups, but little did they care about that. The distinctions now so common to journalists and other outsiders were not even part of their vocabulary. (I heard of married couples who, until the war, weren't aware of each other's ethnic backgrounds.)

All the children were receiving counseling and special attention. After the inhumanity they had witnessed, several were uncontrollable. Others were withdrawn. Some were orphaned, some disabled. Most had trouble concentrating. Many were disoriented, now living in an unfamiliar city. But that hour the boys were focused on a map of Bosnia spread across a table. Suddenly, they had become the leaders of France, the United States, Russia, Germany, and Japan. A prepubescent Jacques Chirac, Bill Clinton, Boris Yeltsin, Klaus Kinkel, and Yasushi Akashi pored over boundaries, arguing about how to divide up the Yugoslav territory.

The young political leaders pounded their fists, their voices increasingly strident and strong. Back and forth they yelled. Finally, as if begrudging their agreement, they violently shook hands.

A litany of individual proclamations ensued as, one after another, they grabbed the mike. Faces twisted in dark grimaces, they seemed oblivious to their audience, caught up in their anger. Shouts, distorted and shrill, pierced our ears.

I looked at my interpreter, who had grown quiet. "What are they saying?" I whispered.

"Those aren't words," she shrugged. "They're just making noises."

38. OUTSIDE: Bombs and Bluffs

The summer of 1995 brought a new military scene. The accident on Mt. Igman had set the stage for action by American officials. As well, it was increasingly evident to the international community that the status quo was not only ineffective, it was deadly: to UN troops, to Bosnian civilians, and to the reputation of multinational bodies committed to peace and security.

Three years of deployment in the Balkans had produced 167 fatalities and close to twelve hundred were wounded in UNPROFOR, the UN Protection Force.[31] That and CNN coverage of peacekeepers handcuffed to NATO targets, such as radar sites and bridges, had forced the UN to acknowledge that it could not protect its own troops with air coverage alone. In June, the UN agreed to a Rapid Reaction Force to give credibility to a badly damaged UNPROFOR mission. The force consisted of ten thousand heavily armed troops, mostly British and French, who entered Bosnia with helicopter gunships, armored vehicles, and field artillery. The United States contributed artillery-locating communication devices, navigation systems using global positioning satellites, night-vision gear, helicopters, and intelligence-gathering equipment.[32]

Of course, US support for military options throughout the war had been little and late. And even when Americans had participated, their formidable resources did not translate into impressive action. I had noted this discrepancy when flying over the Adriatic on a plane used to reequip the US warship *Dwight D. Eisenhower*. Complete with a hospital, hotel, and, obviously, airport, the aircraft carrier was a floating city. Its planes and equipment and the five thousand sailors on board were part of Operation Deny Flight, the NATO enforcement of the no-fly zone over Bosnia. Some credited this operation with containment of the war. But the planes circling over the genocide month after month were failing to take out the aggressors' heavy weapons.

At least now the gravity of the war, brought to the fore by Srebrenica, was sinking into the consciousness of the Western world. Admiral Leighton "Snuffy" Smith Jr., commander in chief of NATO's Allied Forces in Southern Europe, observed that "the fall of Srebrenica . . . for the Serbs, was a tactical victory, but a strategic defeat." Indeed, ten days after the massacre, British Prime Minister John Major announced: "We've reached a turning point. . . . We cannot afford different noises from different capitals."[33] He went on to indicate British support for the US-proposed air strikes, saying that the Bosnian Serbs should be made to "pay a very high price" if they attacked another safe haven.

On 28 August, General Rupert Smith pulled UN forces out of the remaining eastern enclaves. NATO air action was now possible without fear of UN troop casualties from Serb counterattack or friendly fire.

Meanwhile, Croatian President Tuđman had launched a stunningly successful four-day blitzkrieg, taking back the Krajina region of Croatia and reversing the ethnic cleansing perpetrated by Serb forces four years earlier. Tuđman's hands were not unsullied. Some two hundred thousand Croatian Serbs were forced from or fled their homes; many who remained were killed or tortured.

At the same time, Federation troops (the Bosniak and Croat armies) began a similar northward push in Bosnia. Hundreds of thousands of Serb refugees from both offensives streamed into the Serb stronghold of Banja Luka, in northwest Bosnia.

Serb forces in the west were whipped. With desertion rates high and climbing, and morale crushed, they had little capacity to stand and fight.

At this point, Federation troops could have chased the Serb military completely out of the northern part of Bosnia and reunified the country. But such a rout would have produced more Serb refugees. And that tidal wave of humanity into an already strained Serbia would have revealed Milošević's weakness to his countrymen and possibly spelled the end of his by-then brittle regime. US officials were anxious to preserve Milošević as a negotiating partner. (Unlike him, Karadžić and Mladić had been indicted for war crimes on 24 July. They would have been arrested at the border.) The negotiation team was pragmatic: better the devil they knew.

Moreover, the international community had agreed to an earlier Contact Group plan that meant yielding any further gains back to the Serbs. If the Federation was successful in driving out the Serbs, the plan would have demanded that Izetbegović turn over to them much of what his troops had just reclaimed.

Thus, astonishingly, Americans intervened to halt a full Federation victory. Assistant Secretary Holbrooke demanded that the Federation troops halt before Banja Luka. In fact, Izetbegović claimed that the United States threatened airstrikes on Bosnian troops if they marched on Banja Luka.

On 28 August, Serb shelling of a Sarajevo market killed thirty-seven more civilians. Given new resolve by Clinton and Major, that atrocity was the last straw. Two days later, NATO and the UN put behind them years of hesitation and humiliation by launching a "peace enforcement" campaign—with more military engagement than peacekeeping. Breaking the siege of Sarajevo was the centerpiece of the operation. But even if the city were opened, the NATO attacks would continue, Clinton and Major promised, until all parties agreed to come to the negotiating table.

Nearly three hundred NATO aircraft commenced Operation Deliberate Force, targeting Serb storage depots, armories, repair facilities, and command and control nodes. On 30 August, President Clinton fielded reporters' questions about US bombs hitting Serb targets in Bosnia. Instead of sitting at his Oval Office desk, he was interviewed as if in passing, standing in a parking lot in Jackson Hole, Wyoming, wearing a polo shirt. He appeared to be downplaying the seriousness of the US action.

Perhaps that lower key was intentional, given Moscow's objections. Foreign Service colleagues had often reminded me that Bosnia was a B-level crisis compared to the A-level importance of relations with Russia. It seemed to me, however, that robust support for what was right in a lower priority situation would send a clear message of strength to our challengers at any level.

The most vigorous NATO attack was against the city of Banja Luka on 11 September. In addition, the United States launched thirteen Tomahawk cruise missiles at key Serbian military targets. By now, Serb command headquarters and all major defense posts had been destroyed.

Immediately afterward, Russian Ambassador Vitaly Churkin met with NATO representatives in Brussels to emphatically condemn the UN-NATO action. He was not alone in his concern about America's relationship with Russia. In an absurd concession, State Department press guidance on 12 September read: "We share the Russian opinion that there is no military solution." Nonetheless, a mere two days later, the siege of Sarajevo was over. The air operation was proving a success.

I wrote President Clinton, insisting that letting up on the bombing would be, paradoxically, our most violent option. He wrote back on 14 September: "We must press forward with the work of Bob Frasure, Joe Kruzel and Nelson Drew, who gave their lives trying to find a solution to the terrible conflict in the Balkans."

39. INSIDE: Side by Side

With so much focus on extraordinarily bad individuals, some people were, thankfully, also focusing on the extraordinarily good. Svetlana Broz, granddaughter of Josip Broz (Marshal Tito), maintained such a perspective. An author and cardiologist, Broz was thirty-seven when she volunteered her services in Bosnia at the outset of the war. In 2000, Broz moved permanently to Sarajevo—a city that, she said, had "kept its soul intact" even during years of siege. Intent on helping to preserve the country her grandfather once led, Broz became a Bosnian citizen in 2004.

The doctor conceived and now heads the Sarajevo branch of Gardens of the Righteous Worldwide, encouraging the creation of parks, woods, and gardens to honor and memorialize those who resisted evil and saved the threatened.

During the war, as Dr. Broz treated the wounded and ill across Bosnia, she noticed people's need to disclose their stories. She began to collect accounts in earnest, traveling many miles to record the memories of people from all parts of society. What she found were tales of honor and courage amid criminal bestiality. But before Broz was able to publish the book she'd titled *Good People in an Evil Time*, her home in Belgrade was robbed and her manuscript stolen. Undeterred, Broz set out to recompile her material, preserving for history representatives of the good people who defied the suffering and division.

One such individual was Ilija Jurisic, a Bosnian Croat in Tuzla, who told stories of want and generosity:

I'd known Hasib, a Muslim man from Brcko, since 1997. We were inseparable. Both of us were retired school principals, but when the war began, we volunteered to defend Tuzla.

Being in the army didn't mean we had food. Days went by when all we could do was complain and comfort each other. There just wasn't enough to go around. Tuzla was in a desperate state of siege, with terrible starvation. Elderly people rummaged though garbage cans at dawn, looking for remnants. The joy in their eyes when they found a morsel was sad.

One day, a reserve officer named Jusuf appeared at our door, from the village of Koraj. "Do you have anything to eat?" he inquired. We were delighted anyone even bothered to ask.

"Oh, we get a little here or there," we said softly, embarrassed.

"Do you have any corn?"

"No, that's an abstraction," I answered, off the cuff.

"Would you like me to see if I can find some in the countryside?"

"That's really too much to ask. But if you did come up with a pound or two, we'd be very grateful," I said.

He didn't answer but left soon. A few days later, someone brought us a message, "A package has come for you and Hasib." We were astonished. With the city under siege and no one able to get out, where could this have come from? "What kind of package?" Hasib asked.

The times were so crazy. "You think it's explosives, don't you?" I said to him.

We picked up the package. It was a sack, tied with a note: "I'm sending my friends corn so they can distribute it to others. Jusuf."

There were about sixty-six pounds of kernels. A treasure! We were confused, feeling like we were taking something that wasn't ours yet grateful that our new friend had remembered us. There was no electricity in the city, so you could grind corn only at a mill. Since there was no gasoline, we hauled our fortune by foot the eight miles to Bozo's mill, dragging it on a sled across the snow.

While the millstones ground the kernels into flour, we figured how much would be left once the miller took his part. In the middle of our calculations, Bozo interrupted us. "There, it's done. I won't take my part. I can tell that you good people are in a difficult situation. It was an honor to help you out. Well, time for lunch."

I leapt up and kissed him. It was incredible. That man had given up almost seven pounds of flour and left it to us. And what's more, he invited us, who'd been starving, to lunch—two men he'd never met before.

We hurried back to town, thinking how we would surprise our families, and being careful not to let the sled tip over. In front of the sports center we ran into Alma, the wife of a colleague. Her daughter had been on a sled that was hit by a car. She was lying at home in a cast, with a fractured hip. When she heard about our day, Alma burst into tears. "I'm on my way to see my brother. I don't have anything to bring him, because I have nothing myself. And I'm so worried about him. He has no food, no firewood. . . ."

As she was speaking, we remembered the time her son had hidden a piece of bread under his pillow because he was afraid his sister would eat it while he was at school. "Alma, take half this flour," said Hasib.

Stories like this are endless. Still, later I was interviewed by an international team about whether it's possible for different ethnic groups to live side by side in Tuzla. "If we can share our food when we're starving, why do you think we can't live next to each other?" I responded.[34]

40. OUTSIDE: Decisions at Dayton

Wright Patterson Air Force Base in Dayton, Ohio, 1 November 1995. After twenty-two days of NATO air campaign bombing and three years of war, the parties of the Balkan conflict gathered to negotiate a settlement. Making clear their direct involvement in the conflict, Croatia's President Tuđman and Serbia's President Milošević went head to head with Bosnia's President Izetbegović.

The setting was ideal: a heartland city; an impressive collection of American armaments; eight thousand acres of military base; no-frills visiting officers' quarters clustered around a rectangular parking lot; and all of it far from the probing eyes of the press. The process was initiated by President Clinton, guided by Secretary of State Christopher, and carried out by Assistant Secretary Holbrooke.

Part of Holbrooke's strength was his willingness to go beyond sound bite explanations for the war. He was not afraid to label something raw greed. Nor was he blind to blatant politicizing. In his account of the negotiation, he describes "the stupidity of the war." As an example, the three interpreters' booths—Channel 4 "Bosnian," Channel 5 "Croatian," and Channel 6 "Serbian"—all broadcast the same interpreter.[35]

Through Dayton's back corridors of power, Holbrooke navigated the flow of laborious discussions and unashamed posturing. Generals briefed presidents. Foreign ministers vied for the limelight. Perpetrators and survivors alike pored over maps, dazzled by three-dimensional, digitized imagery, courtesy of US intelligence agencies.

Holbrooke, who later reflected on his "Big Bang approach to negotiations,"[36] used his considerable prowess and persuasion to force a deal. But some at Dayton were dismayed as they watched the process unfold. According to their reports, Milošević was such a practiced bluffer that sometimes even Holbrooke was bested. The Serb's diplomatic gaming led to a losing hand for Bosnians for the next decade and beyond—and left Milošević himself temporarily unbruised.

After twenty days of intense talks, the delegates initialed a peace agreement. President Clinton flew out for the ceremony, where an array of colorful flags of the participating countries were displayed behind a long table draped in blood red.

The agreement brought enormous relief as, finally, the shooting would stop. But many who had day-to-day contact with the warring parties considered the result deeply flawed. For example, while there were clauses declaring the "right to liberty of movement and residence" and promising the "prosecution of war crimes," the toothless Dayton agreement established no clear mechanism of enforcement for either.

More specifically, critics noted two striking casualties: a multiethnic society and a unified Bosnian state. The new government would enshrine the three ethnic categories trumpeted by warmongers. Over the dogged objection of Bosnian Prime Minister Haris Silajdžić, the final agreement mandated multiple legislative divisions and a weak troika of presidents. The structure, further burdened by veto-wielding bureaucratic layers, guaranteed political paralysis.

Bosnian ministries and embassies were to be headed only by individuals who identified themselves as Serb, Croat, or Bosniak. This deplorable formula forced those with mixed parentage to declare themselves as members of one group or another, and it froze out smaller minorities, such as Jews. Progressive individuals unwilling to identify themselves by ethnicity were also locked out of the political process. Such a structure played into the hands of ultranationalists, who used their newfound political legitimacy to obstruct the rebuilding of a tolerant, integrated society.

Inside the borders of Bosnia, vestiges of the three separate militaries were allowed to linger for years. And most shamefully, the United States abetted the Serbs in achieving a major war aim: dividing Bosnia. Perpetrators of torture, expulsion, and murder were rewarded with their own political entity on Bosnian soil, brashly declared the Serb Republic (Republika Srpska). Dayton's designers insisted verbally that the area would be ethnically mixed. A Bosniak or Croat survivor who had been forced out of his or her home was legally allowed to return, but into a community now called Serb and controlled by nationalists.[37]

But such were the spoils of genocide. The thief, caught, was punished by having half of what he had plundered taken away.

Collecting initials from Tuđman, Milošević, and Izetbegović was hailed as a diplomatic triumph. However, the United States of America was now in the position of creating an agreement that rewarded villains and set up the subsequent war in Kosovo. Thus, the harsh reality was that although his military operation on the ground had failed, at Dayton Milošević prevailed.

II.
Peace

SECTION 6 After Dayton

41. INSIDE: Morning Has Broken

Two weeks after the General Framework Agreement for Peace in Bosnia and Herzegovina was formally signed in Paris, I wandered into a spacious ballet studio at the National Theater in Sarajevo. My footsteps were the only sound, but my imagination populated the room with lithe dancers, some pirouetting, others with legs stretched up on the barre.

From the corner of my eye I noticed bullet holes peppering the large plate-glass window. I wondered who in the class would never dance again. The studio, so familiar to these young pupils, so much a part of their routine as they filed in for their exercises, had become a place of danger.

Wars are hardest on the young. They lack the experience to give trauma a greater context and the ego strength to process what has happened to them. Though the peace treaty had been signed, declarations on paper could not return these little survivors to where they started. The dislocations were not just geographic but emotional as well.

For guardians, it's especially difficult to reach those who've closed themselves off after seeing mothers gang raped, fathers beaten, playmates shot. Bosnian parents (and caregivers, for orphans) searched for ways to restore their charges' trust and internal stability. But after such a maelstrom, words were not enough. They often turned to movement, music, and theater—even as they had during the war.

An international proverb asserts that "when cannons roar, the muses are silent." But despite snipers and shelling, in Bosnia the arts survived—some even said "thrived"—as citizens sought out unheated theaters and dimly lit galleries for an hour or two of civility. Such brave

I was sustained by spontaneous outpourings of love and life, especially as I was leaving my own children in Vienna for the work in Bosnia.

excursions were an excuse to wear tuxedos and furs, and to pretend that life was normal. Although theatergoers were not certain they could make it home again, the chance to partake of art was too important to ignore. As a professor at the University of Sarajevo's Academy of Fine Arts noted triumphantly, "in Sarajevo, the muses were not silent."[1]

I wondered if that muse took on healing as well, because reliance on the arts continued after the signing of the peace. Granted, sometimes the tone was ironic. At an elementary school, I saw a grand piano—case smashed, strings tangled—with a placard saying only "Civilization 1993." But on a more hopeful note, US Embassy personnel took me to a therapeutic project for children. As guest of honor, I had a front-row seat. Actually, there was only one row for our audience of three. This show was really about the performers.

Suddenly, a dozen girls pranced into the room. With hands on hips, they swayed and danced to raucous music, while one young superstar held a play microphone and cut loose as the lead singer. All were dressed in black and adorned with dramatic makeup, feathers, and glitter. The choreography allowed no wallflowers. When the girls finished, we applauded and whistled our approval.

After such a treat, I wanted to give something back. Looking around for an instrument, I saw a small battery-run keyboard. Putting aside my ambassadorial mantle, I sat on the floor and held the keyboard on my lap.

The children eagerly gathered around me as I sang, "Morning has broken, like the first morning . . ." Their foreheads relaxed, and smiles slowly spread across their faces. One sweetheart asked if she could kiss me. I nodded yes and held out my arms. The young divas surrounded me, smothering me with affection.

42. OUTSIDE: Waiting for Christmas

Back in Vienna, we faced a constant press of problems. They converged every Tuesday morning, as some twenty representatives from US federal agencies and our principal State Department officers gathered at the embassy for a "country team meeting." I encouraged the participants to discuss something from their week, even if it seemed not directly relevant to others. In an hour of reporting around the table, we put together a mosaic of US interests, often extending beyond Austria, since many of the attendees had responsibilities throughout the region.

Jean Christiansen, our immigration and naturalization officer, was a mature professional who had worked with dramatically diverse groups. She always responded to cruelty, whether perpetrated by Bosniaks, Croats, or Serbs. So I weighed her words carefully one Tuesday as she described a recent trip. She had interviewed Serb men kept for three years in a concrete silo without a roof, in bestial conditions. One described how, when his friend's head was smashed against the wall, the brains splattered all over him. "There are atrocities on all sides," concluded Jean.

Helena Finn, our public affairs officer, jumped in. She had served in two Muslim settings—Pakistan and Turkey—and she noted: "Our reports are that 90 percent of war crimes are committed by Serbs against Muslims."[2] Of course, that fact and Jean's statement were not mutually exclusive, but the political analysis was heating up.

Another officer, Mike, added more fuel, defending Jean. Mike was proud of his Greek Orthodox heritage, so, just like the Russians, he felt the Serbs were his cultural cousins. He wanted to be sure they were not slandered.

The officers, it seemed to me, were arguing political positions informed by their backgrounds. But finding people whose views were not colored by personal experience was difficult. Indeed, my eight years of theological studies and work on race relations in the US South were bedrock to my own outlook. If we four were facing difficulties in such a circumscribed situation, it was easy to see why the international community was paralyzed not only by uneven competence but also by conflicting points of view.

At another team meeting, on 19 December 1995, we were passing around Christmas cookies as Jean took her turn reporting. She had just returned from a nightmarish task—interviewing inmates in a Serb-run concentration camp that was to be dismantled, according to provisions in the Dayton Accords.

The eight hundred men from eastern Bosnia in the camp were crawling with lice, Jean told us. Frigid water had been poured on their naked bodies outside for cruel "showers." "Those are the lucky ones," she said. Thousands of others had simply been shot and pushed into mass graves. Of those "lucky ones," she found forty-two who had been set aside for "special handling"—torture, beating, and starvation.

Jean explained that she had been charged with arranging for the immigration of 120 of the men to the United States. They would not be moved until late January, however, because of paperwork. This was Christmas, she explained, and no one would be in to process applications.

Not one of the people around our table registered a reaction. To be fair, her news came amid a string of reports on upcoming press events, elections results, and a dispute over food product labeling. But as I sat listening, I realized that this conversation could just as well have occurred fifty years earlier. In that moment, I glimpsed the psychology—the denial, really—of American diplomats who for years refused to act despite clear evidence of Nazi atrocities. Did they, too, hear repeated reports in their country team meetings?

Jean continued. Forty men were crammed into rooms only ten feet by ten feet. A plastic sack for the belongings of each man hung on a nail. There was no furniture. The men slept on the floor. As she interviewed them individually at a table set up in the room, the others waited outside, barefoot in the winter cold.

The meeting ended, and I asked Jean to come to my office. We telephoned authorities in Washington, insisting that they speed up the men's paperwork. A week later, Jean was away when I received a call from the government agency handling the account, to which my name was now attached. Could I guarantee that all arrangements were in place for the refugees once they left the camps? "Absolutely," I shot back, having no idea what arrangements the official was asking about. The prisoners, I was assured, would be transported immediately.

Even so, some months later, Jean Christiansen reported in another country team meeting that one of the Serb-run camps was again full. Several nations that had pledged to take the former prisoners in as refugees had reneged. The men had been crowded into the worst camp, where they still waited.

43. INSIDE: Serb Exodus

For seventeen long months, US Ambassador John Menzies spent his nights in a sleeping bag on an army cot next to his desk. Accepting the assignment to Bosnia, he was risking his life for a thankless job. He and his few colleagues, a tight team, did the day-to-day work on the ground, while others flew in, detractors said, for photo ops.

Menzies was a hero to me. He'd come to Bosnia through Vienna, where my admiration had taken root. Reflecting my own impressions, Bosnian politicians described him to me as unusually honest and stable. He followed his own moral compass, even when that meant conflict with his superiors in Washington.

The ambassador had invited me to Bosnia several times. When I asked what I could bring, his answer was "space heaters." I put two in my bag. Always a gracious host, my friend accommodated me with an army cot and sleeping bag.

The ambassador also provided an escort and armored Humvee. As we drove through town, my gut tightened when we passed an old warning on a wall, with paint dripping from the large hand-painted letters: "Danger: Snipers." On that stretch of street, more than five hundred pedestrians had been picked off by marksmen in the surrounding hills. Of course, they were just a fraction of more than ten thousand Sarajevans who had been killed.

We continued our drive to the suburb of Dobrinja. Stretching in front of me were long, hand-dug ditches. My driver that morning was from the neighborhood, so I asked him about the trenches. "For soldiers?"

"No," he said in halting English, "for citizens." Through these shadow highways, residents of gutted and burned apartments had run back and forth, bent at the waist and lugging whatever they could to a safer place in the city.

Alongside the trenches was a sad procession of cars, trucks—anything with wheels to carry the mass of Serbs fleeing the capital. The road was clogged as far as I could see. Day after day, panicked families had piled onto trucks everything not bolted down: furniture, bedding, appliances, plumbing fixtures, even the bones of their ancestors.

"Where are you going?" I called out to a driver, through my interpreter.

"I don't know," the man responded.

Despite provisions in the peace agreement, Serbs in the Bosniak-Croat

There was nothing to be gained by using snipers except terrorizing the population of Sarajevo into surrender. It had been centuries since the world had witnessed a city under siege for so long.

Three parallel lines: traffic carrying the fleeing Bosnian Serbs; a trench for Dobrinja residents to run through, bent low, on their way into the city for supplies; and destroyed apartment buildings, targets of men with too many tanks and too little conscience.

Federation were being pressured to flee their homes. Many feared retribution from their returning neighbors. But some who wanted to stay were being told that once Sarajevo was handed over to Federation control, they would be massacred by "Mujahideen." Others heard that any Serb who stayed would be considered a traitor by other Serbs.

Who was spreading that word? Not the Bosniaks or Croats. The warnings were on Serb radio broadcasts from Pale, headquarters of the hardliners. When verbal threats were not enough, Serb thugs beat up those who stayed behind.

Adding to Serb concerns, the Bosniaks who had moved in to secure the area raised the flag of the SDA, the conservative political party that identified itself as Muslim. Claiming Sarajevo as Bosniak territory was a clear abrogation of the Bosniak-Croat Federation agreement. Then, in an injudicious gesture of support, Admiral "Snuffy" Smith, newly arrived from NATO's Southern Command, tried to placate Serb hard-liners by offering to facilitate the evacuation. The admiral failed to understand that their migration would take years to undo, since the homes of fleeing Serbs would be filled immediately by Bosniak and Croat refugees unable to return to their own homes in Serb-held parts of the country. By allowing this shift of population, Smith was purchasing short-term gain at the expense of long-term stability.

Thus, what should have been a period of reintegration was instead marked by ongoing displacement. For months thereafter, ethnic cleansing continued across Bosnia, with tens of thousands of people driven from their lifelong homes.

44. OUTSIDE: Refugees in Austria

I was in an unusual position, viewing refugee policy from both an American and an Austrian perspective. During World War II, Nazi practices embraced by Austria had forced hundreds of thousands from their homes, most of them to their deaths. But since then, that country of only eight million had sheltered more than two million refugees fleeing Communist regimes, with one third settling there permanently.[3] The refugees included 180,000 Hungarians, 160,000 Czechoslovaks, and 33,000 Poles. With the war, some 90,000 Bosnians entered Austria legally, and more came illegally. Almost all would end up staying. In fact, on a per capita basis, Austria accepted more than twice the number of refugees than any other country in Europe. And that ratio was much greater when compared to the United States.

Austria's extraordinary record of hospitality was politically significant. The country was laboring to come to terms with its complicity in genocide against the Jews a generation earlier. In 1993, Chancellor Franz Vranitzky had said at Hebrew University in Jerusalem: "Just as we claim credit for our good deeds we must beg forgiveness for the evil ones, the forgiveness of those who survived and the forgiveness of the descendants of those who perished."[4]

On the other hand, a furor was raging in Austria over the emergence of a political figure accused of "brown" sympathies. Jörg Haider, governor of Carinthia Province, was the son of a Nazi, itself no cause for condemnation. But the anti-immigrant verbiage of his Freedom Party was creating great embarrassment for other Austrian politicians, who cringed at international warnings of a fascist resurgence. They were also determined to do the right thing for a targeted ethnic group—this time through their policies on refugees from the former Yugoslavia.

The policies themselves were not without controversy. Unemployment in most of Europe was soaring, and workplace competition was not looked upon kindly in socialist Austria, despite that country's relatively high employment rate. To protect jobs for *echte Österreicherei* (true Austrians), federal labor policies forbade refugees from working. Thus, Bosnian refugees waited, year after year, unassimilated and longing to return home.

At the US embassy, we occasionally convened Austrian and American government officials to wrestle with the problems of immigration and social absorption. But new ideas regarding repatriation appeared infrequently within our policy community. In one conversation, I suggested the Austrians reallocate transitional housing funds. Some of the recipients were at a camp that had been a way station for waves of refugees in years past. Most were placed in inns scattered across the country. Instead, I asked, why not fund their return to Bosnia and the rebuilding of their bombed-out houses? Other officials quashed the proposal, saying the returnees would be resented for having fled the crisis and then come back with relative wealth. I agreed but wondered if we were not letting the perfect become the enemy of the good.

People with various agendas approached me with proposed solutions to the refugees' employment problem. One Arizona entrepreneur needed laborers for his plantation. Could I help get the Bosnians visas? Knowing how Mexican labor was exploited, I refused to send those I had visited in refugee camps to work in the fields of a new country, where they would not understand the language or their rights.

We needed help finding answers; yet to my knowledge, nobody was convening the refugees for their advice on the policies that would govern their future. My grass-roots connection to the refugee community was Christine von Kohl, a former journalist in the Balkans. Christine founded the Bosnian Cultural Center in Vienna to connect refugees to their new society and to each other. She was a wellspring of ideas, particularly when compared to the stagnant thinking of some officials.

Christine visited my office frequently, always with another request. Would I tell Washington about ethnic Albanian journalists being roughed up by Serb security forces in Kosovo? Could I help find space for her center? Did I have access to cars for Austrian university students to track down resettled refugees, abandoned by authorities after they arrived? One student, Christine told me, discovered a woman who had been living a few miles from her brother for more than a year without knowing it.

Repatriation of Bosnians would remain a sticking point, as host countries designed then rejected one solution after another. Germany insisted on returning Yugoslavs to home communities still controlled by indicted war criminals. Austria refused to follow suit and continued to provide free education, healthcare, and financial support for years. Still, refugees in Austria were unable to work, yet unable to return home.

45. INSIDE: Refugees at the Residence

The home of the US ambassador in Vienna had long been associated with elite settings of war and peace. During World War II, Nazis occupied the estate, formerly owned by a Jewish coal mogul. In June 1961, the eyes of the world were trained on the mansion as President John Kennedy met with Soviet Premier Nikita Khrushchev there for nuclear nonproliferation talks.

More than three decades later, the residence was an unlikely retreat for Bosnians on the run. The hundreds of displaced people who crossed our marble threshold were mostly women and children. Given the grandeur of the estate and the indignity of their situation, the effort to reconcile our lives and theirs would have been morally paralyzing, so I didn't try. Instead, I played show tunes on the piano as Nancy Gustafson, a favorite American star at the Vienna State Opera, sang to the kids sitting cross-legged on our elegant French carpets. As Gustafson ended her medley of Broadway musical numbers with a plaintive Bosnian folk song, tears spilled down the mothers' cheeks.

Another time, when forty Bosnian children came over, I discovered that I had more in common with the other mothers in our backyard than anyone might have imagined. Beside me was my thirteen-year-old daughter, suffering from an acute, life-threatening illness. Every moment, my attention was divided between the needs of my traumatized guests and concern for her.

One teenage boy had brought a guitar. A couple of hours into the afternoon, I pulled mine out and sat next to him. We all belted out Peter, Paul, and Mary tunes that had, to my surprise, made their way into Bosnian pop culture: "How many times must the cannonballs fly, before they're forever banned?" Our harmony lifted to the line: "And how many times can a man turn his head, pretending he just doesn't see?"

On the other side of the lawn, a group of rambunctious boys couldn't resist the pool. Chaperones tried in vain to keep them from throwing each other in. No one knew who could swim, since the kids had spent their summers in refugee camps rather than vacationing on the Adriatic coast. I found inflatable rafts and plastic water wings for those who might need them and a pile of my T-shirts for the girls, so they could take off their dresses and join the boys in the water.

Later, we all posed for a group portrait. My children blended in with the Bosnians. Then out came the soccer balls. Whooping and hollering, the boys ran across the wide lawn, arms flailing for balance. The girls sprawled on the sloping hill leading up to the rose arbor. Cokes emerged from the cooler. Hamburgers were served up sizzling from the grill. There was plenty of ice cream to go around—twice. In the middle of the revelry, one child asked my eight-year-old if our TV worked. Another asked him if we had running water.

The kids could have been from any Austrian or American school, stopping their play just long enough to pose. Our Lillian, with Teddy in her lap, was a gracious host.

46. OUTSIDE: Diplobabble

The State Department sent press guidance downstream to US ambassadors, so we would "be on message." I imagined that the drafting of these
unclassified memos fell to some good-hearted public servant who had
been drawn to the lofty mission of foreign policy. No doubt he thought
he would be at the cutting edge of policy, crafting perceptive, minute-
by-minute accounts of a brewing conflict or nuclear threat. Instead, he
found himself in a bare, unadorned room, spinning fumbling policies
into seemingly credible talking points.

Designed for military commanders, diplomats, or White House officials, the format of the memos was sticky questions we might face, accompanied by snappy answers we were to deliver:

> Q: What is our reaction to the UN report that the Bosnian Serbs destroyed
> homes of refugees who intended to return?
>
> A: We have seen reports about the UN allegations but cannot confirm them.
>
> The embassy protested these bombings to the Bosnian Serb officials when
> they occurred.
>
> IFOR [NATO's implementation force] has increased patrols in the areas as a
> result of the bombings.
>
> Since then there have been no further reports of such destruction.
>
> Signed: Christopher, Unclas[sified]

In short, Secretary of State Warren Christopher was mobilizing diplomats and troops in response to bombings he could not confirm. Perhaps
the reason he was speaking out of both sides of his mouth was because
the department had conflicting goals: keeping a distance and showing
how Johnny-on-the-spot we were. So much for internal consistency.

Meanwhile, buried in the UN reports were calculations of ruined
homes, accounts that reduced whole families to flat, colorless statistics. Brčko: 35,017. Gračanica: 10,558. Gradačac: 17,669. Kalesija: 17,856.
Lukavac: 10,529. Sapna: 8,332. Tuzla: 52,061. Živinice: 16,775.

Numbers, for all their helpfulness, could numb.

47. INSIDE: Displaced

By the war's end, an enormous number of Bosnians had fled or been
driven from their communities. At our embassy, I was privy to aerial
intelligence images documenting the process in wretched detail—hundreds of villagers streaming down a snow-covered road, fleeing friends
who had become foes. The rumble of detonation was the last memory of

their homes. Often, as a coup de grâce, the last blast was the mosque or Catholic church, their spiritual home.

With international forces providing inadequate security, tens of thousands of citizens were displaced in the first six months after Dayton. Modest-sized towns sheltered a flood of new refugees, mostly Bosniak.

Bosnian Serbs had also lost their homes. As the invigorated Federation army clawed its way back across the country, Serb refugees fled to the shrinking territory of Republika Srpska. Some went further, over the Drina River into Serbia itself, where they found that they were not part of the "Serb brotherhood" after all. Resented and unwelcome, they were now competitors in a crushed economy, among those they had been told were "their own."

Wanting to see firsthand how refugees of all sides were actually living, I went to homes for the mentally disabled, damaged apartments, and refugee centers. The attention of an ambassador meant a lot to the people I talked to, although I always feared I was raising expectations I could not meet.

In Sarajevo, I visited a former hotel. Every possible space was filled with refugees. Newcomers were turned away. A wall that weeks earlier had a hole left by a mortar shell was now smoothed over, but the windows, like most in Sarajevo, were still covered with plastic. In the halls, children were playing among small mounds of bright red pellets. "Rat poison" was the casual explanation.

Our guide led me to the cold, unlit basement, to show with pride where five showers had been installed. I congratulated her, then noted that we couldn't actually appreciate them because a chest-high pile of wood was in the way. "It's winter," she said, flustered. "People mostly shower in the summer."

I asked to see a room. We knocked, and the door opened into a space twelve by fifteen feet, which for two years had housed a family of five. The building was allotted gas only every second day, so a small iron stove, piped out the window, could be converted from gas to wood. A tin plate with porridge was bubbling on top of the stove. Laundry hung above it.

Grandma invited me to come in and sit down. She was knitting brightly patterned socks with thick woolen yarn, to be sold for a black-market price of three dollars. The scarf on her head framed a wrinkled but warm face. I could accept the fact that her constant grin was toothless—she'd lived a long life. But her eighteen-year-old grandson, standing by the window, had only one of his six front teeth.

Their home had been in a village in eastern Bosnia. I listened to the story of their flight, a thirteen-day ordeal. Gunmen had stormed the farm town, shooting, raping, and beating unarmed citizens. For three

Every grandmother had a story. And most stories shared a pattern:
Surprise. Betrayal. Hiding. Terror. Torture. Death or flight.

days, Grandma had cowered in the dark, crowded basement of the mosque. Finally, she ran and made it safely to her apartment. With six family members and a neighbor, she hid there for weeks.

One day they heard pounding on the door. Thugs crashed through and dragged off her neighbor, whom they never saw again. Seeing their vulnerability, the family fled, trudging through the nights for two weeks until they reached the relative safety of Sarajevo.

Grandma knew they were lucky to have made it out alive. No talk from her of going home. Or of regaining her life savings. Or of ever living again with her possessions. She and her family at least had the chance to start over.

It was time to leave. I took one more look around as the old woman squeezed my hand to say thanks for my visit. My eyes fell on a picture calendar nailed to the grimy wall, opened to a tropical vacation spot. Perhaps that was her dream—the sunny beaches of Florida. If she could have just one wish, I asked, what would it be? She leaned over and whispered, "To live in two rooms."

48. OUTSIDE: Sowing and Reaping

Some of the impediments to reconstruction were physical—such as armaments and land mines. Others were attitudinal—such as resentment and revenge. I witnessed their destructive power many times, but particularly on two trips through the Bosnian countryside. Most of the population is rural. Thus, getting the farm system back into operation was an important goal during the early rebuilding.

When US troops entered northwest Bosnia following the signing of the Dayton Accords, the *International Herald Tribune* published a picture of a young man standing stork-like, watching their arrival. The assailant who took one of his legs probably did not have a grenade or machete. More likely, the weapon had been planted underground.

Avoiding land mines was a constant preoccupation of international soldiers. Beneath a big "Welcome" sign at Eagle Base, the US military headquarters in Bosnia, was a display of half a dozen models of the plastic or metal devices, with warnings and instructions for defusing them. "Some welcome," I thought, staring at the sign.

Walking into the building, I passed a map covered with hundreds of dots, like confetti. Each represented a field of land mines—six hundred thousand to a million mines—strategically placed to stop advancing armies as well as to terrorize civilians who wanted to return to their homes. The land mines were to have been removed by the Bosnian

A warning of mines for the international troops was as mundane as soap, as routine as mealtime.

troops. That had not happened.[5] And no one appeared to be pushing the commanders to comply.

Granted, there were also financial and technological obstacles to removing the mines. Funding was scarce, and those monies that did come in were sometimes stolen to support war criminals and their protection networks. Adding to the challenge, a new type of mine moved down rivers and thus off maps; locating them was nearly impossible.

The scourge left a broad mark. From a US Black Hawk helicopter, I surveyed the bucolic landscape. Between roofless farmhouses were fields, some dotted with haystacks but others untended. The reason was land mines, explained Colonel Bud Thrasher, strapped in next to me. Through the mike on his helmet, he shouted a story. Driving down a farm road a week earlier, he had come across a father clutching his twelve-year-old son, who had just stepped on a mine. The colonel rushed the boy to the hospital. He lived, but his foot had been blown off.

I thought of Colonel Thrasher as I rode in a military Humvee past rowdy children running, kicking balls, shouting. Which of them might be next? That concern was reinforced when I brought a donation of uniforms to a soccer club. The coach thanked me, then voiced his fear that one of his young players might blow himself up coming to practice.

Land mines made the war stretch on, long after the peace agreement was signed. But then there were the attitudinal challenges, too. As pernicious as a field of mines, the propaganda and intractability of political extremists also hindered postconflict reconstruction.

Dayton had divided Bosnia into two political entities, meant to function as one country. But in Republika Srpska, the ruling nationalists had coopted even the meaning of that new border. Their lies caught hold among fresh—and naive—international workers; unwitting outsiders often were part of a chain of misinformation and resentment. To wit, during a visit to a refugee camp outside Banja Luka, I met a recently arrived young American working for a highly respected NGO. "Welcome to Bosnia," I greeted him.

"This isn't Bosnia. You're in Republika Srpska," he corrected me.

"Well, Republika Srpska is part of Bosnia," I answered pleasantly, feeling a little bad for him, sorry that he was confused.

"No it isn't," he insisted.

"But it is," I countered. "That was the heart of the Dayton agreement. Bosnia remains one state, with two parts." The young man clearly did not believe me.

But there was more. Although he had been on the scene only five weeks, he seemed bitter: "The international community isn't being fair. All the aid is going to Bosnia. These people here in Republika Srpska need it more."

I said that the aid imbalance was due to Bosnian Serb leaders not allowing refugees to return to their homes in Serb territory. Freedom of movement and the right of return were guaranteed in the peace agreement, and compliance was one of the few conditions of economic aid.

"But aid shouldn't be tied to politics," the young man argued.

I understood that conditionality inevitably hurt innocents. But it also provided leverage, however imperfect, toward the fulfillment of justice. If not aid conditionality, I asked, what did he think we might use as an incentive for compliance on all sides?

He and I were not getting very far with that discussion, so I changed the subject and asked what sort of reconstruction he was working on. He said seeds had arrived for the spring planting, enough for seventy-five thousand farmers. They had been supplied by the Office of Foreign Disaster Relief in the US Agency for International Development (USAID).

Given the US-led NATO bombing of the Serb army, how were Bosnian Serb farmers responding to the American gift?

"Oh, they have no idea that the seeds are from the United States. And it wouldn't matter to them anyway," he said.

Surprised, I reminded him of the Marshall Plan, which rebuilt Germany and Austria after World War II. America pumped thirteen billion dollars into a massive recovery program—or about ninety billion in today's dollars. With that generosity, our country reaped what we sowed. "Hardly a week goes by without an Austrian coming up to me to say thanks," I finished.

The young American aid worker was not impressed.

49. INSIDE: Banja Luka Bitterness

US sympathy for all victims, however sincere, provided little help to Serb refugees. As I toured Banja Luka, I wondered how these civilians felt about America.

From the start of the war, many Serbs distrusted outsiders and resented world opinion. After all, even though they had signaled their protest by boycotting the referendum, the international community had recognized Bosnia's resulting independence. Later, the Serbs had watched as Croat and Bosniak military forces arbitrarily arrested or executed Serb civilians, mistreated prisoners in detention, and perpetrated reverse ethnic cleansing.

By the end of the war, Serb deaths numbered almost thirty-one thousand. Their people claimed this was nothing short of genocide. They cited radical Radio Hajat broadcasts that called for the execution of Serbs and the extremist Tuzla newspaper *Zmaj od Bosne* that urged that "each Muslim must name a Serb and take an oath to kill him." More gruesomely, they pointed to the atypical but incendiary Bosniak youth newspaper, *Novi Vox*, which printed a "patriotic song," promising:

> Dear mother, I'm going to plant willows,
> We'll hang Serbs from them.
> Dear mother, I'm going to sharpen knives,
> We'll soon fill the pits again.[6]

Serb belief that such vitriol was commonplace stemmed from a disinformation campaign. While mistreatment was real, the Serb-controlled media made wildly exaggerated claims, resulting in the perception of atrocities and hatreds much worse than actually existed. This brew— resentment of world opinion and fear of abuse at the hands of their compatriots—fortified the Serbs' resolve to kill before they were killed. Some of their worry was warranted. While the world watched, the Croatian army, supported by Federation forces, had come within thirteen miles of the de facto capital of Republika Srpska.

After Dayton, in a bold break with former President Radovan Karadžić, President Biljana Plavšić had officially made Banja Luka the political capital of Republika Srpska. Known as "the green town" because of its many parks, Banja Luka spread across a fertile plain that spanned the Vrbas River. Hunting and fishing were popular in the surrounding

A wife, supported by two sons, mourns her husband. Like others in the crucible of war, displaced Serbs lived under spirit-threatening pressure.

forests, and in this lush setting, the city had thrived, becoming the economic and cultural center of northwest Bosnia and the second largest city in the country.

But Banja Luka's role in the war was hardly idyllic. In 1992, it became the nerve center for nationalist activity on the western side of the Serb-controlled region, as well as a haven for Serb refugees. Galina Marjanovic was a former teacher of the deaf who, during the war, helped children look for their parents. When I met her as I toured the city, she told me how she had witnessed sickening hardships. One day, she left her house with bread to feed the hungriest refugees. As she approached a truck, a man told her, "Forget the bread! There's a woman here we need to bury. And take this new mother to the hospital." On the truck next to the dying grandmother, the granddaughter had delivered a baby. In war, death bled into birth.

Leaving Galina, I traveled outside the convalescing city to visit a school converted into a "collective center"—a strange euphemism for a refugee camp. In the schoolyard, laughing children chased a soccer ball. Women in scarves and aprons hung clothes on a line, with toddlers hiding in the folds of their long skirts.

Indoors, the former classrooms were lined with bunk beds, clothes draped on the frames. Small groups sat around despondently, with nothing to say that had not been endlessly said. A mother told me of fleeing her home and of the death of her husband at the hands of Croat soldiers.

A Serb refugee, stripped of her home, her profession, and her dignity. Even with arms crossed in defiance, this municipal judge seemed lost in a refugee center.

She wiped tears from her face as her two teenage sons held her, their arms around her waist. Several men gathered behind her as she spoke, muttering angry words I couldn't understand.

Across the room, a gaunt, dark-haired woman dressed in red sweat pants leaned against a bunk. Her grandmother, dressed in black, sat on the bed beside her. I asked the younger woman about her life before the war. She had been a municipal judge, she told me, her voice thick with hostility.

"Who are you angry with?" I asked, steeling myself.

"Our local officials have created this misery," she spat.

Overhearing our conversation, another woman added: "America is far away. Tuđman is far away. We don't care what they're doing because we can't change it. But our own Serb leaders—they should be doing something. They're the most responsible."

50. OUTSIDE: War Criminals

In the international community, debate raged over who was responsible for Bosnia's stability. This was true not only inside the Beltway, at The Hague, and at NATO, but also among military personnel on the ground. Among the latter, the most heated peace and security dispute was over the apprehension of indicted war criminals.

The Dayton Accords required that the warring parties surrender those accused of war crimes, allow refugees to return home, and ensure freedom of movement for all. Within several months of the peace agreement, the national Bosnian government turned over to The Hague two Bosniaks indicted for war crimes against Serbs.[1] With less cooperation, the government of Republika Srpska and Croat nationalists in the Federation government protected their accused, which left mass murderers, rapists, and other psychopaths in positions of formal and informal authority. A year after the agreement was signed, the US Department of State noted that indicted war criminals were serving as police in Republika Srpska.[2] For good reason, Bosnian refugees did not feel safe reentering some regions, rendering the promises of returning home and moving freely impossible to keep.

Although Serb President Radovan Karadžić had been charged with genocide and crimes against humanity (even before the massacre at Srebrenica), during an interview in a Sarajevo suburb, Karadžić's wife said her husband would never surrender.[3]

The question remained: What were we going to do about him and scores of other indicted war criminals?

NATO's mandate was to keep order, and having criminals on the loose was anything but orderly. But the organization's approach to this problem was significantly influenced by the selection of Admiral "Snuffy" Smith to head NATO's "implementation force." He was an unfortunate choice, I thought, judging from our meetings at his Naples headquarters a few weeks before Dayton was signed. There, brandishing dueling laser pointers, the admiral and ten of his generals had briefed me on possible intervention operations, known as "Provide Promise," "Quick Response Options," and "Extraction Plan." "Of course, if the famous people in Washington give me the word, I can send my planes in and tear up the ground and kill a whole slew of Bosnians," Smith had drawled—a tone I found surprisingly glib for someone charged with stabilizing a postgenocidal society.

My misgivings about the admiral were borne out in the hallway of the US embassy in Sarajevo, when I came upon a sobering conversation between Ambassador Menzies and Smith's political advisor, Steve Dawkins. I knew the ambassador was intent on removing indicted war criminals from the Bosnian mix. But the staffer conveyed an adamant hands-off policy: "Admiral Smith has made it clear. If he's in a café and General Mladić comes in the front door, he's [Smith's] out the back. It's not NATO's job to pick up war criminals."

Entering the conversation uninvited, I protested that the Dayton Accords promised international forces would ensure security. "No, our mandate is to 'detain,' not 'arrest,'" was Dawkins's explanation. It seemed we had fallen through Alice's looking glass, where words could change meaning at a whim.

Using the embassy's secure phone system, I called Secretary of Defense Bill Perry to tell him he had a problem: two high-level American officials, the ambassador and the troop commander, were interpreting the words of Dayton differently. Perry responded that he was gravely concerned and would take it up with Chairman of the Joint Chiefs Shalikashvili and NATO Supreme Allied Commander General Joulwan. To reinforce the message, I then called Bob Hunter, US ambassador to NATO, and Madeleine Albright, US ambassador to the UN. Both expressed dismay. They said they would attempt to mitigate the problem as it unfolded, although neither was in a position to solve it.

There were other verbal twists. The European Action Council for Peace in the Balkans reported that, in the town of Vitez, international soldiers spotted a man they believed was an accused war criminal. After verifying his identity at their base, they refused to return and arrest him. That would have been a "manhunt," not explicitly required in their mandate.

These two surreal scenes did not flow inexorably from Dayton. They were the result of people interpreting the mandate in the narrowest possible way in order to minimize their own responsibility. As Jim Hoag-

I called officials like Ambassador Madeleine Albright (shown walking out to Air Force One) and Secretary of Defense Bill Perry (shown at the Pentagon) when I realized their determination to end the genocide wasn't shared by those in charge on the ground.

land of the *Washington Post* put it, "After the daring US diplomacy and military strikes against the Serbs that led to the peace accord, the administration has switched to a strategy of avoiding failure—and avoiding the responsibility for failure—rather than taking new chances for success."[4]

It seemed the US military would do anything, including nothing, to stay away from trouble. But it was hard to locate with any assurance the source of the decision. When General Joulwan, who had overseen the effort to break the siege of Sarajevo, was our houseguest in Vienna, I pushed him for several hours to finish the job and apprehend Bosnian war criminals. Joulwan insisted he lacked that authority. "I'm just a simple soldier," he said, repeatedly. "We act when political leaders tell us what to do. I'm waiting for orders, and they haven't come." Did he or did he not have the necessary authority to act? High-level international advocates insisted he did.

But perhaps Washington was indeed giving him a red light. That caution would be, in part, politically understandable. A presidential election was coming up, and media coverage of an American casualty in Bosnia could jeopardize the entire US presence there and reflect badly on Clinton. Adding to the complexity, NATO feared a shootout because it wanted Karadžić alive to stand trial, as the only one who could lead the tribunal to Milošević.

But most of the resistance came from the military sector. Some explanations made apparent sense. "Our soldiers aren't trained to be police," I was told time and again, with the implication that such miscasting was doomed to fail. Other excuses fell flat. Defense Department officials later verified to me that "force protection" was their mantra.[5] When the *New York Times* reported that the United States had dropped plans to arrest Karadžić and Mladić, the Pentagon explained that it feared retaliation against American troops.[6]

Military commanders rotating through with short assignments were loath to send home a body bag from a shootout on the other side of the world. The motivations may have been not only humane but also self-serving. The negative scrutiny of the press, cutthroat culture in Washington, and tight competition in the promotion ladder created an aversion to risk.

Retired Officer Magazine complained: "US soldiers here are seen as obsessed about personal safety." Even the military band at a diplomatic reception played in flak jackets and helmets, with their M-16 rifles next to them on the ground.[7] But there were real dangers. A plot was exposed in which women were positioned along a road south of Tuzla to lure soldiers into an ambush. The policies restricting troops to their bases for months on end were, however, disproportionate to the threat. Com-

When Supreme Allied Commander George Joulwan posed at NATO headquarters with each of the US ambassadors in Europe, little did he know how hard I'd be pushing him to send troops to stop the atrocities.

manders kept soldiers so protected that the number of deaths in Bosnia was actually smaller than those from road accidents, drunken fighting, and other mishaps in Germany, where the troops otherwise would have been stationed.

It was distressing to see how a few Serb bullies could transform their foes into their protectors. Just as, during the war, the Serbs had managed to paralyze the international community by using UN forces as actual—or potential—hostages, now the presence of a huge number of soldiers armed to the teeth became the reason the war criminals could *not* be apprehended.

As Smith's hands-off approach was emulated throughout the military, indicted war criminals felt a new sense of impunity. The *International Herald Tribune* described Karadžić being driven not only in full view, but with a local police escort, to his hideaway headquarters. The (advisory) international police[8] said they called NATO troops, who did nothing. Similarly, while Carl Bildt, the high representative in Bosnia and Herzegovina, was meeting with political leaders in Banja Luka, Karadžić was moving around in the same building. A heavily armed NATO soldier stood outside—but the military show was nothing more than that.[9] On Capitol Hill, at the State Department, in the Oval Office, at NATO, no one straightened out the policy gone awry. Human rights watchers were appalled.

For the most part, the US military was led by affable, garrulous, smart men who could find a hundred reasons not to apprehend a war criminal living right under their noses. Eventually, I urged that a bounty be posted for live capture. My colleagues in Washington rejected the idea as unseemly, as if it were not a common tactic with the FBI. It took an act of Congress (literally) to bring the idea to fruition.[10]

Finally, *USA Today* reported that, "ending 18 months of looking the other way, NATO . . . sent troops to arrest two men accused of genocidal war crimes," an action prompted by the frustration of the leaders of NATO's member states. The paper noted that this "was a dramatic shift for NATO, until now reluctant to get troops involved in arrests."[11]

51. INSIDE: Uncatchable

Balding, baby-faced Blagoje Simić smiled disarmingly. "I'm not uncatchable," he said. "I think someone important still hasn't ordered the arrests to be done." And as far as he was concerned, that someone was "Clinton . . . absolutely."[12]

In November 1996, the *Boston Globe* journalist Elizabeth Neuffer spoke with the indicted war criminal in his mayoral office in Bosanski Šamac.

Thirty-six years old and trained as a doctor, Simić was "every inch the Balkan gallant" when Neuffer and her interpreter appeared at his door, unannounced. He received the journalist smoothly, "ushering [her] in, offering a rickety chair, snapping his fingers for coffee—'for the ladies, please.'" Gray-jacketed and settled in a red velvet seat, Simić went on to explain why none of the sixty thousand NATO forces, including the Americans at their base down the road, had arrested or even questioned him.

Simić had been president of the Serbian Democratic Party of his town before the war. But it wasn't until April 1992 that he became president of the Serbian Municipal Assembly of Šamac—later renamed the War Presidency of the Serbian Municipality of Bosanski Šamac.

How could that overreaching designation apply to a town (population thirty-three thousand) that comprised seventeen Bosnian Croats and Bosniaks? On 17 April, Serb forces had seized control and renamed the place. By May of that year, the new name nearly fit: only three hundred Croats and Bosniaks remained.

Non-Serb residents who hadn't simply fled were killed, forcibly driven out, or coerced into slave labor. It was easy for troops to spot whom to target: non-Serbs had been compelled to wear white armbands. Over the next year, municipality leaders, including Simić, carried out a campaign of purges and torture.

This was the man who, though not "uncatchable," was still living in the open three years after his gross violations of international humanitarian law.[13] Stories like his were common at all levels—from neighbors who stole from the displaced to leaders who devised the expulsions. And among the latter, no story was more galling and no leader more perverse than Radovan Karadžić.

A psychiatrist, Karadžić had studied at the University of Sarajevo. To indulge his artistic streak, he spent a year writing and reciting verse in New York. Later, he published some of this poetry, along with books for children. Perhaps because he was a man of the mountains, from a small and rough Montenegrin village, much of his poetry considered themes of nature. But buried in the lines was violence:

At last I am bereft
Of all benefactors
I glow like a cigarette's ember
Touching neurotic lips:
While others search me out
I wait in dawn's hiding place
This glorious opportunity
To suddenly forsake all

That this epoch has bestowed upon me
And I hurl a morning hand-grenade
Armed with the laughter
Of a lonely man
With a dark character.[14]

In 1985, Karadžić had been convicted of embezzlement and fraud; he was sentenced to three years in prison. He never served his time—a foretaste, perhaps, of his evasion of capture a decade later and beyond. But many refused to see his "dark character." On the Bosnian Serb St. Jovan radio station in 1998, the indicted war criminal was lauded as a man of "Christ-like virtues."[15]

And no wonder. He deftly explained away even the most barefaced atrocities, easing the collective Serb conscience. After the winter 1994 marketplace bombing that killed sixty-eight Sarajevans, Karadžić was ready with a fanciful account: the Bosniaks had taken bodies from a morgue and placed them in the market in order to cry foul. When a journalist asked him how he knew this, he said: "Many had ice in their ears." The journalist countered that he had seen the bodies, and the psychiatrist persisted: "Yes, but did you check their ears? You didn't? So how can you be sure?"[16] Even the subsequent siege of Sarajevo was transformed from an atrocity perpetrated against the encircled city to a brave attempt to keep the Bosniaks from attacking Serbs outside of Sarajevo.

Undoubtedly Karadžić played a key role in events that pushed the conflict to new levels. In April 1992, thousands of Sarajevans marched for peace through the streets of the city. As the demonstrators approached the office of Karadžić's party, his bodyguards fired from the roof into the crowd. Six people were killed.

How had this peasant boy, whose neighborhood was fully integrated (Alija Izetbegović, Bosnia's wartime president, lived around the corner) and who chose a Bosniak as godfather to his son, evolve into a war criminal eluding capture?[17]

52. OUTSIDE: Evenhanded

NATO leaders were determined not to incite an uprising. They saw "neutrality" as essential to the safety of their troops. But many in the military also believed that all sides were equally guilty. If five Serbs were sent to The Hague, five Bosniaks and five Croats needed to go as well. One military officer clarified this view for me: the fact that so few Bosniaks were indicted was evidence that the ICTY was biased.

This issue of fairness was complicated by the brilliant showmanship of the Serb leader. Milošević was fond of crying foul, as if he were the victim in the conflict. It was a tactic consistent with the stereotype that Serbs saw themselves as targeted and oppressed. On the eve of the hand-over from UN- to NATO-led troops, melodramatic TV broadcasts from Banja Luka proclaimed that NATO would have to "regain the trust of the Serbs," who "can forget" but "will never forgive" the air strikes.

The rift between diplomats and military was deep when it came to placating such resentment. Admiral Smith had asserted to me earlier in Naples that the United States was being too hard on the Serbs. True to form, one of his first actions was to go to the Bosnian Serb stronghold, Pale, against Ambassador Menzies's request. There, Smith told Serb leaders that he would consider extending the deadline for handing over some of the areas they held. Menzies, understanding the psychology of the players, was furious. That effort at appeasement, he said, would be interpreted by the aggressors as a faltering commitment to justice.

Not all the military leaders I encountered were of one mind. At the US European Command in Stuttgart, General Chuck Boyd had warned me that I had fallen prey to Bosniak propaganda and should have had more Serbs over for dinner.[18] But his replacement, General Jim Jamerson, had a different tone. When he stayed with us in Vienna, I pressed the case that we needed assertive action by the US military. It was not true that Balkan people had never been able to live together, I told him. Jamer-son said he had often heard the same and realized that outsiders were sometimes unwilling to distinguish among the combatants or to see the difference between a policy of systemic atrocities and individual wrongs committed during wartime. I wished he had been assigned to Sarajevo instead of Stuttgart.

A third US general was pivotal in developing the military's version of evenhandedness. William Nash was commander of the peacekeeping operation for the northeast sector of Bosnia. (The country was divided into three sectors, under the Americans, British, and French.) I asked him for troops to protect high-level visitors coming to commemorate the Srebrenica massacre and press the international community to address the needs of survivors. In turn, the general requested my assurance that, as we planned the event, I would invite Serb and Croat women still look-ing for their missing.

Like Ambassador Pickering had at the diplomatic gathering in Brus-sels, General Nash made it clear that he did not want to upset the Rus-sians. He wanted to know how many Russians we had on our interna-tional host committee. And would our handouts also be printed in the Cyrillic alphabet used by Serbs and Russians? We spent more time hash-ing out those details than we did worrying about the thirty thousand–plus survivors.

Major General William Nash, commander of the northeast peacekeeping operation headquartered at Eagle Base, was confident that, despite the genocide, all sides of the conflict should be treated the same.

As we talked, I realized the commander's quandary: how to face up to a tragically inequitable past while laying the groundwork for an equitable future. How to recognize the overwhelming complicity of the Serbs, while establishing a new order that would protect their rights.

In broad terms, General Nash described the challenge facing his officers: "We don't have the intuitive grasp of this situation in our professional souls." That was a powerful admission, since NATO was providing de facto law to the region. Without a clear moral foundation, it would be easy to collapse into confusion.

Case in point: When a few disoriented Bosniak men who, amazingly, had survived Srebrenica came stumbling out of the woods months after the massacre, they were taken into custody by IFOR troops. Unable to reach their command center, the young soldiers consulted their handbooks' all-purpose evenhanded guidelines. Per instructions, they turned the long-traumatized men over to local authorities — Serb nationalists — who immediately imprisoned them.

The internal State Department report was terse: "Re. Turnover of Bosnian Muslims to Bosnian Serb police. The IFOR troops who did this followed local procedure. The intent of the procedure was to bring all local military forces under the control of local authorities. The procedure did not foresee a situation where military personnel from one of the war-ring parties remained in another party's sector after the deadline for the movement into respective zones. [Major General] Nash, US Sector Commander, has put measures in place to prevent situations like this from re-occurring."

Months later, the escapees were still languishing in a Serb prison. Unable to find anyone willing to force their release, I asked General Nash what he was doing to free the men. "As soon as I realized what happened, I started banging my head against the wall," was all he said.

53. INSIDE: No Justice in Srebrenica

After the guns stopped firing and the peace was signed, life remained blocked for the refugees from Srebrenica. Several natural leaders emerged to organize the survivors. One was Fatima Huseinović, a petite, energetic woman with an infectious smile. Sitting at her kitchen table, she tried to help me understand:

> One day I was walking down the street with four other women. We passed another, dressed real nice, walking her dog. When he started to sniff us, the woman frowned and yanked on his leash. "Stop it! Those are refugees!"—as if we were dirty.
>
> I lost my home, my family, my work. But no loss hurt me more than when I lost my identity. I felt so degraded, being just a "refugee."

Fatima was organizing collective action among the survivors so that, with a stronger voice, they wouldn't be ignored. Together, they pushed for accountability, the arrest of war criminals, and assistance to the children among them. As "speaker of the women of Srebrenica," she signed a resolution stating that "the worst crimes committed in Europe after the fall of the Third Reich must not be rewarded."[19]

The women couldn't go back to their homes in or around Srebrenica, she told me, as long as indicted war criminals were free to swagger through town. It was too risky, physically and mentally. This was, after all, the region where Karadžić was said to be living.

Fatima's own home was empty. She had two daughters. (For the first time in this patriarchal society, she said, having daughters was considered a blessing. It meant you might have a child still alive.) Yet she hadn't seen her daughters for four years. The younger one had been in Germany, studying to be a doctor when the war broke out. But even her life had been derailed: she'd dropped out of school and become a nurse so that she could send home money for the other seven members of her family.

As she showed me pictures from the purse she fled with, I asked Fatima Huseinović how many men in her family perished in the massacre at Srebrenica. "I haven't counted," she answered. "I don't have the courage."

Like her mother, the eldest daughter was a refugee, having fled with her husband and children to nearby Macedonia. As Fatima talked, she began to cry. She longed to see her family, but her son-in-law was a Serb. Because of all that the Serb troops had done, she was afraid he wouldn't survive if the family came to Tuzla as planned. Besides, she added, so many homes had been destroyed. Where would they all live?

Fatima pulled out her purse to show me pictures. She had left home with only that purse, so the pictures were among the few remnants of her life in Srebrenica. There was her husband, holding their grandchild. He'd been a hospital administrator, while she'd worked in a warehouse. She pointed to their home—a small, middle-class, white-framed structure. "We went for ski vacations in the winter and to the beach in the summer," she recalled.

Another family photograph showed four men sitting around a table with bottles of wine, two holding guitars and grinning. One had left at the beginning of the war, she said. Then Fatima covered three of the men with her hand. They had stayed behind in Srebrenica. All were missing. She said:

> Sometimes, in the long years we were under siege, I kept thinking about how it would be just to brew some coffee, like we always had before the war. It may seem silly, but I couldn't get it out of my mind. Then when I arrived as a refugee in Tuzla, I was finally able to go buy a kilogram, brew it, and fix myself a

cup. But it meant nothing to me. I had no husband to drink it with. I had no son. Were they still back there, hiding in the woods? Or in forced labor? Wherever they were, were they craving this coffee?

If only they could have the chance to return to civilization, to a normal life . . . to sit around a table and share some food. To live for even a little while, life as it was before. Then maybe it would be okay if they died.

"If I knew he was dead, I wouldn't suffer," agreed Kada Hotic, a plainspoken, formerly middle-class wife and mother who also led a group determined to find answers about the missing. Kada was aware that the news might be horrible. But speaking of her teenage son, she said: "The kindest thing someone could do is tell me the truth. It would be over. Everything else would be bearable."

How could survivors move past such paralyzing uncertainty? For Kada, the solution was justice. Though she insisted that the ICTY should not be prosecuting ordinary soldiers, she was equally firm that commanders should be taken to court. Maybe then, she mused, reconciliation would be possible. Kada was careful to insist on justice, not revenge, saying that if she hurt someone who wronged her, "I wouldn't be me anymore."

But she went even further than nonretaliation, transforming her victimhood as she took on the perspective of the very soldiers who had killed her son and husband: "They must have flashbacks all the time. . . . It must be so hard for them." Moving beyond sympathy, Kada explained: "The commanders were awarding medals to whoever committed the worst crime, to the one who killed the most people in the fiercest way, or raped the most women. . . . That soldier who killed my son believed he was doing good for his people and for his religion. I'm sure he's not aware even now that he was committing crimes."

The simplicity of her vision was humbling: "If nothing else, we can at least try to be sure that all we experienced in Srebrenica isn't covered up." To press for the truth, Kada turned to street demonstrations and other activism. She expected no help, and she asked for no compassion. That would make her feel like a beggar, she said: "I feel better when I'm protesting."

54. OUTSIDE: The Tribunal

Nuanced politics did not always lend themselves to complete honesty. Publicly, I sometimes had to ignore the obvious, most pressing subjects. For example, I had to resort to weak, State Department–crafted statements extolling the humanitarian aid that the United States was sending to the Balkans—even as I was advocating to the Oval Office that we take much stronger political and military action to bring war criminals to justice at the International Criminal Tribunal for the Former Yugoslavia in The Hague.

That being said, the more we learned about the ICTY, the more discouraged I became. At a country team meeting, we discussed how computer records of abuses committed by the Croatian army had been stolen from a UN office in Zagreb. It was unfathomable to me that such important information would not have been backed up for safekeeping.

Someone then asked about the Bosniak prisoners now leaving the concentration camps that Jean Christiansen had visited. Had they been interviewed for the ICTY? Surely they must have been, I declared, dismissing the question. My team members, long-term career officers, shook their heads: "Assume nothing."

The idea of a war crimes tribunal was, of course, not new. The model grew out of the aftermath of World War II, when the victorious powers established military courts to try leaders of the Nazi and Japanese regimes. The UN Security Council's authority to convene such tribunals was even written into the UN Charter. International courts, sponsored by the UN or by a national government, were to be established when there was no local capacity for trying war criminals.

From 1945 to 1949, a series of trials in Nuremberg, Germany, prosecuted high-level Nazi officials for crimes against the peace, conventional war crimes, and crimes against humanity. Whereas most conflicts end with conditional surrender, Germany's was unconditional, and victors were free to choose how they would mete out justice. Five decades later, the ICTY and a contemporaneous tribunal for Rwanda were the first instances of such justice mechanisms since World War II. As in Germany, the tribunal set up for Bosnia was ad hoc. Despite the considerable expense, there were many important benefits of this approach.

From the victim's perspective, the process could return power stolen during the violence, as someone who suffered could stand up in court and relate his or her experience. A string of testimonials meant that fewer crimes would be forgotten and that a full picture of the war could be assembled. On the national level, the tribunal could provide a valuable experience of the rule of law in a place striving for democracy. Seeing the law upheld even against the leaders behind the atrocities would encourage people at every level.

But transitional justice measures are inevitably flawed. In terms of deterrence, frenzied hatred for another group is not lessened by the specter of a future trial. After the fact, many top criminals never face trial or are acquitted due to legal niceties that may outrage victims—for example, inadmissible testimony or unclear chains of command.

But foremost among the concerns is "victor's justice." Who decides whom to indict and prosecute? How will the victors acknowledge the suffering of the defeated? Postgenocide tribunals can so inflame the populace that they cause a return to conflict.

President Clinton was mindful of history's weight: "We have an obligation to carry forward the lessons of Nuremberg. Those accused of war crimes, crimes against humanity and genocide must be brought to justice. They must be tried, and if found guilty, they must be held accountable. . . . There must be peace for justice to prevail, but there must be justice when peace prevails."[20]

In the context of the Mladić and Karadžić indictments, Judge Fouad Riad described the carnage as "scenes of unimaginable savagery, thousands of men executed . . . hundreds of men buried alive, men and women mutilated and slaughtered, children killed before their mothers' eyes, a grandfather forced to eat of the liver of his own grandson. These are truly scenes from Hell, written on the darkest pages of human history."[21] Still, leaders of the international military forces refused to apprehend the accused and bring them to trial.

55. INSIDE: Waiting for the Truth

Trying to capture the personal dimension behind the court proceedings, I interviewed a woman whose husband had been indicted. Back at home, Zlata was a politician active in the Bosnian Croat nationalist party.

Ten days before my interview, she'd gone to The Hague for the start of her husband's trial. We spoke after her return to northern Bosnia. I tried not to lead her, to be dispassionate both in my questions and in my responses to her. But I was fully aware that the scene in Ahmići that she described was very different from that of Ambassador Drago Štambuk, who had felt such shame as a Croatian diplomat in London.

> Z: Unfortunately, a great tragedy befell the Muslims of our town. That's why my husband is at the International Court at The Hague today.
>
> I was born in 1954, one of six children. I married twenty-five years ago, right after secondary school. I was a fighter, and my husband liked that. I built a house and, to tell the truth, I really bore the burden of our family. We lived a good life.
>
> I started working in the municipal government, even while I was studying management and organization. Then I started a business that now employs ten people.
>
> *SH: What happened to you during the war?*

Z: Throughout the war, my family and I didn't move away, even though our neighborhood had more Muslims than Croats. Let me tell you about my relationship with my neighbors. My children were closer to their children than anyone else. Nothing could separate us. Every day, I drove to work and back with two of them—both Muslim. One night, we sat in my home until 11:30, talking about everything. None of us knew what would happen in the morning—that our community would be terrorized. When it happened, my husband and I spent two days with Muslim neighbors. That's why I live where I live, and that's why I haven't left.

But in 1995, a lot of Croats in our town were charged with crimes. My husband was on the list. For the next year and a half, he hid from the international troops and police, but I still stayed in my home. When we—not just him but also our children and me—couldn't bear his hiding any longer, we decided he should surrender. If he went to the court, the truth would come out. If he didn't go, he wouldn't have a chance to prove he wasn't guilty.

We're all relieved that at least the process has started. As a woman, as a mother, and as a wife I'm glad—obviously not because my husband is in prison, but rather because he went of his own accord. He's been there a year. After a lot of testimony from witnesses, he's accused of fifteen murders, ethnic cleansing, and other crimes. But we need to be strong and carry on. Many people haven't testified yet, and they'll tell the truth. Truth will prevail.

SH: What caused the tragedy of the war?

Z: The election of 1990 proved that Serbs, Croats, and Muslims wanted a change in the political system. No one was happy with just one party as we'd had before, and I was thrilled when I saw the first elections with multiple parties. Where I live, we all accepted the results. Nothing changed. We were the same people—neighbors, friends, and colleagues. We just organized the government to reflect the elections, so that we all had our rights.

We'd entered a new era, and I felt the Croatian people needed my help. So I got involved with a political party—the Croatian Democratic Community (HDZ)—and I've been a member ever since. As a Bosnian Croat, I was overjoyed when the referendum for an independent Bosnia and Herzegovina passed a couple of years later.

Before the war, our town was 45 percent Muslims, 52 percent Croats, and a few Serbs and others. It hasn't completely changed, but about five thousand Croats from places under the control of the Muslim army fled to this area, and vice versa with Muslims who were forced out of our town. A lot of people died on both sides. Things happened that we didn't know about—not only the citizens, but also those of us in government.

As complex and difficult as this time is, at least people aren't being killed. My neighbors are returning. Muslims are coming back to Ahmići. And I'm still there. It doesn't matter that many of them left, or that my husband is accused of this or that. We'll all live together again.

SH: What's it like to be a wife in your situation? What do you think about in the middle of the night?

Z: I was the only one of the wives who stayed in our village. Some left out of fear for their children's safety, but I have no fear. Except for criminals, people are just people, no matter their ethnicity.

Still, there were terrible times. We were surrounded by hostile troops for eight months. Three of my sisters are refugees, driven from their homes. My thirty-five-year-old brother was killed. My sister's twenty-five-year-old son. My other sister's twenty-two-year-old son. In my extended family, more than twenty people died, and lots of others were wounded.

Sure, we have scars. Horrible things happened on both sides. You know, when someone kills your child or brother, it takes a lot of time and strength to recover. But we have to keep going, hoping that one day . . . You know, for years, I simply haven't had time to cry. I'm afraid if I start, something could awaken in me and knock me off track. I have to be strong. My greatest support is belief in myself and in God, even though I'm not a great believer.

My family's very important to me, but we all make mistakes. I think I did as much as I could, but I still wonder where I went wrong. Then I ask my husband, in prison, how he bears all this. He says, "Thank God I have a wife who takes care of everything, and I don't have to worry about problems at home." I tell him he should just tend to his health and nerves and leave everything else to me. God knows how long all this will take.

The most important thing for me is that when he leaves prison—when he's found innocent—I want him to be healthy and have the rest of his life with our children, enjoying their successes, and enjoying the town and country we live in.

SH: How are you raising your boys to learn tolerance and reconciliation?

Z: You asked a lovely question. God wants it to be that way. Many people tell me my children set an example. It's not easy for me to take them to The Hague every month. We go to the cell to see their father for eight hours. There's no window and no fresh air. How do they stand it? They hold onto the truth. They're a hundred percent convinced that their father is innocent, and that gives them strength.

I have them studying foreign languages. They surf the Internet and take computer courses. They play sports. My oldest son drives, and he goes out with his friends. I hope one day you'll meet my children. But their souls are full of sadness. Can you imagine when they hear, "Your father's a war criminal"? It hurts. That's why I hope you'll write about this conversation—and that they'll be proud of their father and their mother.

SH: I'm struck by your calm and your intelligence.

Z: I'll tell you now, woman to woman. Since my brother and other members of my family died, I've had to be there for everyone else. My mother, my children, my brother's children—everybody saw in me someone who could help.

As a mother and a wife, I wanted to go into politics. There aren't many women, but I hope I'll motivate others to become politicians, whatever their parties. Politics isn't incidental. Instead of killing, we should talk. Especially mothers—we love our children more than anything in the world. I'm stronger than my male colleagues, because they aren't grounded as I am, as a mother is. It's important for women to be in Parliament, where decisions are made.

If women had been the leaders, we might not have had this war. Men think they're so smart, but really they're just stubborn. A woman can be intelligent, a businessperson, *and* a mother and wife. A man could never do what I do. Men think women should be at home, have babies, and wait on their husbands. I cut that out a long time ago.

Now I'm running for Parliament, and when I win, we women will fight for people who are vulnerable, especially mothers and children. I'll defend not only the rights of my own people but also the rights of all others.

SH: Some politicians want to see Bosnia divided.

Z: There's only one Bosnia. All three ethnic groups should live here. Dayton mandates that everyone can return home. Minorities need the same rights as the majority. But people also need money to rebuild their houses so they can return to where they can speak their own dialect, express their own culture, and practice their own religion.

Before, when we were mixed, we didn't even need police. Now, we have tanks. I know they're here to protect us, but they remind us of the war. I can't wait for them to go—that's when we'll really have peace.

I also don't like the world being here through humanitarian agencies; I'd like you to come as our guests, as tourists visiting our beautiful mountains and rivers. We're hard-working and creative. We shouldn't need charity.

Instead, what we need is for the world to stand behind all three peoples of Bosnia and Herzegovina. There have always been differences, and there always will be. But about one thing there's no difference: we all want a good life.

56. OUTSIDE: Intelligence and Political Will

Since becoming ambassador, I had come to know a lively shadow world I had seen only in movies. Given the size and scope of our Vienna intelligence operation, when in Washington I frequently dropped by the organization we called "Langley," "Across the River," or "The Agency." Often on these visits to CIA headquarters, I was impressed with how well practiced people there were in secrecy.

A month after the Srebrenica massacre, a visibly shaken agent handed me satellite images of a football field—one showing men lined up in rows, another with the men gone, but with new mounds of freshly dug earth. Nine months later, I was asked by a reporter if I knew of the existence of such photographs, which had never been acknowledged.

At another Langley meeting, I found myself caught up in a loop of illogic, as six specialists and I debated the importance of picking up war criminals. "Why does the timing matter?" one asked. "Let's work on getting the government infrastructure in place and then pick them up."

"But the war criminals are doing everything they can to stall the building of those institutions," I countered.

"If we pick them up now," another added, "the Serbs will say we're not impartial." I recognized the argument.

"Wouldn't it be more impartial to say that *everyone* must turn in their criminals, and then actually enforce it?" I asked.

"But if we go after the Serbs, they won't cooperate with the Dayton Accords."

"You think they're cooperating now? What about freedom of movement, and handing over the war criminals?"

"Well, except for those things . . ."

"This was 'intelligence'?" I thought angrily. I had enormous respect for CIA operatives who risked their lives to uncover drug rings, trace nuclear smuggling, and locate terrorist cells. But not all CIA personnel were upright. I was well acquainted with the first CIA station chief assigned to Bosnia; he had come directly from Vienna, where I had threatened to fire him for obfuscation. (The ambassador, by executive order, has the right and responsibility to know everything the CIA uncovers in-country, except "sources and methods.") That conflict earned him not a demotion, but the Bosnia portfolio, where he continued withholding information from the ambassador. I wondered what headquarters was thinking. Was his placement the result of inattention—or intention?

Aside from the station chief's insubordination, his new war-region assignment was challenging. And given the global spread of terrorism, he was charged not so much with understanding the dynamics among the parties to the war, as with assessing extremist Islamic activity taking root in Bosnia. But it also appeared to me that the CIA's scrutiny was directed not only at radicals from outside, but more broadly at Muslims within Bosnia.

Intelligence officers rotated through assignments worldwide, and they were accustomed to interacting with violent Middle Eastern groups like Afghan Mujahideen or Egyptian Islamic Jihad. This seemed to create among the spies an anti-Muslim inclination that extended to Bosniaks. A significant bias was exposed when an analyst handed me a six-page report on the purported perils of picking up indicted war criminals— overwhelmingly Serbs who had perpetrated genocide against Bosniaks. It was hard to know if the analysts were more blindly pro-Serb or anti-Muslim.

I tried to rationalize their attitude, recognizing that at the same time that we were taking a tough stand against "rogue states" like Libya, Syria, and Iraq, we could not be soft on "Mujahideen" who had infiltrated Bosnia. But the intelligence needed to be independent and not tied to a political agenda. I was therefore distressed when, yet again, more intelligence officers passed on to me what I had heard in military briefings earlier about "Muslim extremists"—whom I well knew, and had reported, were nothing of the sort.

That anti-Muslim bias was interfering with the meting out of justice: the enemy of their enemy was their friend. I told the analysts about accounts from human rights workers and reporters documenting sightings of indicted war criminals, and I described how Karadžić had been seen in his jeep, his wavy silver hair blowing in the breeze. Then I recounted the description of a journalist friend who had looked up several men on the list from The Hague and simply gone to their homes. One answered the door but gave a false name; another made no pretense.

My interlocutors made no response. I could not assess whether their stone-faced stares were signs of caution, apathy, or lack of understanding. I hoped it was not more nefarious. A high level State Department official told me that when Secretary of State Christopher asked to see the latest intelligence on the former Yugoslavia, it was eleven days old. That official spoke of "collusion" between the US intelligence and military to weaken the State Department's insistence that the United States apprehend war criminals.

With a tone that seemed to me to be coming from the top, the CIA maintained this line during yet another meeting with me. At breakfast on an upper floor of CIA headquarters, Deputy Director George Tenet insisted that the agency had tried indefatigably but could not locate Karadžić and Mladić. I said that notion was ludicrous. I knew the methods we had available. If we did not know where they were, it was because we did not want to know where they were.

Not so, Tenet assured me: "We're doing everything we can. We have a hundred people trying to find them."

Surely he would not lie, I thought. Then I remembered where I was.

I felt both frustrated and vindicated when, later, the CIA's lead Balkan specialist admitted to me: "We basically know where Karadžić is. Picking him up is just a matter of political will."

57. INSIDE: Professor, Perpetrator, President

Biljana Plavšić didn't have much to work with when, as heir to the regime of Radovan Karadžić, she became president of Republika Srpska. That and a few dinars might buy her a shot of *slibovic*.

Karadžić, Mladić, and Plavšić had been the evil trio running the war. A member of the Supreme Command of the armed forces of Republika Srpska, Plavšić was an unabashed Serb nationalist. Yet even toward her own people, she was pitiless: "There are 12 million Serbs and even if six million perish on the field of battle, there will still be six million to reap the fruits of the struggle."[22] A former biology professor at the University of Sarajevo, Plavšić was reviled for statements asserting Bosniak inferiority. To her, Bosniaks were genetically abnormal Serbs. Speaking of Ejup Ganić, she said: "I have never met a more deformed person than him in political circles, which abound with such deformed people."[23]

Plavšić particularly deplored intermarriage. "We are disturbed by the fact that the number of marriages between Serbs and Muslims has increased," she complained, "because mixed marriages lead to an exchange of genes between ethnic groups, and thus to a degeneration of Serb nationhood."[24]

Her solution? "I would prefer completely to cleanse eastern Bosnia of Muslims. When I say cleanse, I don't want anyone to take me literally and think I mean ethnic cleansing. But they've attached this label 'ethnic cleansing' to a perfectly natural phenomenon and characterized it as some kind of war crime."[25]

In fact, one of the war's first acts of ethnic cleansing was led by one of the president's heroes. Željko Ražnatović, better known as Arkan, headed a paramilitary group called the Serbian Volunteer Guard,[26] later dubbed Arkan's Tigers. Plavšić raved about the soldier's April 1992 attack on a mixed Bosniak-Serb town: "When I saw what he'd done in Bi-jeljina, I at once imagined all his actions being like that. I said: here we have a Serb hero. He's a real Serb, that's the kind of men we need."[27]

The best-known woman in the war, Plavšić was despised by most of the Bosnians I respected. She elicited, at best, ambivalence in the international community. When Karadžić was indicted by the ICTY and barred from public office, he clearly expected his former co-conspirator to become his puppet. But when she unexpectedly moved the Parliament to Banja Luka, far from his presumed hideout on the eastern side of Republika Srpska, he was furious. This defiant gesture of independence signaled a split from the Serb hard-liners in Pale (near Sarajevo), who had orchestrated much of the war. Unlike Karadžić, Plavšić was turning to the West.

My initial meeting with the president of Republika Srpska was the brainchild of Brigadier General John Abizaid, which he shouted to me through helicopter headphones as we flew over the US-controlled northeast sector of Bosnia. Even though Plavšić had been part of the inner circle with Karadžić and Mladić, the general pointed out, she had not been indicted and was now in the top position of authority. Better to have a woman, like me, develop a relationship with her.

I agreed and decided to visit her office in Banja Luka—a lengthy drive through Serb-controlled territory. I told the president I'd seen her on TV and in international papers at least once a week: "You've assumed semi-star status. It's a lot of responsibility."

"Too much," she replied. "Don't expect so much of me. You in America don't know how expensive democracy is, because you were born into it. The problem in this region is that there has been no continuity." She commented that her ninety-five-year-old mother remembered five conflicts: two Balkan wars at the beginning of the century, two world wars, and now this one: "We must have one generation that doesn't know fighting."

The next time I met President Plavšić was at negotiations in Vienna. The question of authority over the strategically placed town of Brčko was so contentious that it had been excluded from the Dayton Accords. The evening of the first day of the negotiations, Plavšić came to our embassy residence with the rest of the negotiating teams. As a diplomat, I put aside our differences and greeted the president as she entered our home.

"How are you?" she responded, then, taking me aside, plunged in with a personal question: "How do you and your husband manage a marriage where you're both professionals with large responsibilities?" I couldn't imagine two men starting a conversation that way.

To ease the tension of the negotiations, I'd invited a jazz piano player

President of Republika Srpska Biljana Plavšić (second from left) — later an indicted war criminal — at the table in her Banja Luka office. She was a terrible mix: hateful professor spouting poison; betrayed partner of Radovan Karadžić; and the best hope of the West. At this meeting, Bosnian Serb women leaders asked for a more prominent role so they could soften the tone of hard-line officials.

to join us. Choosing the repertoire for a few group songs was complicated. We could divide the room, I said to the pianist facetiously, and sing antiphonally, "This Land Is Your Land, This Land Is My Land." Not good. We tried "Swing Low, Sweet Chariot," until we got to the end of "comin' for to carry me. . . ." When I turned to the group for ideas, Plavšić offered enthusiastically, "It's Good to Touch the Green, Green Grass of Home." So much for singalongs, I thought. There's a reason diplomats stick to démarches.

On another occasion, Ambassador Robert Frowick, head of the OSCE mission to Bosnia, gave me a ride to Banja Luka on his plane. We both had business with Plavšić. Frowick wanted to discuss election timing and arrangements with her. My goal was to introduce the president to other women in her area who might play a strong role in a moderate government.

President Plavšić was polite but not warm toward the other women as we held our discussion, her aides (all burly men) looking on. But as we walked from her office into the hallway, she whispered to me, "You changed the whole ambience! You can't imagine what it's like for me. We women always have to prove ourselves. I'm completely surrounded by men, all the time. They have a strange way of seeing things. The men in Pale can't believe they have to deal with a woman."

On a subsequent visit, the president and I wrote notes to each other as we sat at her table, since her office most certainly was bugged by Karadžić's goons. She then suggested I ride in her car to the cemetery where her mother had recently been buried. There we could speak openly, she said, as we walked through the gates.

It was a cold but sunny day, and we were bundled up. She pulled out candles, which we lit and put on the grave, "so someone watching thinks we're talking about my mother," she explained under her breath. In answer to my question, Plavšić replied that she could not go after war criminals, even minor ones, without putting herself in physical danger. She described Pale as an enclave of criminals: "I have no power there, but we can isolate them. And I can be everywhere else."

As we sat on a nearby bench, two women strolling along the street in heavy winter coats called out to her: "You're our only hope!" With an 80 percent unemployment rate, Banja Luka was desperate. For many, Plavšić was a tough leader for tough times.

Given the constant surveillance the president was under, Secretary of State Albright suggested that the president call her on any trips out of the country. I understood Albright's interest, and perhaps pity. Even after I received reports from our embassy personnel that thugs had been sent by Karadžić to eliminate Plavšić, she would not cooperate with having her former partner picked up by us and sent to The Hague. But she was tormented by his turning on her. "I'm so disappointed. If I'd known how difficult my life would be, I wouldn't have taken on this job," she told me, in a wistful voice.

Only at the end of her tenure as president did she give me a go-ahead signal, over the phone from Banja Luka: "You Americans know how to deal with terrorists in Iraq. It's a problem money can solve." At first I was puzzled; the United States was not engaged in Iraq at the time. Her comment made no sense—until I realized she was not talking about Iraq. She was asking us to pay someone to pull the trigger (literally) on her erstwhile accomplice.

I asked Plavšić once if she would be indicted as a war criminal. She insisted disingenuously that her work had been only humanitarian, overseeing Serb refugees. She maintained that she knew nothing about what had happened in Srebrenica but assumed there must be some sort of evidence or the international community wouldn't be making such a claim. When I gave her a summary, she asserted that she had been preoccupied with the Croat offensive outside Banja Luka and, in fact, had wondered why Mladić was not there. She finished by saying that she did remember seeing him on television from Srebrenica.

It was a less than convincing argument. So I was not totally surprised when Mike O'Connor, from the *New York Times*, came by my Vienna office to raise a question. He'd heard that we invited President Plavšić to our "Vital Voices: Women in Democracy" conference of 320 women leaders across Western and Eastern Europe and North America. "Do you think that's smart?" he asked. "You're going to have a war criminal on the same stage with the American first lady." I explained the basis of our inviting her, as the highest duly elected woman in Bosnia. "And she hasn't been indicted," I added. O'Connor maintained a journalistic skepticism.

Was I making nice to a war criminal? The question gnawed at me.[28]

SECTION 8 International Inadequacies

58. OUTSIDE: The Fourth Warring Party

The romance of peace was already fading as I sat at breakfast with Bosnian Foreign Minister Muhamed "Mo" Saćirbey in the dingy café of the Hotel Bosna. Already the international community—"the fourth warring party"—was starting to antagonize locals. Over eggs, feta cheese, and fatty cold cuts, the smooth-talking Saćirbey confided his fears.

First, he said, local expertise in Bosnia was stretched. Although Sarajevo was still a city of three hundred thousand, half were refugees out of their rural element. Most students and professionals who could escape had done so, resulting in a debilitating brain drain. What was more, Communist education had been short on training for the new, competitive market economy. All this resulted in a mind-boggling mismatch of tasks and talent on the local level, which in turn led to an influx of international talent to compensate. "Can you imagine what this does to the momentum of a citizen's movement? And that's the core of democratization!" said Mo, who had grown up in the United States.

Compounding that problem, Saćirbey knew his country was becoming overwhelmed by hundreds of well-intentioned organizations pouring in to deliver aid, from knitting yarn to construction materials. The help often was not on target. Long after the world should have known better, agricultural aid seemed to dominate humanitarian programs, as if all Bosnians were farmers. "The international community will give us a tractor before they'll give us a computer," an Oxford-educated Bosnian woman remarked to me sardonically.

Such off-the-shelf programs were being implemented by a dozen foreign aid departments, agencies, and NGOs. Bosnians were swimming in an alphabet soup of institutions: UNICEF, UNHCR, OSCE, USAID, EU, ICRC, and so on. And each organization or country had its own regulations, so "dates certain" were most uncertain, as delivery delays stretched from weeks into months. Some donors had nonsensical procurement rules. They missed valuable opportunities to help Bosnian society, as supplies already available in Bosnia had to be flown in instead from home countries, thus stunting local enterprise.

Even among the internationals, the different styles of leaderships grated. Responsibility for coordinating international groups fell to the Office of the High Representative (OHR), mandated by Dayton. But that goal was unattainable.

Former Swedish Prime Minister Carl Bildt was selected for the knotty task of leading the OHR. Bildt had a careful manner as he went about untangling donor countries' interests, resources, and approaches to aid. In contrast, Americans working within the OHR pushed for bold action. The quintessential enthusiast was Jacques Klein, a major general in the US Air Force and a career Foreign Service officer. His actions produced sparks, such as when he sacrificed free speech and ordered troops to seize radio transmitters of hate-mongering broadcasts, in violation of agreements to stop the airing of incendiary speeches.[1]

A larger-than-life, robust character, Klein was determined to drive the rebuilding of Bosnia. He clearly thought that little would happen without American efforts, but Europeans derided him as a "cowboy." Still, as he became the longest-tenured outsider, he developed keen insight into the region. "The tragedy," he once opined, "is that the people of Republika Srpska have been led into one historical cul-de-sac after another by extremely poor leadership."[2]

At other levels of the OHR, many staff members loaned from a host of countries were highly talented, experienced stars; but they often worked alongside unimaginative, low-energy bureaucrats whose home offices were more than willing to send them off on far-away assignments.

Compared to international military operations in the area, the OHR was underfunded. But its budget was still larger than the federal budget of Bosnia. Civilian aid organizations' large staffs filled the hotels and choked the streets with well-equipped jeeps, while local residents did not have money to rebuild their destroyed roofs, much less buy a car. Of course, the organizations employed Bosnians, but they paid them a fraction of the salaries foreigners got, even when the locals were more qualified.

The politician Ejup Ganić illustrated the situation for me by drawing a large bag of dollars, next to a tiny bag of pennies:

The first is the payroll of the OHR, OSCE, UN, and NATO forces. Their job is to get refugees back to their homes. The second bag is the money actually given to refugees to rebuild their homes so they can return. The refugees haven't returned, because there's no funding for their houses or to start businesses. There are enough reports from these organizations to fill all the shelves at Harvard. They all talk about the progress they've made. But the refugees aren't back in their homes.

Organizing the assistance became an industry in and of itself. After surviving three years of shelling, Ganić had a particularly laconic interpretation of the absence of outside intervention during the war and the subsequent deluge of helpers during the peace: "When we needed a doctor, they sent us a priest. When we needed a priest, they sent us a doctor."

59. INSIDE: City Signs

Sarajevo was recovering. In peacetime, given the Serb exodus and the influx of Bosniak refugees, the population had become increasingly mono-ethnic. This was hardly the Bosnian ideal of multiculturalism. But on the upside, alleged Serb and Croat war criminals were keeping their distance. Scenes in the capital were hopeful.

I remembered how, during my first visit, I was forced to run off the ramp of a cargo plane to avoid snipers. Now, the airport was still controlled by French soldiers. Sandbags and rolls of barbed wire lined a narrow passage leading out from the tarmac with a sign: "Champs Elysées." But passengers were at least able to deplane without flak jackets.

"I didn't know this city for the first two years I visited, because we were always running"—that's how Livia Klingl, an Austrian journalist, had introduced me to her wartime Sarajevo. She'd also described how she'd brought in several pieces of fruit and given them to the family hosting her. After she interviewed a series of people over several days, the same fruit was offered to her, as the guest. It seemed that even *in extremis*, Sarajevans would rather be generous than fed.

Now life was moving quickly back to its prewar bustle. Open markets boasted fruits, pastries, and sausages. Street hawkers shouted out names of newspapers and cigarettes. Horns honked and brakes screeched. Every few minutes, a modern red tram rumbled by, a gift of the Viennese.

Sarajevans were proud of their rebuilding, and rightly so. On my first postwar visit, I marveled at each new sign of reconstruction. For the first time in my life, I found myself admiring smooth walls. But to a visitor,

Tobacco on the streets was a peculiar indicator of Sarajevo's returning health.

the destruction was still extraordinary. Every time we drove from the airport into the city, we passed a reminder of war's effect on an economy. A large, boxy yellow building, whose sign read "Yugocommerce," greeted us on our left. Almost every one of the facade's 150 windows had been shot out, like rows of targets at a carnival. Elsewhere, a chic woman with a cigarette, draped across a billboard, gazed at an apartment building with one side crushed by shelling.

Some of the symbols were mixed. In one building, pure white snow had fallen quietly on the shell-shredded metal roofing, now hanging uselessly into the empty space. And everywhere, as workers plastered over the scars of three and a half years of war, dump trucks hauled away loads of debris, and new structures rose up in cleared lots.

There were other signs of revival. Another shop opened every day. Between crumbling walls and shattered windows was a makeshift artist's gallery. Its neighbors were a perfectly restored boutique with designer shoes, historic shops with rows of gold and silver items, and a tourist souvenir stand sporting baseball caps with bright yellow embroidered mosques. Down the block were sweaters and rugs, knitted and woven by refugees—and the ubiquitous athletic shoes with outlandish prices.

But behind the veneer, the basic infrastructure to sustain a true market economy was lacking. There was no currency. Purchases were made in Deutschmarks, with change in chewing gum or worthless Yugoslav dinars. Efforts to create a central bank had failed. Meetings produced agreements, which shortly fell through. There was no integrated phone system. No telecommunication was possible between the Federation-controlled capital and the Serb-controlled half of the country, Republika Srpska. And the dysfunctional political system, combined with the old Yugoslav experience base, was a considerable obstacle to starting up businesses.

Unemployment and underemployment were astronomical. Mechanical engineers drove taxis. Professors waited tables. People trying to start businesses encountered inefficient or corrupt bureaucrats who sat on permits for months. The most robust growth was in the purported black market in cigarettes and alcohol that Karadžić was building from his hiding place.

Perhaps the most stubborn sign of hope, however, was that in spite of a 10:00 p.m. curfew, coffeehouses dotted the town, filled with young people's conversations as animated as those in the cafés of Vienna. Cappuccino machines hissed, and tables spilled out onto the streets.

In one coffee bar, a thin, wan man approached our table. He was a Sarajevan journalist who had been in Vienna when the Federation agreement was negotiated in our embassy, almost two years earlier. "That was the first real step toward this peace," he said.

I remembered something he had said. "You told me at dinner that you hadn't had a full meal in two years."

He smiled: "I was your guest then. Now please be mine." It was a significant gesture. Most people appreciate being rescued, but few want to be dependent indefinitely. So at his bidding, I drank one more cup of strong coffee, then spent a sleepless night, with plenty of hours to divide up and sort through all I had heard and seen of the city.

60. OUTSIDE: Out of Step

The NATO-led military operation kept vigil over the transition to stability. But coordination among the organization's many contributing countries was tricky. They had different allegiances, varied styles, and non-interoperable equipment.

At the outset, it was clear that nations were planning their IFOR deployment in isolation. They conducted independent surveys and assessments, failed to share the resulting data, and separately determined the needs of the mission. In part, the problem was lack of central planning; however, the challenges went deeper. With different cultures and histories come different notions of what a peace operation entails. Attitudes and customs shape doctrines, which in turn shape the approach to the mission. In Bosnia, this principle at best meant scattered efforts and disunity. But at worst, cultural clashes among the many participating nations dragged down the mission.

The problem was not just among military forces. Lack of cooperation between the new civil structure and military operations led to further incoherence. These failures stemmed from civilian implementation delays, turf battles, and lack of formal unifying mechanisms.

First, ramping up civilian efforts depended on a secure environment. Because security in turn depended on implementation of the military provisions in the Dayton Accords, delays in setting up the civilian sector plagued the process. Even when the environment was deemed secure enough, creating, funding, and staffing the efforts took time. Given the terrible privations that Bosnians had endured, I was dismayed when the newly named High Representative Carl Bildt announced that he would begin his work in a few weeks—after, I noticed, a long, European-style Christmas vacation.

In the year-long gap left while the Office of the High Representative struggled to become operational, IFOR came under pressure to assume roles better left to the civilian side—such as ensuring the provision of gas and water. When at last the OHR was developed enough to take on those roles, military "mission extension" contributed to confusion about

It was amazing to think that grinning young men on the streets had just ended three years of grim battle.

Checkpoints, limited fuel, broken up roads. It was slow going as the country began to advance.

who was taking the lead on projects. The resulting turf battles sometimes led to ugly incidents, such as when a success-starved UN civil
agency disparaged a reconstruction project undertaken by the military.

Part of the discord was systemic. Military leaders were determined
not to get entangled in the many difficulties on the OHR side or to have
their hands tied by a decision process dependent on civilians.

Delays and conflicts were, however, only symptoms of a greater, overarching failure: no unified command structure existed to integrate and
synchronize civilian and military apparatus. Part of the problem was
political. The high representative himself had no UN authority. Without
that widely accepted political backing, he was unable to provide direction to a combined operation. Consequently, civil and military components strived for cooperation but fell short of deep integration: the two
spheres were neither formally nor informally stitched together. Dayton
did not even require that the civilian and military authorities consult
each other. Meetings of principals occurred only from time to time, not
on a consistent basis. And without support from the top, midlevel coordination was certainly not strong enough to produce a cohesive effort.
The result of this disunity was that the civil and military operations fell
far short of what they could have achieved together. Their failure could
be measured not only in wasted budgets and ineffectual work plans but
also in frigid apartments and fearful returnees.

Complications aside, for the most part Bosnians appreciated the stabilizing effect of international troops. An American officer described to
me how "IFOR" was showing up on more than just NATO tanks and vehicles. Astute civilians had started putting emblems on their cars and
trucks to bluff their way through the illegal but numerous paramilitary
checkpoints. One day, the officer had passed a horse-drawn cart, loaded
with hay, with "IFOR" painted across the back.

61. INSIDE: By a Thread

The emotional pitch of survivors across the country was sky-high as they
begged for information about what had been done to find the missing,
whether their missing family members were alive, whether there were
secret detention centers holding prisoners, and whether remains had
been decently buried.

They were alienated even by the legal jargon crafted to help their
cause: "A missing person is a person about whom his family has no information and/or, based on reliable information, is reported as missing
as a consequence of an armed conflict that happened in the territory of
the former SFRY."[3]

By the end of the conflict in 1995, about thirty thousand people were missing—out of a population of 3.4 million.[4] But all those unaccounted for had multiple other people who were frantically trying to find them. The effects were reflected in workplace disinterest, unending emotional suffering, and civic withdrawal. Acknowledging these far-reaching impacts, former US Senator Bob Dole declared that reconciliation projects were essential for bringing "closure to thousands of families who have been locked in the torment of the past."[5]

When people approached me with their searches and their questions, I wished I could give clear answers. But so many promises had been made, only to be followed by betrayal. In several cases, international military leaders insisted that they couldn't secure an area that contained mass graves, so that the bodies could be exhumed and identified. To underscore their demand for information, a group of women publicly vowed that if answers weren't forthcoming within fifteen days, they would instigate civil disobedience and "spread rebellion." The threat was credible: on the Serb side, women in Banja Luka held two senior diplomats hostage for twenty-four hours at the office of the OSCE. The price for their release was information about some two thousand missing Serbs.

But hearing the information did not mean accepting it.

Mark Steinberg, a California attorney who helped those searching for loved ones, described to me a scene that was only one among millions. A forensic pathologist was attempting to identify the remains of a young child who had died in the war. Was the girl the daughter of the woman waiting outside his laboratory? The mother had given the pathologist her child's height, weight, and hair color. The doctor found a match in all respects. He emerged from his lab to report to the woman that her daughter was, indeed, deceased.

The woman said he was wrong, and that she could prove it. She said she had forgotten to mention that her daughter's appendix had been removed. The doctor returned to the laboratory and found that the girl's appendix was missing. He came back to the woman, saying he remained certain the dead child was her daughter.

Still she resisted. She asked the doctor to see if the personal effects delivered with the body included a red coat. He went to the effects room, checked the appropriate locker, and found a red coat. He returned to the woman and told her she now needed to go home and rest. She wouldn't leave. She said he had to do one more thing—just one more. He had to check if the button on the coat had been sewn on with homemade thread.

Once again, the doctor returned to the laboratory, took out the coat, looked at the thread, and saw that it was, in fact, homemade. He sighed, then went back to the mother. Looking into her eyes, he said nothing, took her arm, and guided her out of his office.

62. OUTSIDE: Missing

Mark Steinberg and Ambassador Menzies met with a diverse group of women who had created an Association for the Missing, to exhaust every means possible to find their loved ones. According to Principal Deputy High Representative Michael Steiner, who called me in Vienna requesting my support, this was the first group to cross conflict lines. If they could do it, surely others could follow.

The Bosnian women were upset but organized, while the outsiders trying to help them were composed but in chaos. Six months had passed since Article 5, Annex 7 of the Dayton Accords mandated an effort chaired by the International Committee of the Red Cross to address the thirty thousand to forty thousand missing Bosnians. Yet the ICRC still had not determined its own governing rules. After six more months, multiple ventures had been created by the exasperated international community, with titles such as "Working Group on Enforced or Involuntary Disappearances," "Working Group on the Process for Tracing Persons Unaccounted For," and "Expert Group on Exhumation and Missing Persons."

At the G7 summit in 1996, President Clinton had established the International Commission on Missing Persons to address the situation.[6] But the initial stages were slow and unequal to the task of satisfying so many searching families.

For its part, the UN had appointed Manfred Nowak, a professor of international law in Vienna, as the "expert in charge of the special process on missing persons in the former Yugoslavia." Nowak came to my embassy office to explain his goals and to ask why he did not have the support of "the Americans." "The Americans" in turn complained to me that Nowak was not equipped for the job and in fact was naive. Having never worked with Nowak, I had no way of assessing the charge against him.

Since most of the missing were dead, Nowak's search was closely tied to exhuming mass graves. His plan thus began with an antemortem database comprising dental and hospital records and other identifying information from family members. Those data could be compared with information collected as graves were opened. Still, he cautioned, after an expenditure of some six million dollars for the first year of operation, the identification rate might not be higher than 10 percent.

After the Red Cross had said for eight months that they could get no information, Steinberg prevailed on them to do the obvious—cull from witness testimony at the ICTY names of those already known to be dead. They could then pass that basic information on to anguished families. Meanwhile, a group of experts set up by the ICRC met in Geneva. I thought it would have been more fitting, though less convenient, to have held the meeting in the town hall of Srebrenica.

Complicating efforts to identify bodies, the Serbs were still reneging on the "freedom of movement" guaranteed in the Dayton Peace Agreement, and international troop commanders were still no help. Thus, women survivors of Srebrenica were unable to get to the corpses left lying in the woods around their town (still under Serb control) to identify and bury them. It took a year before UN Special Rapporteur on Human Rights Elizabeth Rehn arranged for the Finns and Dutch to fund forensic specialists to deal with those "surface remains."

Booby traps were another obstacle for the families. So were land mines. But the NATO commander was adamant that removing mines around mass graves was not in his mandate. Nor would he provide security for the gravesites as they were being exhumed—his tens of thousands of soldiers had to stay on base "for their own safety." If the dead had been American soldiers, I wondered, might the commander have found a way to retrieve and bury their bodies?

Almost two years after Srebrenica, Professor Nowak resigned, "based on the experience that there is not sufficient political will to establish the fate of the missing by all possible means, including exhumation and to create an unambiguous mandate of the special process based on a clear division of labour with the ICRC and other relevant organizations."[7]

Indeed, one of my most disheartening evenings was at a Sarajevo restaurant, with representatives from the ICRC, the ICTY, and Physicians for Human Rights. Since I worked closely with survivors, I frequently interviewed those who controlled a vital part of their lives. But this time, I stayed silent as the three argued heatedly about whether and how bodies could be excavated from mass graves.

One advocated exhuming large numbers of corpses, to convince survivors that their loved ones were likely dead and not in forced labor in an underground mine in Serbia (a rumor that kept many people's hopes alive). The next insisted that the skeletons not be disturbed, because doing so might destroy evidence of war crimes. The third argued that although DNA testing would be slow and expensive, identifying bodies was the real goal. His organization was proud of its response to the challenge, and they were hiring a public relations professional to explain why that year they could identify only fifty out of fifteen thousand unnamed corpses.

Reports of depression mounted as the tense peace wore on. In some cases, this epidemic took the form of suicide, domestic violence, and extreme lethargy. Many of those who had hung on heroically through years of fear now ended their lives in the postwar malaise.[8]

Psychologists also reported a sharp upswing in family violence and anxiety disorders. At times, this aggression included sons against mothers. In others, husbands of many years would become violent without warning, causing women to consider taking their own lives. But the numbers were uncertain. Not only were there inadequate statistical agencies, but women greatly underreported being abused. Speaking about such matters was taboo: Bosnia was still a patriarchal society, which made mistreatment a private matter and the preservation of a marriage paramount. In short, women were taught to obey, not speak out.

Whether due to post-traumatic stress disorder or the depression that follows a three-and-a-half-year adrenaline surge, the emotional dip in Bosnia was palpable. Formerly energized leaders, suddenly mired in hopelessness, were hardly able even to attend meetings. Civic guidance from these influential citizens disappeared. The brain drain contributed to the problem, with young people feeling there was no future for them in Bosnia.

Doctors gave myriad psychological reasons to account for the steady increase in depression and violence. After years of racing past snipers, cowering in basements, enduring rape or mutilation, and watching loved ones suffer, most of the population was left with deep psychological wounds. Yet few dared ask for help. Agony was widespread and professional treatment scarce and poorly distributed across the country; moreover, they might be labeled "crazy," and mental illness was stigmatized.

Some observers blamed the failed economy for the change in mood, as well as other economic and social factors. Unemployed and coping with newly changed family structures, men in particular struggled to reclaim their past identities. They were expected to provide and care for their families, but violence and poverty had taken their toll on men's sense of self-worth. Many simply could not go on.

The widespread availability of weapons meant that uncertainty easily could translate into violence. The legal system was unequal to dealing with this trend. Before the massive displacements, family and friends could have stepped in to mitigate such domestic problems. But the war had destroyed those networks, leaving women and children without support. The unresolved refugee crisis left families divided and disconnected from their homes, adding to the lethal mix.

In Republika Srpska, the suicide rate jumped immediately after the end of the war; 77 percent of the suicides were men. A sociologist theorized: "Aggressive impulses that were present during the war are now returning like a boomerang. Maybe that is the reason why more men commit suicide than women."[9] The return of such impulses was often unexpected. Ljilja, a thirty-year-old Bosnian Serb, was finally settling into life after the war. Her family's lot was improving. Then one morning while their baby slept, her husband went to the front of their home and draped his body over a live hand grenade. He left no note and had given no indication of distress. His wife lamented: "I never saw it coming, that he was thinking of killing himself. We had a baby, things would have gotten better I am sure, we could have been happy, but it is too late now."[10] During the war, the aggressors had been told they were heroes as they killed, raped, and tortured for glory. Day after day, those ideals of valor were reinforced by fellow combatants. Afterward, when their band of brothers dispersed, these soldiers were left to their own thoughts. Outside their collective, perpetrators had to cope with their guilt alone.

Among all groups, another kind of guilt was claiming lives—the quiet guilt of having survived when so many others had perished. Thus the war took its toll among perpetrators and victims alike, long after peace was proclaimed.

64. OUTSIDE: Press Tour

The news media are chronically oriented toward fearful, negative accounts, whether rumors, scandals, accidents, or destruction. In the Balkans, reporters who tried to buck the trend had trouble getting encouraging stories placed after the war. Editors dodged the blame, saying publishers were calling the shots. Publishers claimed they were just responding to market forces; their readers wanted disasters, not champions. And finally, given the tragic stories they had been covering for three years, it was personally hard for media professionals to shift to an optimistic mode.

Touring a heavily mined community in a van, I sat behind a seasoned *New York Times* reporter. We looked out the windows at a dozen houses along the road. Eleven were damaged and uninhabited, but one had been restored. In front, the house boasted a bed of purple and blue irises in full bloom. The woman who lived in the house, I was told, was determined to care for her irises. So she had returned, searching her yard inch by inch on her knees with a fork to be sure there were no land mines.

"Crossing Borders," we called our press and funders tour,
organized by Valerie Gillen, Carol Edgar, and Sarah Gauger.

The reporter and I each wrote up our observations for publication. Yes, there were setbacks, arrests, and beatings. And sorrow was fertile ground for frustration—or worse, inaction. But the Balkans could not afford more years of paralysis. Courageous people were in fact moving back to their homes. Thus, my article called on readers to overcome the negativity that only compounded the challenges of rebuilding.

A few days later, I opened the *Times* and read the story of my fellow passenger. It was a tale of hopelessness, positing that because of real and figurative land mines, the region would never be resettled. When I looked further into his work, I found one article after another under his byline reporting corruption, disappointments, and hurdles in postwar Bosnia. None described the signs of promise I was beginning to see. To hear him tell it, nothing was going right.

I would not have cared so much had I not realized the influence such a barrage of negativity had on policymakers who held the purse strings to development funds. The negativity was self-fulfilling. Why should the world support economic development in communities run by corrupt politicians or too dangerous for resettlement?

Lonely (and self-doubting) in my optimism, I invited several American journalists to join me for a tour across the Federation and Republika Srpska. We spent four days in Tuzla, Banja Luka, and Sarajevo. From that trip, seven articles were published over the next year.

One young reporter on our tour was eager to interview refugees in a collective center outside Banja Luka. With pen and notebook in hand, he approached a Bosnian Serb grandmother. She was sitting on the side of a bunk bed, her head in her hands. Her skin was furrowed from years of weather and war.

"Hello, Grandmother. Will you tell us why you're here?" I asked, sitting down next to her on her bed.

In a deadened voice, she described her resolve not to leave her village. Then one day her house was shelled. Her home burst into flames, burning to death her seven grandchildren. "Croats did that," she said, with revulsion.

"Will you ever be able to forgive and forget?" asked the young reporter standing next to me. I found the question callow—disrespectful of her grief. Her retort was in kind.

I took the young man aside and said: "Ask if she can imagine ever living next door to a Croat woman and her children." We stepped back over to where she sat, and he asked the question. Her look went right through him.

"Of course," she answered, as if he were a simpleton. "We always have."

The freelance reporters said later that they had never had such a difficult time getting stories placed. One told me that her piece on strong Bosnian women was ranked lowest in interest by readers. In fact, it was exactly this concern that Bosnian Prime Minister Haris Silajdžić had expressed to our group. "I'm afraid of what will happen when there's not enough blood," he said simply. In the parlance of American journalism, "if it bleeds, it leads."

65. INSIDE: Organized for Action

Prime Minister Silajdžić asserted that the conflict would never have happened if 51 percent of the policymakers had been female: "Before she commits to war, a woman decides if the goal is worth the life of her child. And she doesn't try to be a hero at the expense of other people's children." Was he right? The Bosnian women I knew were convinced he was.

Week after week during the war, these sophisticated, highly educated women had dodged bullets across sniper zones to collect water in plastic jugs. Still, one woman told me that every morning she put on her lipstick as an act of defiance.

Her words were on my mind when I spoke to about forty women leaders, whom I'd met with half a dozen times before at Žena 21 (women of the twenty-first century). The small club, situated near the river and up two flights of dank, dark stairs, had been started by Nurdžihana Đozić—who had written the stirring letter to Lord Carrington early in the siege. Like so many other professional women, the fifty-year-old journalist had worked without a salary during the war; she had managed a monthly magazine by using the occasional electricity in the café across the street from her apartment. A team had distributed the papers across the city, braving snipers. Estimates were that each of the six thousand copies was read by ten women in Sarajevo. In places dense with refugees, the readership was fifty per copy.

Surrounded by Nurdžihana's colleagues, I was midsentence in a rousing homily of encouragement when the lights blinked off, then on, then off again. My hosts didn't seem to notice. There was no stir, no

In sixteen years of work in Bosnia, I witnessed no group as consistently focused and determined as the women, rebuilding their country.

commotion. Candles simply appeared and were passed down the table as the meeting continued. Suddenly we were joined by another forty— shadows on the walls.

As I closed, repeating what I'd been told about the new meaning of makeup, I poured tubes of American lipstick onto a silver tray. The women laughed. They understood the symbol. Rather than buying into the masculine world of war, they would trade on their feminine force to wage peace. As I passed around the tray, I pointed a flashlight on it so they could choose their weapons.

Soon after, I invited members of that same group to our embassy residence in Vienna. That meeting was one in a series I'd been hosting with women across imploding Eastern Europe. In addition to offering respite, we always included strategic planning sessions and training in pressing needs, such as post-traumatic stress disorder. With every group, raw personal stories led to bursts of energy as the participants plotted to restore their societies. These Bosnian women envisioned a breakthrough conference to reunite their divided country. This was not my diplomatic bailiwick. Further, many colleagues at the State Department had serious reservations, warning of both physical danger and political failure. Nonetheless, I decided to support the plan with my personal funds.

Back in Sarajevo, the organizers worked without pay for two months, never stopping. In my office, Valerie Gillen tried to help, but phone service was erratic, and it often took us two days to get a fax through to them. For that matter, everything was difficult, including having no bank that could cash checks from supporters like me. But for these women, that was business as usual.

Although they planned the conference for 250 attendees, twice that number showed up at the rented Army Hall. Women in postwar Bosnia were stretched beyond comprehension, but these hundreds came because they realized that if they could create enough forward motion, they might prevent a slide back into war. Representing more than fifty women's associations from every corner of the country, they united in a city that had been under siege without lights, heat, or running water only a few months earlier.

Many Bosnian Serbs or Croats braved retaliation by paramilitaries when they returned from the conference to their "ethnically pure" towns. More troubling, they were putting their families at risk: going to Sarajevo, they left their children unprotected; and returning home, they would mark their families as collaborators with the enemy. Still, an amazing 35 percent of invitees braved scavenging soldiers at military checkpoints to come from Republika Srpska.

When the women arrived at the gray, pockmarked building, they were greeted by a huge banner announcing: "Women Transforming Ourselves and Society." That mission was fulfilled; the meeting was both life-changing and historical. It produced a legion of energized women who decided to fan out into electoral politics, business, and academia. And it was the first postwar conference encompassing all Bosnia-Herzegovina.

As the buses from newly opened regions pulled up, exhaustion gave way to apprehension. The women from outside Sarajevo didn't know how they would be received by those who had survived the siege. After all, who knew what son or brother had manned the tanks and snipers' nests in the hills?

But the State Department's expectations of infighting proved wrong. For one thing, we worked hard to keep each woman feeling integrated into the whole. During the war, those from the outskirts hadn't had the same voice as those from within the capital. In a gesture unusual for Bosnia, the organizers put a microphone in the center aisle, giving all the women an equal opportunity to have their say as they planned priorities for their new state.

At one point, a woman from Srebrenica started talking about her experience and sobbing. That opened a gate. A Croatian who'd suffered tremendously started to do the same. But that path was well worn, and the moderators knew it was time to move into the future. So they introduced the next set of speakers, who would cover several broad themes. In small rooms and hallway clusters, the women crafted concrete proposals for each area. Conjuring up a new future, in which all interests would be represented, the women created a platform of action covering human rights, elections, lawmaking, work equity, media, family matters, education, and health. But the underlying message of this conference was that working together, they would break through psychological and social barriers that would block any one of them alone.

Given the uncertainties of the local political situation, Bosnian women had seized an extraordinary opportunity to stabilize their society. It was such an obviously smart move, and one that, if left to international powers, well might have been overlooked.

66. OUTSIDE: Lyons

The women of Bosnia needed much help to assume the leadership their country required. But it was easy for their activities to become marginalized rather than recognized as on a par with traditional political and military affairs. That needed to change, and I had to go straight to the top.

On 12 April 1996, I wrote to President Clinton, offering two pieces of advice. The first was: "We must come up with a more solid approach to the war criminals living within a few miles of the troops." And the second was: "We need a strongly targeted effort now to strengthen the role of women in Bosnia. . . . The structure is there, the talent is there, and our long-term interest is there."

The president wrote back in May: "I would be very interested in your thoughts on raising the profile of women in Bosnia and increasing our efforts to deal with women's issues in the process of rebuilding civil society in Bosnia. In the meantime, I will have my staff look into ways to improve our current outreach program, and I will look for an early opportunity to speak publicly on the matter."

The president had sent my letter to the State Department, with a note to the undersecretary of state for political affairs. The ball was rolling. An assistant secretary of state called and asked me to help design an initiative that could be announced at the upcoming G7 meeting in Lyons, France. On 9 June, I convened three trusted embassy personnel with a few State Department officials who were passing through Vienna.[1] None of us had time during the next day to meet, so—sustained by brownies and wine—we stole some hours from the middle of the night to dream up what we dubbed the Bosnian Women's Initiative.

The evolution from design to practice needed shepherding. The president had put his initials in the margin of my letter, which meant "make it happen"; even so, with the crush of competing priorities in Washington, an untended effort would quickly be lost. With this in mind, I shifted my priorities to this venture. Colleagues at the State Department helped me create a Bosnian women-run network to distribute funding and technical support through nascent NGOs stimulating women-owned businesses. The department committed to fund the first year of the project. Other nations would be asked to contribute as well.

On 23 June, I spent my morning working on a public statement from President Clinton establishing the Bosnian Women's Initiative. That afternoon, Sandy Vershbow at the National Security Council, who was working on the president's G7 trip, informed me that no announcement of the initiative would be made—there would just be a press release. This one was worth fighting for, and I lobbied hard until, on 25 June, I received a call from Vershbow asking me to be in Lyons a few days later. I was to brief President Clinton before he introduced the initiative at the end of the G7 summit.

It was terrible timing. I was due on stage in Bosnia a mere twelve hours before that presidential briefing to keynote a conference. In the absence of commercial flights to Bosnia, there was no physical way I could make both events as planned. So my colleague Valerie managed to get me moved to the beginning of the Sarajevo program, ahead of President Izetbegović's welcome. I delivered a rousing message and then was rushed in an armored vehicle to the Sarajevo airport for a ride on an all-terrain C-130 transporting NATO soldiers to Naples.

On the four-jet-engine plane, Val and I got out our earplugs and strapped ourselves into seats against the wall, wedged between charming Italian soldiers and netted heavy cargo. We landed in the middle of the night at the Naples military base and an hour later were on a highway headed for Rome. After a few hours of sleep in the residence of the US embassy's deputy chief of mission, we caught a 6:00 a.m. flight to Brussels. After a layover, we flew on to Lyons. Arriving crumpled and weary, we were whisked from the airport to the Pavilion du Parc, a central hotel that was the headquarters of the US delegation to the G7 meeting. As we walked in, a young White House organizer asked impatiently why I was so late.

I gave the bellman my luggage and proceeded straight to the National Security Council Operations Room. The president's speech writer, Dan Baer, and his assistant were crafting words for the press conference an hour or so later. "Do you mind if I take a look?" I asked the assistant, who was startled by the request.

"It's okay; she's a writer," Dan said. I mentally congratulated myself for sending him a newspaper column I wrote each month. Then I sat down at the computer to reshape (and lengthen) the description of the Bosnian Women's Initiative for the president's remarks.

Mounted on the wall behind me, a closed-circuit monitor showed the empty "situation room" at the White House, where specialists argued military strategy. I felt like I was in that room. Indeed, advancing the role of women in a postconflict society *was* the stuff of war and peace, whether traditional security experts recognized that or not.

Some midlevel White House staffers complained that they were held up as French police in the complex rustled through their documents. I thought about the women's meetings I had been part of in Bosnia. What a contrast. No police secured their hall, despite the danger in which they were putting themselves by crossing former front lines.

The G7 delegation included not only Secretary of State Warren Christopher, but also Treasury Secretary Robert Rubin, pushing his macroeconomic policies and structural reforms, including debt forgiveness for the poorest countries. Those issues were only several on an agenda crammed with environmental protection, Russian elections, UN reform, job creation, terrorism, crime, narcotics, arms trafficking, and nuclear smuggling.

This was the very complicated backdrop of my briefing with the president just before his concluding international press conference. When I arrived at the Pavilion du Parc, Clinton was in his Russian bilateral meeting. I used the time to rehearse my points in a "pre-brief" with White House Press Secretary Mike McCurry, National Security Advisor Tony Lake, Deputy National Security Advisor Sandy Berger, and Deputy Chief of Staff Harold Ickes Jr.

As he walked out of the bilateral meeting, President Clinton caught sight of me standing on the side. He greeted me with a broad smile and big hug, and a surprised "What are *you* doing here?"

"I'm here to brief you," I began, somewhat disappointed. Just then, Secretary Christopher walked up and began reviewing developments in Syria.

We continued upstairs to a small holding room, where the president rehearsed answers to tough questions the press might throw out: the whereabouts of Mladić and Karadžić, an explosion in Saudi Arabia, sanctions for Milošević. To conclude, Berger described the successful deployment in Bosnia of tens of thousands of NATO-led troops.

The meeting appeared over when Vershbow, standing against the back wall, reminded the president that I was there to tell him about the Bosnian Women's Initiative. I quickly described the conference in Sarajevo I had just attended: "These women are working together—across political fault lines."

Clinton glanced up at me as an aide handed him several aspirin and a glass of water. "Like the women in Northern Ireland?" he asked.

"Yes, sir, Mr. President," I said, "and they're the best story you've got."

President Clinton and Secretary of State Christopher met me in the hallway, as White House Senior Director for European Affairs Sandy Vershbow looked on. Sandy went on to a brilliant career as ambassador to three posts (NATO, Russia, and South Korea), as well as assistant secretary of defense for international security affairs.

Berger was clearly irritated. Out in the hallway he pulled me aside. "I've been telling him our troops are a great success," he said tersely.

There's always some reason women shouldn't be the story, I thought. I told him, "You've got the troops in, but you'll need to get them out at some point, Sandy. These women can create the stability to make it possible." From his look, I knew we were not going to resolve that argument in the hallway.

Ten minutes after we briefed him, I watched President Clinton stride out into the sun and stand in front of a beautiful swan-graced lake, before scores of international reporters. He followed his prepared speech word for word, and I smiled as he read my expanded announcement of the Bosnian Women's Initiative, "established with an initial US contribution of five million dollars to spur economic development with training and equipment and business loans."

Then he looked up and gazed out at the press. His voice picked up energy as he departed from the text. I found a transcript later: "Women today are meeting in Bosnia—*today*—on this issue. Muslim, Croat, and Serb women are meeting in Bosnia today, with multiethnic, cooperative determination to regenerate the capacity of the Bosnian economy through the efforts of its women. This has real potential to make a difference!"

For President Clinton, the empowerment of Bosnian women represented a welcome step forward. For Bosnian women, the president's announcement in Lyons meant the world was listening.

67. INSIDE: "What's an NGO?"

As Bosnians shifted from war to peace, Communism to capitalism, tyranny to democracy, a cultural change was also occurring. By choice or necessity, women's roles were evolving. Because so many men had been killed or wounded, the collective contribution of women had become even more vital to society. As individuals, however, many were now the sole providers for their families. With that increased responsibility, they grew in strength, endurance, and resourcefulness—qualities essential to building not only a family, but also a business and a country.

In Tuzla, one entrepreneur received a Bosnian Women's Initiative loan of one thousand dollars for equipment to manufacture sugar cubes. She moved her family upstairs and converted her three downstairs rooms into a small factory, where blocks of sugar on her wide worktable were laboriously cut by hand into thousands of uniform pieces. I visited her the day she repaid her start-up loan and took out another two thousand dollars to expand. In a region with almost no remaining business infrastructure and 60 percent unemployment, this entrepreneur already had six employees—five women and one man—mostly Bosniak like her. Her bookkeeper, she wanted me to know, was a Serb.

Beba Hadžić, another entrepreneur in Tuzla, was typical of many. First a math teacher, then a high-school principal, Beba was used to organizing. She managed to procure carpet looms for a project to engage refugees who otherwise would be sitting at home with only their memories. Now, in one large room, they sat talking as they passed shuttles through brightly colored warp and woof.

Tall and sturdy, with a quick smile, Beba was a paragon of resilience—and a woman of action. One evening over coffee she explained: "I'm not a pessimist. I'm an optimist. If I weren't an optimist, I'd be a terrorist." Beba wasn't playing with words. And she was too careful for hyperbole. She was speaking from four years as a refugee.

During the war, the humanitarian organization Bosfam—an affiliate of the British Oxfam—supplied basic support to refugees. When the group

In Tuzla, Beba Hadžić brought me to meet her rug weavers—refugees from Srebrenica whose work helped them survive past loss and present chaos.

Beba Hadžić from Srebrenica always had a new idea, from a bottomless well of hope.

announced it was pulling out because of danger to its personnel, Beba protested vehemently. The organization's leaders told her: "If you have someone to take over the NGO, we'll turn it over to you and fund it."

"*I'll* run the NGO," she responded immediately—then added, "What's an NGO?"

As the new leader of Bosfam, Beba helped Srebrenica survivors secure food, find shelter, search for the missing, and eventually rouse the world's conscience with a historic commemoration of the massacre. But she was also counselor and comforter, absorbing a daily litany of testimonies and emotional breakdowns. "Sometimes you need three shoulders to bear it all," she said.

68. OUTSIDE: Skewed

Consistent with microlending worldwide, funding Bosnian women's economic activity was a remarkably safe bet. Without the rule of law, corruption among male leaders—former Communists and others—was skyrocketing. Many had become pure opportunists. Among women, however, corruption was almost unheard of. Still, international support that went into women's commercial activity was infinitesimally small compared to aid that poured into more traditional male-led parts of the economy.

Despite repeated official assurances, all was not well with the Bosnian Women's Initiative. Some six months after President Clinton's public announcement that the funds were forthcoming, not a penny had appeared. One day, the Bosnian women leaders called me in Vienna. I had been the one to convey the president's promise to them, so it was fitting that they approach me about the delay. We all knew that these were not superfluous grants to give a few individuals more satisfying employment. The projects were strategic to the international goal of jump-starting postconflict recovery. Furthermore, the prospective recipients were destitute. Such delay was unconscionable.

The UN High Commissioner for Refugees, charged with administering President Clinton's promised funds, had allowed bureaucratic ineptitude and delays that transformed this US gesture of help into one more disappointment. The first staffer sent to Sarajevo to establish the program eventually was deemed incompetent and removed. The next was tapped for the position months before he finished his assignment in Indonesia.

When we finally had our first meeting, the new project leader expressed astonishment that someone had questioned his being selected to run the program because he was a man. "I was the objector," I said, adding that I had nothing against him personally but thought it sadly illustrative that UNHCR had appointed a man to run an empowerment program for women.

The hindrances were not just bureaucratic. Needs were enormous and dollars woefully limited at headquarters. A cable from the US embassy in Sarajevo reported: "UNHCR has been focused on making its ends meet this year, given funding shortfalls. . . . UNHCR will continue to expect the US Government to take the lead in educating other potential donors to UNHCR/BWI [the Bosnian Women's Initiative]."

Taking up that mantle, I made an appointment in Washington with the assistant secretary of state for population, refugees, and migration, Phyllis Oakley. I offered to visit other governments to ask for contributions to the initiative. She expressed concern that such action would undercut the Department of State staffer responsible for expanding the program. But the staffer, who was relatively junior, had little success in adding new donors. Meanwhile, when I did secure grants for projects with Bosnian women, there was so much red tape that I had no choice but to route the funds through NGOs outside UNHCR.

Finally, a year and a half after the Lyons announcement, the initiative's director in Sarajevo informed me that scores of grants were beginning to flow in. Now hope is alive, I thought. But a pamphlet from

UNHCR read as follows: "Operational objectives provide the basis for the development of appropriate activities and work plans to support implementation of UNHCR's Policy on Refugee Women. These are: to develop mechanisms to ensure that the resources and needs of refugee women are addressed in all stages of programme . . . planning, management and evaluation systems. . . ."[2]

There was no bold vision. No inspiring mission. No sense of urgency.

The words came alive only at the grass-roots level. Eventually, I reviewed a report on the initial five million dollar US contribution. Eighty-seven organizations throughout Bosnia were helping women get back on their feet, support their families, and fuel local economies. In Banja Luka, seventy-two disabled women received computer training; 180 widows in the Tuzla area, with six hundred family members, now had farming tools, seeds, and fertilizer. All over Bosnia, women had been trained as tailors, horticulturists, and in a dozen other professions.

Despite those developments, I soon heard rumors from the women that the initiative was being discontinued. Alarmed, I made yet another appointment with the project director in Sarajevo, who also had authority over a wider expanse of UN humanitarian funds. He told me frankly that he did not know why there should be a program focusing on women. His intent was to "mainstream" the funds into his overall budget. I protested that it was too early for that move; women's needs were often different from men's, and a program focused on their situation would be most effective for now. Since we already had a working program, I suggested we should expand it instead. I volunteered again to look for additional funding. Could he provide me with fuller descriptions of grantees I could use to solicit potential donors?

"Let me think about that and get back to you." His reply sounded strange, given my offer. Several weeks later, he wrote to say that after careful thought, he had decided he did not want more funding for the Bosnian Women's Initiative. It might, he said, skew his budget.[3]

69. INSIDE: A League of Their Own

There was so much in Bosnia that needed to be set straight. Rolling up their sleeves, thirteen women leaders (including Beba Hadžić) traveled from all parts the country, by jeep and helicopter, to Eagle Base. The two-day retreat, made possible by NATO and organized by Valerie and me, included women from Srebrenica as well as Serb strongholds, politicians and journalists, and believers of all faiths.

When the women arrived, we all had lunch with our military hosts. I

Our accommodations at Eagle Base were hardly posh: sandbag-lined tents, in the snow.

Diverse women leaders created out of whole cloth the League of Women Voters of Bosnia and Herzegovina. We replicated the model many times in the following months and years.

remarked to myself on the juxtaposition of such a diverse group of soldiers with the Europeans who reputedly could not coexist—because of their ethnicity.

After the first banana cream pie of their lives, the women divided into pairs in a room not far from the mess hall. Each woman listened to a description of the other's wartime experience, then returned to the group to introduce her partner. Next, each individual spent time alone making a list of the three things she most wanted for her country. We collected their aspirations on flip charts. Their hopes centered on major tenets of the Dayton Peace Agreement, particularly the right of refugees to return to their homes.

To turn those dreams into action, Val and I presented several models of American groups that might be replicated in Bosnia: Neighborhood Watch, the New York Women's Foundation, and the League of Women Voters. The participants discussed all the models in depth before they voted on which one they wanted to create. After two days of hard work, they emerged with the League of Women Voters of Bosnia-Herzegovina, replete with governance structure, mission statement, and first-year work plan. This civic vanguard was one of the new democracy's first organizations to cross war lines.[4]

I found the women's aptitude and optimism dazzling. Their ability to agree on long-term stability measures was due in part to a trust-fostering exercise we built into the first evening of our program. In the near darkness of a lantern-lit tent, some sat on bunk beds, others on the floor. All were tired from the day of travel. The simplicity itself was calming, softening defenses. But the goal was not only to help the women bond. Each needed to be understood in the starkness of her individuality and as much more than a war-forged stereotype.

Holding a shallow box filled with everyday objects, I led an exercise in which each woman, without looking, picked one of them and then told what it evoked for her. The first pulled out a pair of scissors; she described how she was cut off from the love of her family and the comforting familiarity of her home. The second ended up with some film. She said she wished someone had still had a camera when her brother was being buried. One woman had a candle:

> I used to think of candle-lit dinners as romantic. Then, after being mostly without electricity for the last three years, I told my friends and family I'd never, ever burn another candle. But I'm going to hold onto this one to say that I can appreciate the beauty it will bring. That's what today with all of you has meant to me. Tonight I'm rejoining the world.

The Eagle Base meeting had been conceived in a candle-lit bistro in Brussels when my husband, Charles Ansbacher, and I joined General Wesley Clark and his wife, Gertrude, for dinner. We had flown up from Vienna to meet the Clarks, since Charles and Wes had been friends for decades. Wes had done his part by ensuring privacy; NATO bought out the entire restaurant for the evening.

Wes had been named NATO's military head—Supreme Allied Commander for Europe, or SACEUR. Having witnessed the accident on Mt. Igman as part of Holbrooke's negotiating team, he was profoundly committed to peace in the Balkans. That meant keeping US troops in Bosnia until the country was stabilized.

Pulling in the opposite direction was Senator Kay Bailey Hutchison, a Republican from Texas, who introduced resolutions on the Senate floor calling for the troops' withdrawal. Gert had worked in the senator's office, and so the Clarks knew how smart—and how resolute—she was. In fact, Wes told us, he would be taking her in his plane to see the situation on the ground within a few days. The general spontaneously asked if I might convene some female leaders to meet with the senator. Perhaps woman-to-woman they could convince her that Bosnia was worth further investment. I readily agreed. Her inspection thus had become the action-forcing event that led to the Eagle Base meeting.

When the general's political advisor, Michael Durkee, called me in Vienna Monday morning, I laid out my plan: "I've made a list of about a dozen women. I'll need jeep transport for some and a helicopter to pick up others farther out or in danger spots. We'll want space for two days and nights on Eagle Base. Let's have flip charts, an interpreter, and two soldiers on call to help. Oh, and I'd appreciate a lift between Vienna and Tuzla."

"That must have been some bottle of wine at the bistro," Mike replied dryly.

The military came through, as militaries do, coordinating the conference logistics. For their part, after their hours in the tent, the women were eager to work together. They spent the second day coming up with detailed plans for their League of Women Voters. I found their aptitude and optimism dazzling. As Val and I worked with the women, we received periodic progress reports on the SACEUR's plane, which was bringing the senator and general from Brčko to Eagle Base. The women had to be prepared with a honed message by the time the skeptical senator walked into the room.

At last, General Clark arrived, escorting Senator Hutchison. He excused himself and went into a side room to return a pressing phone call. The senator and I took seats facing the women's group. I asked the participants to introduce themselves using their professional identities (journalist, political leader, educator) rather than ethnicity. They then presented their plan to create the league.

The senator nodded her approval but asked no follow-up questions. Instead, in an odd non sequitur, she launched into her conviction that US troops needed to come home immediately. Disturbed but undaunted, one of the women replied: "Our country is in its infancy. We're just now starting to stand, and our legs are wobbly. Please, keep the troops here until we can walk." She received no response.

Another woman spoke up: "We come from different ethnic groups, but we know we must implement the Dayton Agreement. And, Senator, every one of us, no matter our background, wants universal freedom of movement and return of refugees."

The senator may have agreed in principle. But in fact she offered no US support for the essentials that could make those ideals a reality, particularly apprehending war criminals. Instead, she advised the women to abandon plans to restore their communities and instead "concentrate on the future and just forget the past."

"You're asking us to validate the ethnic cleansing," my friend Beba countered.

Taking no heed, the senator went on: "I think it may be hard, but you just have to invite your enemies into your kitchen to sit down and have a cup of coffee."

Beba looked at me. I looked back and nodded slightly, although I had no idea what she might say:

With all due respect, Senator, I'm from Srebrenica. I was a math teacher and later head of the school. My husband had a good job. We owned a car, had a nice sound system. We had a comfortable home and a vacation cottage. Now, simply because of my last name, I'm a refugee. And, Senator, I can't invite my "enemies" into my kitchen for a cup of coffee. I don't have a kitchen.

SECTION 10   Recreating Community

71. INSIDE: Beethoven's Fifth

Sarajevo was a center for music, which was enjoyed in living rooms as well as concert halls. Even when life was most dismal, hope was practiced by the musicians. One of the most evocative symbols of defiance was the cellist Vedran Smajlovic, who played on the sidewalks even during shelling. Formerly with the Sarajevo Opera Orchestra, Smajlovic wore formal tails for his pavement performances. On one street, where shoppers had been hit by a mortar while waiting in line at a bakery, the musician played for twenty-two days—one day for each neighbor killed.

During one pause in the barrage, the famed conductor Zubin Mehta came in to lead the remnant Sarajevo Symphony Orchestra in Mozart's *Requiem*. The tenor José Carreras was part of the ensemble. For a concert hall, they used the bombed-out ruins of the Sarajevo National Library. The setting was too dangerous for an audience, so they played to an empty hall, but their performance resonated around the world by satellite.

With similar intent, a year before the peace agreement was signed, my symphony conductor husband decided to produce a concert in Mostar to encourage the troubled Bosniak-Croat Federation. Flak jacket and helmet in hand, he rented a car in Split, on the Dalmatian coast. Handing him the keys, the attendant asked where he was heading.

"Mostar."

"Good luck," the man said wryly.

Charles navigated the tortuous roads of Herzegovina throughout the night. He saw no other cars—only strips of demolished houses. When the road took a steep incline, he stopped and looked more carefully into the dark. Something wasn't right, so he backed up and found another road.

In Mostar, Charles met with the EU administrator of the town, selected the site for the concert on a former front line, then headed back for the coast. In the daylight, he saw that the incline he'd started up then abandoned was a blown-up bridge spanning a ravine.

Weeks later, the concert was scuttled when a nearby kindergarten was shelled. The authorities decided it was too risky for citizens to gather.

Eventually, a few weeks after the peace was signed, Charles produced a landmark concert in Sarajevo—the first since the war. Although the players hadn't been paid for four years, they had rehearsed whenever the shelling let up enough that a substantial number could make it to the theater. Summers weren't as hard, but winter after winter they practiced in bitter cold during the few hours of daylight, with no electricity or gas. They insisted on playing, despite clumsy down coats and wool gloves, to keep up their skills.

Every musician had a story. The orchestra was managed by a clarinetist whose instrument was taken from him by soldiers, put under a tank, and crushed. Out of some seventy players, seven had been killed: some after being drafted into the army; one by a sniper, as he walked to a rehearsal. Many others had left as refugees. The remaining thirty-five players thus included former retirees and students. The army band also lent its talent.

When Charles led the orchestra for the first time, I watched from a box above the stage of the National Theater. From my vantage point, I could take in the orchestra, the audience, and the passion of my husband as he conducted. One musician sat on a stool upstage right, behind the trombones. From her perch, Sonja seemed to reign over the oboes and violas. Her small, dark eyes were riveted on the conductor. Sonja had been dividing her time between kitchen kettles and kettle drums for at least forty years. Thin, almost gaunt, her frame seemed frail beside the huge instruments, until she started swinging her mallets. The sequins on her sleeves glittered as her arms flew in a pattern, crisscrossing, then thrashing like the wings of a bird. In her blend of frailty and strength, Sonja embodied the contradiction of Sarajevo.

The hall was a small jewel box of Hapsburg elegance. Slate blue, trimmed with gold, then dusty rose and floral designs as the eye moved upward. For a reason no one seemed to know, this structure had been spared. Still, it required a management decision to heat the building that night, because oil was precious. At least the string players, for a change, weren't in overcoats; and with the minister of energy in the audience, the musicians could count on light throughout the concert.

The performance started twenty minutes late. It took everyone time

From the back row of the orchestra, Sonja on the kettle drum was a symbol of resolve. Charles led, and encouraged, the decimated orchestra in this historical concert.

to get past the soldiers in camouflage uniforms, who were waving metal detector wands across each elegantly dressed guest—unheard of in the pre-September 11 world. Every nook of the building had been searched for bombs by a special team with long-handled mirrors. Even my husband's music case was examined. But as I searched the crowd from the first pounding chords of Beethoven's Fifth Symphony to the triumphant conclusion, I saw few dry eyes.

I particularly noticed the mayor of Sarajevo, Tarik Kupusović, and his wife, Essena, with whom Charles and I had visited that morning. Sitting in their living room, we'd discussed the political morass, the damaged society, and the significance of the concert. Then they asked if we would like to hear their daughter, Mirha, play. She gave us a simple, quiet piano piece by Bach. As I listened to the familiar musical development, my eyes wandered to a shattered glass balcony door on one side of the piano and small holes in the wall and sofa on the other.

This was not Tarik and Essena's original home. That one, in Dobrinja, had been totally destroyed. Essena told us how she'd run through the long trenches I'd seen from the NATO Humvee during the Serb exodus. Like others, she'd braved snipers to salvage the few sentimental items she could. With a bittersweet smile, she held out a linen napkin embroi-

Mirha seemed pleased to play for Maestro Ansbacher and me. The family had been in the kitchen, her mother explained, when bullets riddled this room. Mirha hadn't been practicing just then.

dered by her mother, retrieved from the shambles. Now, in the concert hall, I watched her face, wondering if she was thinking of the past or the future.

72. OUTSIDE: "Neither Free Nor Fair"

To provide a sense of forward movement and coax the society toward normalcy, many international leaders advocated quick elections. Secretary Christopher opined that putting even a flawed election in motion would "give all the people of Bosnia a chance to shape their future."[1] But there were strong arguments against holding a vote so soon. *New York Times* columnist Anthony Lewis laid out a devastating comparison: "Suppose that at the end of World War II, Heinrich Himmler and Adolf

Eichmann had remained in control of a large zone in Germany. They were supposed to be removed and tried for war crimes. But the United States and its allies decided to hold all-German elections while the Nazis still ruled the zone, suppressing and murdering opponents."[2]

Although acknowledging the need for the "best possible conditions," a State Department spokesperson said it was too much to ask that indicted war criminals be arrested before elections—those would not be the "best possible" but rather impossibly "pristine, ideal conditions."[3]

Some high-level American policymakers made damning statements about the early elections, urging postponement. Speaking from Dayton, Ohio, the Republican presidential candidate Bob Dole called the forthcoming elections "a fraud, but a fraud with the American stamp of approval. . . . Many Americans, regardless of party, think it's a big mistake to pursue what would, in effect, be a sham election."[4]

Former Secretary of State Henry Kissinger, a disbeliever in a unified Bosnia, added that each side "suppresses dissent and seeks to use the elections to solidify its ethnic base for the ultimate showdown with hated rivals."[5]

In addition, highly respected international groups like the Helsinki Federation for Human Rights strongly opposed the OSCE policy of holding unfair elections, claiming they "destroy[ed] any possibility to restore the . . . pre-war multi-ethnic character."[6]

Within Bosnia, as well, moderate voices called for delay. Among defenders of the multicultural dream, Prime Minister Silajdžić was one of the most outspoken, pointing out that preconditions called for in the Dayton Peace Agreement—freedom of press, movement, and expression—had not been met. Soon afterward, he was attacked while campaigning, hit with a steel pipe. "I can't even go to the Serb stronghold of Banja Luka, much less campaign there," he protested to me. "So what kind of election will that be? Why the hurry?"

The OSCE, charged with laying the foundation for representative government in Bosnia, thought differently. Ambassador Frowick saw the vote as essential to stabilization. But he took the iconoclastic step of admitting publicly that, given the circumstances, the vote would be "neither free nor fair."

Silajdžić threatened to boycott elections that he felt would install hard-liners in key positions, set back reunification of the country, and stymie the return of hundreds of thousands of refugees. "Why bother taking war criminals like General Mladić and President Karadžić to The Hague? If we accept the [ethnic cleansing] they carried out, they should get a medal instead," he told a CNN reporter. Despite the prime minister's warnings, the first national elections took place on 14 September 1996, only nine months after the final signing of the peace agreement.

In addition to charges of intimidation and fraud, political dysfunction created immense logistical barriers. The electoral process was necessarily convoluted: few displaced people felt safe going back to their towns. Thus they were given the choice of voting for the candidates running where they were living as refugees or of casting long-distance ballots for candidates running back home. With the refugee vote split, there was greater likelihood of extremists winning in towns from which those voters had been expelled. Even if a moderate were elected because of the refugee vote, a hostile community could physically block that person from assuming office.

The question was not only how people were being elected, but also which people were being elected. Although Karadžić was a fugitive from justice and had been barred from public office, his picture was displayed prominently next to campaign posters for other Serb nationalists. Clearly, he was running by proxy.

Consequently, as Silajdžić had predicted, in most cases hard-liners were elected. But a rough piece of democracy was in place, and the international community was taking responsibility to guarantee at least some modicum of fairness. This was a success in its own right, as the country lurched toward stability.

The OCSE had opened the door, and people flooded through. The turnout was enormous—so large, in fact, that charges of double counting spread immediately.[7] The International Crisis Group, a highly respected NGO, compared the votes that were tallied with demographic statistics from UNHCR and declared that voter turnout was 106 percent, demanding that the OSCE not validate the election. But the OSCE disputed the underlying population figures and claimed the count was actually 90 percent.

In fact, measures had been taken to ensure that there was no double voting. Officials had stamped hands with ink. One old farmer ruminated: "Some foreigners came, and they marked us like calves."

73. INSIDE: Sarajevo Red

My Vienna mentor, Viktor Frankl, whose wisdom derived from the Holocaust, once said to me: "Sometimes it's only through ruins that you can see the sky." I remembered his words when I returned to the Sarajevo National Library to pause in the silent grove of pockmarked granite columns. Built on the deep foundation of Bosnia's complex culture, the ruined edifice, longing for reconstruction, had assumed a spiritual quality for me.

After endless shelling, one chaotic night during August 1992 it was targeted with napalm and burst into flames. The fire consumed nearly 50,000 feet of wooden shelves, the atrium, and the stone lacework of the balustrade. Irreplaceable, centuries-old manuscripts and "Bosniaca" were lost. In all, more than a million books were turned to ash.

The energetic director, Enes Kujundžić, was adamant that Sarajevo have a functioning library once again. The city gave him empty army barracks in which to begin restoring the collection. People assumed the former library would be rebuilt—they just didn't know when. As a first step, fire-engine red scaffolding would rise to the new roof under construction, a gift of the Austrian government. No state was coming up with the millions of deutschmarks needed to renovate the historic building, but at least a roof would slow the deterioration.

One winter day, I returned with Charles to a favorite room of mine on the second floor, where we poked through the ruins. I admired the traces of patterns in red, blue, and gold, still discernible on fallen chunks of pale stone wall. Turning to my left, I looked through two rooms, hollow with destruction. Through a stone doorway with neo-Moorish trim and an icicle fringe, we noticed a card catalogue, sitting cockeyed on the rubble.

It began to rain on us through the gaps. We moved more quickly than usual around the room, stepping through the crushed ceiling lying in a heap on the floor. In the center, a lone weed had sprouted. Living things had taken on crucial meaning to Sarajevans. I understood a small bit, remembering a mature rose bush I'd passed in a military Humvee. Seeing the shock of red blooms through the thick, bulletproof window, I thought, "Thank God, now there's peace, and the roses can bloom again." Then it dawned on me: those roses had been blooming every year—even amid the violence and decay. Nature had defied the march of war.

I had the same thought when I passed an apartment building with its entire end collapsed, as if it had melted. The balconies were twisted and hanging. Yet in a window of this ghost house was a tended flower box with brilliant red geraniums.

The flowers had prevailed, yes. But flowers in Bosnia were not just a romantic symbol. Walking through the heart of the city, Charles and I stopped to examine bright crimson splashes on the pavement. A local artist had stained some mortar red and plastered grenade holes in the streets and sidewalks.

Some people hated the reminders of pools of blood. For others, these "Sarejevo roses" were symbols of a personal grief yearning for public acknowledgment.

With snipers gone, a new flower appeared on the streets of the capital, provoking debate over the importance of remembering the past or reorienting toward the future.

74. OUTSIDE: Re-leaf

Reconciliation develops organically. With time, new memories are grafted onto old; with tending, pain recedes and hope takes root. Ambassador Menzies, an informed and insightful man, understood this process. Given his background, I was not totally surprised when John broached with me a notion that became part of his legacy. His career had been launched in the US Information Agency (USIA), the cultural arm of the Foreign Service, rather than in the political and economic State Department "cones" that yielded most ambassadors. I frequently found the USIA professionals more down-to-earth and imaginative than their State Department counterparts.

Our seminal conversation took place at midnight in his Spartan office building right after the peace was signed. Charles had just gotten into a sleeping bag, and John and I wanted some news, so we had gone down to watch CNN. The satellite dish must have shifted; the TV gave us nothing. Instead, we sat across from each other in the bare room, sipping lukewarm hot chocolate from white Styrofoam cups. "You know what I dream of?" he said. "That field across the road. It used to be a park. But during the siege, people had to cut down the trees and burn them, green, to keep warm. I'd like to replant the park with a tree for every child from Sarajevo killed during this war—sixteen hundred of them."

John was right about the importance of trees. When I later crossed paths with a Bosnian employee of the embassy, she pulled me aside and whispered: "You know, for all the meetings, visits, and reports we're producing about starting a central bank, or setting elections, or amending our constitution, it's the replanting of the trees that Bosnian people appreciate most."

Kemal Kurspahic, editor in chief at the prominent daily *Oslobodjenje*, had voiced that sentiment in an impassioned plea: "Do whatever you can to stop the killing, to bring about peace, and then bring us trees." Trees had become Sarajevo's "most precious commodity," he said. Citizens had braved sniper fire to chop them down. Once the parks were destroyed, people went for the stumps. Kurspahic reported that "an entire day of cutting and digging would yield a few bags of wood for cooking and winter heating." But trees bore other dire significance. During the war, the paper published two dark cartoons: A man searches in vain for a tree from which to hang himself; and Jesus carries his cross up a hill, joined by Sarajevans bearing trees.[8]

Soon after my midnight conversation with John, I took his dream to my embassy's agricultural attaché, Alan Mustard. He, in turn, approached Global ReLeaf, an American NGO that had replanted trees in Ukraine and Belarus after the Chernobyl nuclear disaster, as well as in blighted neighborhoods in the United States. Some months later, the Sarajevo director of parks came to our embassy. With landscaping plans spread across my table, he described how desperate citizens had denuded beautiful parks and boulevards for firewood.

When I went on the radio, asking listeners to fund a tree in a child's memory, Austrians responded generously. A year and a half after John's vision, the planting began. I officially launched the project in front of a partially restored elementary school in the shell-pounded Sarajevo suburb of Ilidža.

Just outside the door of the building, a large willow had been cut down for firewood. Our new tree was to be planted in that spot, in the name of a child who would never climb its branches. The principal, teachers, and students were energized, anticipating the ceremony. They had spent days clearing rubble, scrubbing, and painting. In the process, I was told, workers digging a hole for the new tree unearthed and detonated three land mines.

Next to the school was a large garden planted by refugees. The school director told me he hoped it would become a park in the future, where the students could play. As a mother, I wondered what it would take for me to feel safe about my child chasing a ball that went bouncing off a playground here.

75. INSIDE: Watermelons

Compared to Sarajevo, most of the country was moving much more slowly toward normalcy. That was especially true of the eastern enclaves, the former "safe areas." Similar to Srebrenica, Goražde was formerly home to about fifteen thousand Serbs and Bosniaks. But during the war, most of the Serbs had left, and the city harbored about fifty thousand Bosniaks. Now, after the war, since the Serbs had not been allowed to "tidy up the map" (as one British official referred to the proposed massive expulsions), Goražde was linked by a roadway to the rest of the Federation.

In this town, the devastation was apocalyptic. As the peace was being negotiated in October 1995, UN vehicles were able to pass through Serb checkpoints for the first time in more than three years. (The town was only an hour's drive from the capital, but through Serb territory.) Accompanying journalists described a desperate situation, with so little food that there were sores on children's faces from lack of vitamins.[9]

The first peacetime passenger bus entered Goražde ten weeks later. Hundreds of people, many weeping, lined the streets to welcome the fifty-five passengers from Sarajevo. The crowds were held back by police as they pushed forward to see who was on board. Could it be family members taken out over the years by helicopter for medical treatment, with no way to return?

A year later, I made the trip in a car accompanied by two armored vehicles and guards with AK-47s. Along the road between Sarajevo and Goražde, I saw few signs of physical reconstruction. In Goražde itself, packs of dogs swarmed around our vehicles as we slowly drove past families living in still-destroyed buildings. Laundry hung in the cold rain next to concrete foundations where dwellings once stood. Many apartments had no glass in the windows. A pulley system hauled water to the upper floors of a fourteen-story apartment building, whose makeshift wood-burning stoves emitted a dozen columns of smoke. I noticed a woman standing in her fourth-floor apartment, now open to the sky.

A foursome of farm women walking along the sidewalk allowed me to take their portrait. "We're wearing clothes from you!" one said with a wide grin, tugging on her woolen jacket, donated from America. For a moment I felt our commonality. But visitors like me couldn't understand Goražde without the backdrop of life before the war.

To give us that perspective, Sabina, once a journalist and now an entrepreneur, reminisced about her town's musical ensembles, theater, and school, where her daughters learned piano and guitar. She insisted that Goražde was historically a cultural crossroad and had been for centuries: "When other people didn't know who Mozart was, we were playing his music."

I talked with Sabina again a year after that first trip. She described her hometown, still in shambles:

> There's not one major factory operating now, and still no clean drinking water. Maybe five hundred people are employed, and we don't have the road they promised. People are frightened, and they're still surrounded by war criminals. There's no real communication between Sarajevo and Goražde. I travel there three or four times a week, and I still shake when a policeman stops me and says, "We're the police of Republika Srpska, not the 'Turkish' police."

But not all of Sabina's story was discouraging:

> One day, I pulled over to buy a watermelon from some Serbs and handed them one of our new Bosnian bills. An old man said to me, "Why are you giving me this Turkish money?"
>
> "Sir," I said, "This is the currency of your country and mine, and the name of our country is Bosnia and Herzegovina." He ignored me.
>
> The next time I stopped again to buy a watermelon from him. When he made a remark, I tried to be polite but told him he was wrong, that I'm a Bosniak, not a Turk.
>
> The next time, he said nothing to me. He just took my money.
>
> The fourth time, he smiled at me.

76. OUTSIDE: Arizona

In a military helicopter, hovering over the former northern front line, a US general told me a story of reconciliation, Bosnia style. The mechanism was not a religious rite, official policy, or personal gesture. It was a makeshift market. The general noted that after the war, wherever there was physical safety, free enterprise was bringing together former adversaries. But the setting of this particular market gave it added importance.

Brčko was strategically positioned: all road, river, and rail links that connected the western and eastern parts of Republika Srpska passed through its narrow corridor. Thus it was perceived by Serbs as crucial to the security of their "political entity." With the city under Serb control, Bosniaks and Croats would be unable to reach Croatia and the Sava

River, which links the Danube River and the Black Sea. Hence it was a negotiation sticking point at Dayton. There was a moral component as well. More than three thousand unarmed Bosniaks and Croats in the town had been murdered by Serb troops, while other non-Serbs had been driven out of the city and into a squalid tent city. Giving control of Brčko to the Serbs would be a warped reward.

Four years after the Dayton Accords were signed, special arbitration awarded Brčko multiethnic status and self-governance under an international supervisor. By an agreement hammered out after Dayton, the municipality had been restructured as a "neutral district." Both the Federation and Republika Srpska surrendered control of territory to a new, multiethnic district government, initially under an international administrator. In theory, the agreement allowed refugees to return to their homes. In practice, however, that option was not fully viable. By day, Bosniaks were rebuilding their properties. By night, Serb extremists were blowing up the reconstruction.

For security, NATO stationed troops nearby. In the shadow of their military checkpoint, Bosniaks began passing messages across the line to Serb friends, families, and former teachers—who soon marshaled their courage to cross over and join them for Saturday picnics. Before long, a resourceful Serb concessionaire brought refreshments to sell at the rendezvous site. Other enterprises spontaneously appeared in the sprawling, muddy fields. Farmers began bringing homemade brandy and livestock. Soon a giant open-air market sprang up near the NATO watchtower—a psychological safety zone. Buyers came from a hundred miles in all directions, and merchandise came from even farther.

When nationalist local authorities attempted to shut down the gathering spot, NATO troops stepped in. They negotiated protection, coordinated with the local police from all ethnic groups, and brought in dogs to detect bombs. For a while, the biggest problem was traffic jams: in just a few weeks, a Sunday crowd averaged one thousand people. Eventually, weekends were drawing some four thousand to the market, many from hundreds of miles away.

Much of the trade was wholesome: light fixtures, soccer balls, and skewered čevapčići. But some was toxic. The area became a hub of organized crime, including sex trafficking. Unwilling women were auctioned off like livestock. Afterward, they were coerced into local prostitution or transported abroad, where their passports were taken from them to keep them from escaping.[10]

Equally ugly, an entrepreneur and former soldier in his midthirties remarked: "I am quite ready to sell brandy to Serbs in the morning and shoot them in the afternoon. There were plenty of people who did this during the war. First we take their money, then we get rid of them. Most Muslims will never allow the Serbs to hang onto the town of Brčko, no matter how friendly we are when they hand over their cash."[11]

Was the market just one more venue for exploitation, or did its existence also show that Bosnians were willing to bury their differences? Whatever the chances of conflict in the future, the pull of the market was stronger than the fear of ethnic strife. Initial and tentative social exchanges had given way to bartering between consumers and suppliers. Along with merchandise, market goers exchanged information and hope. This was camaraderie *in extremis*.

At the time of my visit, more than 166,000 people each month were crossing the lines separating Serb from Bosniak and Croat territory. It seemed like a miracle to our pilot. Looking over the bustle of a Saturday afternoon, he remarked: "Used to be, we'd fly to Tuzla and not see a single light on the ground for miles. The only thing moving was us."

77. INSIDE: Three Hundred Gold Coins

In Bosnia as anywhere, faith could offer solace in the dark, but there were times when religion became the darkness itself. Respected as a source of values and connection, religion elevated the human experience. But politicized as a means of profit and control, it debased.

Politicized religion takes on many guises. For their own purposes, perhaps, the Saudis described Izetbegović as a "fighter for Islam, sent by God to lead the Muslims along the true path," and King Fahd awarded him a medal for contributing to the spread of Islam.[12] For the thousand Bosnians of the Seventh Muslim Brigade, faith was a strong basis for identity. Members of this unit wore green bands around their foreheads, often with Koranic inscriptions.

In the southern part of the country, hate spewed from pulpits. Passive during the massive expulsions of non-Croats, some Catholic leaders in the Mostar area now resisted the return of refugees of a different faith, and they actively and publicly opposed the rebuilding of non-Catholic sacred sites.

Karadžić spoke for radicalized Serbs. "Our faith is present in all our thinking and decisions, and the voice of the Church is obeyed as the voice of supreme authority," he declared. And at a rally in Sarajevo's Zetra stadium, he proclaimed, "Tonight, even God is a Serb!"[13]

Among the dozen religious leaders I knew across Bosnia, I found activists and fatalists, saints and sinners. I'd heard that religious life was particularly tense in Biljana Plavšić's hometown of Banja Luka. To ex-

The destruction of religious symbols, including houses of worship, was widespread. Above, the site of the razed Ferhat-Pasha Mosque in the Serb stronghold of Banja Luka.

Opposite, the crumbling doorway of the Serb Orthodox church in Sarajevo, shelled by Serbs themselves.

COURTESY OF TARIK SAMARAH

plore why, I made appointments with the leading clerics there. Both the Catholic bishop and the Muslim grand mufti had stayed throughout the war, even though their congregations had been more than decimated.

The mufti's worn polyester suit hung loosely on his bony frame. It was Ramadan, so we had nothing to eat or drink. He pointed out his window, to where the grand Ferhat-Pasha Mosque had stood—the revered symbol for the city's 224,000 Muslims. After 450 years, it took only five minutes for the Serbs to bring it down, he mused. Fifteen other mosques had been blown up, yet he was determined to rebuild.

The bishop, a white-haired philosopher-theologian with a heart as big as his intellect, echoed the mufti's despondence. "During Communism, our people lost our humanity," he said, commenting ruefully on the reasons for the violence. Of eighty thousand Catholics in the city, seventy-five thousand had been expelled. Several priests and a nun had been killed, others imprisoned.[14] Only five of seventy-five churches still existed. Still, the bishop remarked, "I am certain we have been witnesses to a struggle between good and evil. But just as the spirit of evil was ever present, so was the spirit of good."

I wanted to hear the experience of the Serb Orthodox priest, too. After arriving at his residence, I was taken upstairs to a dark but spacious chamber and seated on a leather chair in a room cluttered with books and icons. The priest entered. With his angular features and ill-kempt beard, he reminded me of pictures I'd seen of the enigmatic Rasputin. Somewhat unsettled by his hypnotic stare, I tried to strike up a conversation but could find little common ground—either in content or style. Although it was before noon, his form of hospitality was to offer me a series of hard liquors.

I tried not to be disrespectful, but I was struck with how the Orthodox Church in Banja Luka remained a hold-out of hate. Or so it seemed, when the mufti died a few months after my visit. Recalcitrant Serb city officials refused to let him be buried on the site of the mosque he had vowed to rebuild—which was still an empty, flat field in the middle of the city.

There were clerics who resisted such venom, but needed bolstering. First, as they led their congregations, they could be vital to reconciliation. Second, they could expose to the rest of the world the fallacy that this had been a religious war. Landrum Bolling, a saintly American Quaker, came to my office in Vienna with a plan to address both approaches. I would invite Sarajevo's four religious leaders—Orthodox, Catholic, Muslim, and Jewish—plus one assistant each, to our residence for three days of discussion to create an interreligious council. In a fresh setting, the leaders would be more independent, and they could better see their potential for cohesive action.

In Sarajevo, the lead up to this meeting was uneven. Each leader had reservations. The reis ul-ulema,[15] Mustafa Čerić, who had a Ph.D. from the University of Chicago, met me in the bullet-riddled building next to the mosque. The walls of the room were lined with traditional cushioned benches that seemed designed for distance rather than relationship. I asked Čerić if he had a special wish while in Vienna. "Yes," he said, "libraries . . . and McDonalds." I said I could deliver both.

"I'll come, but no show business," he warned. We agreed there was no place for joint public prayers as families were still being driven from their homes by church-condoned violence.

I continued my individual visits, paving the way for the Vienna meeting. At the Catholic cathedral across the river from the mosque, a stained-glass Christ hung on a cross with his heart blown out by a shell. Before agreeing to come to Vienna, Cardinal Vinko Puljić spent an hour scrutinizing me. Saying he had survived a visit from the pope, he presented me with a commemorative gold coin. On one side, the Madonna held her child lovingly. On the other side was a date several years earlier, meant to commemorate the visit—postponed because of shelling, he explained.

A stone's throw from the cathedral was the Serb Orthodox church, mustard-colored and adorned with white graffiti. I walked the grassy perimeter of the locked building, unsure if I should be wary of mines. Father Dušan Jovanović, the deputy metropolitan, explained that his superior was living thirty miles away. "What is a metropolitan without a metropolis?" I inquired aloud. Shouldn't he be in the capital, not in a village? The Sarajevo church offices were heavily damaged, the priest countered, failing to mention that the damage was from shelling by Serbs, who acted with at least tacit support from the Orthodox Church.

Orthodox Metropolitan Nikolaj always had a reason not to join when I hosted collaborations among religious leaders. It's no wonder that he refused to be moved. One Easter, Nikolaj pronounced that those who aligned themselves with the indicted war criminals Karadžić and Mladić were "following the hard road of Christ."[16] (Granted, on one occasion several months later, he was willing to drive in for a one-on-one breakfast from his nearby refuge in Republika Srpska. When he walked into the Hotel Bosna, I felt like I'd fallen into a storybook. His long white beard hung over a black robe, and a cylindrical black hat topped his fierce-looking face. As soon as our coffee was poured, he plunged into an energetic polemic, describing how he'd urged President Plavšić not to cause trouble with the other Bosnian Serb leaders, nor to disband the Parliament in the new Republika Srpska. "You may intercede with God—but I'm not God," was her reply, the president told me later.)

Some weeks after my round of Sarajevo appointments, each religious community leader plus an assistant arrived on the same flight, excepting one: the Orthodox assistant came by himself, with apologies that the metropolitan "wasn't feeling well." Landrum Bolling and David Little, an expert on religion and nationalism, also joined us, to facilitate the formal sessions.

After tens of thousands of hours burying the slaughtered, consoling distraught families, and trying to help millions of destitute people, the seven religious leaders found some levity in each other's company. They also found depth: Dušan commented that as he'd flown over Bosnia en route, he looked down on his destroyed land and thought how heavy God's heart must be as he viewed his creation.

But within a few hours of the leaders' arrival at our residence, stories, laughter, and memories of a once kinder culture began to emerge. There were as many tales of multireligious Bosnia as we had hours to spend telling them.

The result of our Vienna meeting was the finalization of the Inter-Religious Council, a clear statement to the outside world that the Bosnian conflict had not been a religious war. Laboring to avoid politically charged words, and leaving accusations aside, the newborn Council penned a unified statement encouraging all religious leaders to speak out against violence targeting any group. Upon the leaders' return from Vienna, they called a joint press conference to announce the formation of the council.

When they later assessed just what had made the agreement possible, the men cited the trust we began in Sarajevo and built in Vienna. With smiles, they also mentioned our eight-year-old Teddy racing through the house and rolling on the floor with Isabella the dog; the long, serene walks along paths of the Schönbrunn Gardens; and duets with me on the piano and the vice president of the Sarajevan Jewish community on a violin borrowed from the Vienna Philharmonic.

I added that our conversations were easier because we set aside titles, using only first names. (It must have been decades since the cardinal had been called "Vinko.") We also made our talks intensely personal, describing childhoods and remembering shared heritage. One evening, with everyone sitting around our table, Dušan had told a tale. A Muslim selling his house asked for three hundred gold coins. The prospective buyer protested that the house was worth only a hundred. The seller readily agreed, but added, "I have an Orthodox neighbor on my left, and a Croat neighbor on my right. Each of them is worth one hundred coins, too." The reis ul-ulema, cardinal, and Jewish community president broke into smiles. They understood exactly. In Bosnia, value wasn't measured just in bricks and mortar. It was a joint tally that computed the richness of diversity.

The success of the Dayton Peace Agreement depended on all stake-holders buying into the Bosniak-Croat Federation, the joint administration within the area of Bosnia not controlled by the Serbs. In fact, a solid Federation was assumed by the document's drafters. The weighty policy implications of that assumption were reinforced by Secretary of State Christopher, who declared the Federation to be "a sharp rebuke to all of those who would say that we must carve up post-war Europe along ethnic and religious lines."[17] Yet two years after Dayton, no real progress had been made in creating a unified administration. The process was foiled by authorities with nothing to gain and much to lose in a power-sharing agreement. Politicians could sign, but documents did not quell the ambition of nationalists intent on breaking the country apart, nor did they elevate the voice of moderates, committed to maintaining an integrated society.

Recriminations were thick between Bosniaks and Croats. Ever since the creation of the Federation, the relationship had been tense. Ambassador Daniel Serwer, with his international meetings of "Friends of the Federation," had tried to increase international pressure by dangling twenty million dollars that the United States would spend in central Bosnia on projects jointly orchestrated by the recalcitrant parties. Meetings had been organized in Munich, St. Petersburg, and Vienna to bring together Federation politicians, with hopes that neutral ground would enhance the chance of cooperation.

My interlocutors in the Austrian government were lukewarm to the idea of involvement in the US effort, reflecting the growing disillusionment of outsiders toward the Balkan peace process. Moreover, unease toward all things Islamic was once again in the forefront when the Clinton administration pushed through a postwar "train and equip" program for the Federation. In particular, the participation of Turkey and Malaysia raised apprehensions. I responded to Austrian officials that if they and other Western states were not willing to help, they would share responsibility for growing Islamic influence in Europe. Still, even US support was withheld until Izetbegović replaced a deputy defense minister with close ties to Iran.

Eventually, half a billion dollars[18] worth of training, equipment, and facilities was provided to the Federation to bring its forces up to NATO standards and correct the internal military imbalances that threatened to destabilize Bosnia. But European diplomats remained critical, noting that the program might alarm the Serb military, which might respond by refusing to comply with arms reduction provisions of the peace agreement. Despite those cautions, the European Union did attempt a more assertive unifying role in Mostar. That was, after all, the city that Bosnian Croat separatists imagined as the capital of the region they wanted to control, for which they created the name Herzeg Bosna and received the support of President Tuđman.

Before the war, Mostar comprised nearly equal proportions of all three ethnic groups. Then Serbs shelled the city from the east. After being defeated, Croats shelled Bosniaks from the west. The result was a city and governance structure largely in shambles. Despite Dayton's assurances of unity, West Mostar was administered by Croats, with East Mostar left to Bosniaks.

Hans Koschnick, formerly mayor of Bremen, came to the city as EU administrator to try to unite the two sides. After pouring many deutschmarks into the community, those involved in the international effort could point to a small demilitarized protection zone, functioning primary schools, and a regular dialogue with the leadership of both Bosniak and Croat communities—but no real security for most residents.[19] Koschnick himself was not safe; his hotel was attacked with explosives when he was unexpectedly away. Upping the ante, the German threatened to withdraw EU support from Mostar if local Croat authorities did not let citizens move freely and did not form a joint police force with the Bosniaks.

Despite great effort on the part of outsiders, no significant agreement on strengthening Mostar—the weak link in the Federation—was forthcoming. As late as February 1997, a piece by Anthony Lewis for the *International Herald Tribune* described the expulsion of thirty more Bosniak families from the city, as well as the firing on of Bosniaks visiting a cemetery.[20] Hoodlums and organized crime figures dominated the western part of the town. East and West Mostar each now had its own mayor, its own license plates, its own politically sponsored radio station.

Thus, Mostar remained a symbol of division rather than a model of integration, raising questions about the viability of the Federation and, ultimately, a unified Bosnia.

79. INSIDE: New Bridges

More than a century earlier, the Hapsburg victory over the Ottomans had led to a massive Muslim exodus out of Bosnia. During this tumultuous time, an ethnic Serb in Mostar named Aleksa Šantić spoke out. In his poem "Stay Here" ("Ostajte Ovdje"), he begged Muslims not to leave, despite political repression, but to remain with their "brothers":

The sun that shines in a foreign place
Will never warm you like the sun in your own—The bread has a bitter taste
   there
Where one has no one, not even a brother"[21]

Over the post-Ottoman decades, Mostar continued to be a hallmark of multiculturalism. One fundamental symbol was the revered Stari Most, the white limestone bridge whose beautiful arch reached across the Neretva River. Commissioned by Suleiman the Magnificent and completed in 1566, the bridge once connected the Ottoman East and Christian West. Tradition has it that the builders used eggs instead of water in the mortar, to make the bridge stronger. Earthquakes, Ottoman-Hapsburg conflicts, and two world wars failed to bring it down. So its destruction by Croat guns on the sixty-fifth anniversary of the infamous Nazi *Kristallnacht* signified that ruin had triumphed, at least for the time. The bridge's collapse was a crushing psychological blow to the town and to all who cherished a unified Bosnia.

Looking down on the stone remains, I crossed the river on a narrow steel structure. The temporary bridge was open to women, children, and elderly. No men between sixteen and sixty were allowed across. Even a visit to family and friends took courage.

I walked past long rows of buildings pounded with mortars. Little was left but exposed steel and broken concrete. I could imagine children as they once played in a now-gutted apartment. Only a bright red fire extinguisher remained—a cruel joke left by an evil genius.

Indeed, as political leaders quarreled and sulked, it was the children who seemed most mature. They didn't distinguish between minor differences in vocabulary; laughter was their common language. The kids weren't letting labels like "Serb," "Muslim," or "Croat" keep them from swims in the river and classes in the youth center on the dividing line between East and West Mostar. Rebuilt by the European Union, the center provided an oasis of calm in a devastated part of town.

I was the honored guest at the youth center one day, and television cameras followed me as I went from one room to another, looking at an exhibit of my own photographs of children. At the end of the visit, I sat down on a wide step and invited about thirty teenagers to sit with me, on the floor. They were in good spirits as they gathered into an impromptu audience. Dressed in jeans and T-shirts, the kids looked like they could easily have been from Dallas or Boston, yet they'd endured loss, uncertainty, and terror that few in my country have known.

"What do you think is the future of Mostar?" one asked, as if she were a reporter. The young people realized that Mostar was stuck in distrust. I thought, before answering, that civilization doesn't inevitably move forward. The drive for destruction is born again with every generation. But, then, so is the impulse to hope.

"The future can only be you," I answered, "because you're the bridge. Like it or not, there's nothing else. You're the connection across East and West, past and future, chaos and clarity."

80. OUTSIDE: Air Force One

President Clinton faced a dilemma. Although he believed in a strong US role in Bosnia, he had promised, when the troops went in, that their stay would be brief. As 1997 wore on, Balkan advocates became increasingly nervous about the troop pullout, slated for the middle of the following year. Granted, many Serb weapons had been destroyed, and four airports had opened to civilians. But Clinton knew that implementation of the Dayton Peace Agreement was already a year behind schedule. With nationalists empowered by elections, foreign investment discouraged by corruption, and the judiciary and media limited by bias, a military withdrawal would risk disaster for the Bosnian people. That in turn could embarrass American politicians, who would have squandered the opportunity to stabilize postconflict Yugoslavia.

Various administration voices began a contrapuntal refrain. Clinton's press secretary, repeating assurances that nothing was changing, asserted in the *International Herald Tribune* that the president was committed to the 30 June troop withdrawal date. "Administration officials made it clear . . . that [National Security Advisor] Berger was not setting new policy. Many in Congress would oppose such a change," the reporter wrote.[22] Yet on 24 September 1997, Berger began to mention publicly the possibility of NATO having "an extended stay" in Bosnia.

By December, the administration had shored up support for letting some of the troops stay. NATO's defense ministers determined that they would probably leave twenty-four thousand of thirty-four thousand soldiers, and the US contribution would shrink only from eight thousand to six thousand.[23] But there were disagreements within the organization. General Clark wanted a stronger civilian component to complement the next military deployment, whereas the French opposed further NATO involvement altogether. Elizabeth Neuffer reported that "rather than address these questions . . . NATO may opt to keep troops in Bosnia indefinitely under current rules of engagement."[24]

The time seemed right for a presidential visit to highlight the importance of the US troops' presence in Bosnia. I had left Vienna a few weeks earlier, to take up a new position at Harvard University's John F. Kennedy School of Government. The president invited Charles and me to

On board the cargo plane to Eagle Base outside Tuzla to show US resolve in Bosnia, President Clinton confers with General Wes Clark, supreme allied commander Europe (NATO); and General Hugh Shelton, chairman of the Joint Chiefs of Staff.

fly to Bosnia with him. On 22 December, we gathered at Andrews Air Force Base. Our group included General Hugh Shelton, chairman of the Joint Chiefs of Staff, as well as Secretary of State Madeleine Albright, National Security Advisor Sandy Berger, a congressional delegation, and Bob Dole, whom Clinton had just defeated in the 1996 presidential election.

The twenty-four-hour visit was a study in contrasts between tense hours with stubborn politicians and warm encounters with their constituents. The president, as was his custom, set out to talk with whomever he found, including people in a café near the theater. "Make us your fifty-first state," one man suggested with a smile. Clinton left, enthusiastic about his considerable political investment in the tiny Balkan state.

That warm reception was mirrored in a meeting I attended with the first lady.[25] Hillary Rodham Clinton sat in a small room, surrounded by eight women. One by one, the civil society representatives introduced themselves, describing how they were rebuilding their country.

We gathered at the National Theater to hear the Sarajevo Philharmonic—for President Clinton, respite from the tedium of hard-liner recalcitrance. The front row includes Clinton's chief of staff, Erskine Bowles; the Clinton family; Secretary Madeleine Albright; Bosnian President Alija Izetbegović; Federation President Zubac; and Mustafa Čerić, the reis ul-ulema.

The different parts of the Clinton delegation met up later at the National Theater. As principal guest conductor, Charles was directing the Sarajevo Philharmonic for the president's visit. The crowd waited for more than an hour for President Clinton to arrive so that the concert could begin. Finally, Charles decided to proceed, if only to help time pass for the high-level audience. The stage was decorated with red, white, and blue flower arrangements, against a backdrop reading "Sarajevo," with flame-like letters in orange and yellow. Walking out from the wings, Charles passed a thought-provoking sign: "No weapons on stage."

As the orchestra stalled, the president tried unsuccessfully to resolve a stalemate among the trio of Bosnian co-presidents. True to their modus operandi of the past year, the three were stuck. One was intent that the western half of Bosnia be annexed to Croatia; another was determined that the eastern half be annexed to Serbia. Their intentions pointed in opposite directions. Even Clinton could not spin this straw into gold.

When the president finally entered, the formal portion of the event began. After the brief concert, the president walked to the stage. Putting the onus of rebuilding and reconciling on Bosnians, Clinton told them: "The world, which continues to invest in your peace, rightfully expects

President Clinton was always at his best with a crowd, this time US soldiers sent in early December 1995 to stabilize the fragile Bosnian peace.

you will work for it."[26] In such work they were not alone; America, too, faced the challenges of reaching across differences. In June, he had launched an initiative calling for a national conversation on the sensitive and volatile issue of race relations in the United States. Now, he told the audience, 180 racial and ethnic groups in America were in dialogue and finding strength in diversity. The war, he said, had done violence not only to the Bosnian people but also to the Bosnian history of tolerance.

Later, I found the president and the congressmen from our delegation shaking their heads in frustration at the meeting with the three obdurate politicians. Senator John Kasich said to the president: "I wonder if we're talking to the right people. Maybe we ought to be going through the neighborhoods with a megaphone on a pickup truck." Clinton turned and put his arm around my shoulders. "That's what *she* does," he responded. I was grateful for that awareness, at the highest level, of the importance of voices from the ground.

From Sarajevo, we flew to Eagle Base. The American troops had crowded into a large hall to be addressed by their commander in chief, along with Korean War veteran Bob Dole, for whom many had just cast their vote. Dole had accepted Clinton's request that he chair the International Commission on Missing Persons, many of whom were victims of massacres. Fittingly, the meeting hall was near the Tuzla tarmac, to which the Srebrenica survivors had been bused.

As the soldiers were gathering, a press conference in a side location was being led by Albright and Berger. International reporters waiting for a take on the day's events had little spark in their eyes. It was, after all, two days before Christmas; and while the president's visit was timed to encourage the troops, Berger and Albright's report to the journalists was wearying. Berger spoke first and had nothing good to say about President Clinton's meeting with the heads of state or about Bosnia's prospects. When Secretary Albright went to the podium, Berger came over to the side, where I stood watching. "Tell them about the meeting Hillary had with the women," I whispered. "It was fabulous." He looked at me indulgently. Albright finished her remarks. Berger went back up to the mike, asked for a few questions, and closed the press conference.

I wondered about Sandy Berger's passing up a full description of the day, and a more hopeful one at that. Then I recalled the 1994 Federation negotiations in our embassy, when no women had appeared on the negotiating teams among the dozens of lawyers, experts, and political leaders, even though Yugoslavia had the largest percentage of women Ph.D.s of any country in Europe. Similarly, women were only one out of nine of the new Constitutional Court judges, while they constituted 80 percent of lower-level judges. Women had their fingers on the pulse of their communities, yet they became invisible when it came to negotiations, constitutions—or press conferences.

Later that night on Air Force One, the president and I reviewed the day. I told him about the discrepancy I had observed between the Bosnian politicians and civil society leaders. "We've got to find a way to have more grass-roots input into our foreign policy," he responded, with urgency.

Such an aspiration seemed as hopeful but far-fetched as the notion of Slobodan Milošević in custody in The Hague. Yet the months and years would bring many surprises—some tragic and some promising. The tragic would create flurries of action that drove our policies in directions we had not anticipated. The promising would give us energy to keep moving forward. All of this push and pull would test our fidelity in building bridges between worlds disconnected but part of the same grand reality.

Still, we had to keep at it; the stability of our future was in the balance. Those of us on the plane touching down at Andrews Air Force Base would not be in the center of the policy establishment forever. It would be a shame if the lessons of Bosnia were lost as we left.

Six Lessons from Bosnia

Before Air Force One touched down, I approached National Security Advisor Berger, telling him that President Clinton was enthusiastic about integrating more information "from the ground" into our foreign policy. My hope was that Sandy would not only feel obliged to act but also be persuaded that we needed to expand our fundamental approach to foreign policy.

Standing with me in the aisle, Berger nodded and muttered a noncommittal response. I was disappointed; but his lack of interest was understandable, if not excusable. He was, after all, preoccupied with hunting down the then little-known Osama bin Laden, monitoring North Korea's nuclear program, and urging the creation of a Palestinian state. No one would argue that the National Security Advisor should ignore those priorities. But those were discrete topics, and I was remarking on the process by which we were addressing them.

In the coming years, more crises would emerge—particularly Iraq, the war that has devoured the resources of the United States, obliterating other significant foreign policy objectives while curtailing vital domestic programs. The tragedy of Iraq clinched the case for recasting our security paradigm. As we look for the structural flaws that allowed that debacle, we find a gulf between distant policymakers and the people on the scene: Iraqi politicians, Coalition soldiers patrolling the streets, and everyday citizens. Their worlds are separated by a dangerous conceptual void.

In conflicts throughout the world, six lessons from Bosnia, distinct but interrelated, form a bridge between these spheres:

1. Test truisms
2. Question stereotypes
3. Find out-of-power allies

4. Appreciate domestic dynamics

5. Find fault

6. Embrace responsibility

None of these by itself would have been sufficient, but together they might well have prevented or stopped the Balkan war. Likewise, none by itself can solve any current security problem, but together they can transform the making of foreign policy.

1. Test Truisms

> When Condoleezza Rice explicitly invoked soft power in the US's new approach to Iran, it seemed to signal that attraction and persuasion were being added (or restored) to the political toolkit of the west. But as the crisis in Lebanon demonstrates, when conflict erupts into zero-sum violence, it takes a different kind of courage to persist with these new tools over the familiar hard-power options. . . . Given that the issue which has most damaged Blair's leadership has been his use of hard power in Iraq, might soft power be a concept worth developing and championing? —INDRA ADNAN, "Men, Step Aside: Tackling Terrorism is Women's Work," *Guardian*

A truism is an obvious assumption, so self-evidently valid that it hardly bears consideration. But what seems self-evident still needs outside review. For example, the concept of "soft power" was coined by the political analyst Joseph Nye as an alternative to the truism that led to a US foreign policy defined by swagger and threat—the view that military might is the foundation of peace. Instead, Nye proposes that the United States focus on "the ability to get what you want by attracting and persuading others to adopt your goals. It differs from hard power, the ability to use the carrots and sticks of economic and military might to make others follow your will."[1]

Nye's formulation is not only creative, it also provides a practical, fresh approach. In the psychologist Abraham Maslow's well-worn adage, "If the only tool you have is a hammer, you tend to see every problem as a nail." At least two drawbacks come from having only hammers and seeing only nails. The first is ironic: Hard power is so expensive that policymakers sometimes are too reluctant to deploy it. Thus a challenge may be left unmet, only to grow into a crisis. Second, when conflicts are reduced to black and white, evil met by force, they will be addressed inadequately. Soft power requires a more nuanced understanding of the social and psychological aspects of the adversary. It involves new tools that make our responses more efficient and more effective.

In Banja Luka, de facto capital of Republika Srpska, a Bosnian Serb refugee unloads her history as the Blessed Virgin watches over her. But as she and five other displaced women poured out their stories, none mentioned religious faith. Like thousands of everyday Bosnians I met over the years, they didn't echo the words of a few radical clerics that this was a religious war. In fact, in my experience—aside from demonstrations where religious slogans are used to buttress political cries—faith is almost never the fundamental reason for war. The "fault" is not a line, but the clash theory itself.

Concepts of hard and soft power refer to ways of forestalling or addressing active conflict. Other popular foreign policy truisms, however, start with the subterranean reasons why conflict erupts. But though unsubstantiated formulations may help organize our thinking, they are not sufficient to predict or explain the complexity of actual conflicts. When accepted through incautious secondhand analysis, they easily take on the patina of inevitability.

As a case in point, Samuel Huntington's motif of a perilous collision of "civilizations" (discussed in section 3) exemplifies at least four weaknesses of truisms: they can be self-fulfilling, have a paradoxical effect, betray bias, and miss other important factors.

The first weakness is that assumptions can create the very reality they purport to describe. Huntington adopted the idea of a clash of civilizations from Bernard Lewis, who coined the term in 1990 when he warned of an approaching confrontation with Islam. After Huntington's 1997 book had become a foreign policy phenomenon, Lewis was invited by the strategist Karl Rove to the George W. Bush White House to brief administration leaders. Indeed, Lewis has been called "perhaps the most significant intellectual influence behind the invasion of Iraq."[2]

Earlier Huntington works were negatively synergistic with Lewis's idea. In *The Soldier and the State*, Huntington observes that while "actual personalities, institutions, and beliefs do not fit into neat logical categories," such constructions "are necessary if man is to think profitably about the real world in which he lives and to derive from it lessons for broader application and use."[3] He goes on to generalize in his best-known work, arguing that Americans must reinforce their Western identity ever more insistently in a civilization-divided world. Unsurprisingly, just as it was the favorite book of the Croat separatist President Tuđman, *The Clash of Civilizations* has been described as "the top reference for all Islamist militants, thrilled by the cultural rift that gives credence to their confrontational ideology."[4] The assumption of conflict in Huntington's truism "brings grist to their mill: the two civilizations are incompatible."[5] Even declaring that a clash exists fueled those who would make it so.

That thought was frequently on my mind in the 1990s, as anxiety over Islamic fundamentalism spread across Europe. In a cause célèbre, schoolgirls in France were expelled because they wore headscarves. Rather than quelling tensions, that denial of religious rights fed more Islamic fervor. Similarly, since September 11, the US restriction on visas for students and scholars from countries deemed dangerous has been handled by the Department of Homeland Security rather than the State Department. As a result, it took eighteen months for a feminist writer in Tehran to obtain clearance to attend Harvard University's prestigious

Nieman program for journalists. Likewise, in June 2008, the highly pub-
licized Israeli refusal to let seven students leave Gaza to accept Fulbright
fellowships in the United States drew international dismay. "Face-to-
face exchanges have proven to be the single most effective means of engaging foreign publics while broadening dialogue between US citizens
and institutions and their counterparts abroad," according to the fellow-
ship announcement that Fulbright used for years.[6] But reason was inadequate to overcome the truism-induced fear.

Building on the first, but at a higher level, the second danger of Huntington's truism is that the clash model plus a hard power modus operandi
may cause political leaders to pull back from, rather than engage with,
despots. Overly wary of provoking an entire civilization, the policymaker may fail to form high-level bonds that could prevent the very conflict feared. In fact, the question of whether to sit down with a "bad guy"
was hotly debated in the 2008 presidential race. Senator Barack Obama
insisted that he would "engage in aggressive personal diplomacy" with
Iran and Cuba, consistent with his belief that openness to "the other"
is preferable to isolation.[7] Senator John McCain, a hawk, attacked the
Obama statement, calling it naive.

McCain is not alone. Many American policymakers find it distaste-
ful to engage diplomatically with unsavory leaders. Opening a dialogue
with such characters may be seen as capitulation or, worse, indiffer-
ence to evil. Better to do nothing. But this strict rule itself may be naive,
rather than strong. When abuses are soaring and deaths mounting, we
must create opportunities to intervene. Policymakers must steel themselves for the simple job of talking. Only in rare cases, such as genocide,
is military action warranted. Otherwise, we need to draw from other ar-
senals—such as diplomatic and economic action.

A third reason truisms are unreliable is that sweeping pronouncements
may betray personal, institutional, or national bias. Although Huntington himself is careful to acknowledge the violence of non-Muslim cross-
cultural conflicts, he refers repeatedly to Muslims' fighting among themselves and having "bloody borders," and he downplays the intergroup
violence and warmongering applicable to Western Christianity's crusades, inquisitions, wars, and witch hunts.

Bernard Lewis is more obvious in expressing what seems to be a personal distaste for Islam. During his acceptance speech for the 2007
Irving Kristol Award—which honors "individuals who have made extraordinary intellectual or practical contributions to improved government policy, social welfare, or political understanding"[8]—he framed
migration and terrorism as the latest forms of the "cosmic struggle
for world domination between the two main faiths—Christianity and

Islam."[9] That struggle, he said, could not be circumvented with constructive engagement. Beyond highlighting Islamic violence, Lewis also excused aggression carried out by what he regards as the other side in this perpetual conflict. Though claiming not to justify atrocities, he expressed shock that Pope John Paul II apologized for the crusades, which he dismissed as a proportional response to the Islamic jihad against Europe.

Fourth and finally, models that purport to explain reality with universal application are usually incomplete, ignoring the unique tangle of factors contributing to any one conflict. For example, the clash proposition understates the influence of an individual whose personal character may lead a country into prosperity or ruin.

The clash theory focuses on violence, allowing policymakers to ignore injustices within, between, and among nations. It fails to account for the resulting resentment and socioeconomic deprivation, which, left to simmer long enough, are politicized and recast as cultural. The instability of government or civil society infrastructure may cause a political implosion. State interests also play a role, as when poor nations become the battleground of greater powers fighting over natural resources or strategic position. During the cold war, the world was pocked with countries like Afghanistan, Angola, and Cuba, where the United States and Soviet Union engaged in proxy wars between not only national interests but also ideological models.

A small stone in the global political mosaic, the former Yugoslavia was just one more setting in which these four weakness of the clash truism played out. First, it is true that, until near the end of the war, a cultural divide was indeed evident: Serbian and Croat aggressors were on the same (Judeo-Christian) side of the hypothetical fault line as the American and European observers. But labeling these divides a "clash of civilizations" only exacerbated the problem, making it more difficult for parties to cross the lines, as if they were betraying their own side.

The second weakness, discussed above—the reluctance of political leaders to confront each other because they fear so much is at stake—was evident in President Carter's admonition to President Clinton not to get involved in a "religious war" that was bigger than our foreign policy apparatus could handle. The possibility that the conflict in Bosnia was a struggle between two civilizations made intervention seem like a lost cause.

And third, bias. Sitting in an audience with European military officers, I was amazed to hear British General Michael Rose—who was commander of the UN troops in Bosnia in 1994 and who was subsequently knighted—say: "For people in the Balkans, to speak is to lie. The local politicians don't give a damn about the people. They're all scoundrels." It seemed hardly coincidental that for more than three years Western policymakers failed to stop the genocide against the Muslim population. Had they been a Christian minority . . .

The fourth weakness of truisms, oversimplification, was blatant. Many other factors permitted the unchecked aggression, beginning with Western leaders, who feared domestic political consequences if their countries lost troops on Balkan soil. But inside Yugoslavia, poor leadership was probably the most important contributor neglected in the clash analysis. The country was distressed but not splitting apart before Milošević took advantage of the chaos brought on by the implosion of Communism. In his 1989 speech at the Kosovo battlefield, he was able to excite his Serb base, warning that their disunity was making them inferior. As Roger Cohen put it: "Milošević and the ideologues of his Serbian revolution took their people back to the womb of their unreason. A place where defeat was victory, death a kingdom of heaven, suicide redemption, suffering vindication, and exile a homeland." This nationalism gave Serbs the "solace of a glorious past and their mirage of a glorious future."[10]

In times of such social strife, identity conflicts can spiral. As the opportunistic Milošević dredged up old nationalism, religious differences seemed to prove the clash of civilizations argument. In Vienna, we were wedged between Vaclav Havel, the underground playwright released from prison to become president of Czechoslovakia, and the calamitous Milošević, both of whom rose during uncertain political and economic times to lead socialist countries with comparable industrial development, education levels, cultural heritages, and natural resources. One led his country into stability that could weather a political split. The other led his country into violent disintegration and ruin.

Some political leaders now are trying to undo the damage caused by truisms. Jorge Sampaio is, as one observer puts it, "trying to defuse the mine laid 12 years ago by Samuel Huntington."[11] Sampaio is the UN High Representative for the Alliance of Civilizations (AoC), launched in 2005 by Spain and Turkey under the auspices of the UN. After the attacks of September 11, UN leaders wondered what it would take to prevent a world war of civilizations. The resulting AoC was charged with improving interreligious and cross-cultural understanding and cooperation.

More than eighty countries have joined the alliance, along with international organizations such as UNESCO and the Arab League (the United States is only an observer). One AoC project aims to produce movies with realistic portrayals of religious and cultural minorities instead of simplistic stereotypes. According to Sampaio, "far too often we hear statements from politicians and media people that only exacerbate the situation."[12]

Repeating a truism does not make it true; building a foreign policy on a foundation of faulty assumptions does not make it sound. The Iraq fiasco came about in part because policymakers started with hard power presumptions and never looked back. Dangerous tension with Iran has continued because leaders shut down creative problem solving. In these and all cases, we must have the rigor to stop and question the framework of our perceptions.

2. Question Stereotypes

> During the Vietnam War it was reported that cynical US lawyers working in that country had coined the phrase "the mere gook rule" to describe the very lenient treatment given US military personnel who killed Vietnamese civilians. . . . the Vietnamese were voiceless in the United States and their pain and material and human losses were politically irrelevant and largely unreported here. —EDWARD S. HERMAN, *Beyond Hypocrisy: Decoding the News in an Age of Propaganda*

The number of US soldiers killed in Vietnam—some fifty-eight thousand—is well known in America. But that small Southeast Asian country lost more than a million soldiers and two million civilians out of a population of twenty-two million, more than 14 percent of the population. It's easy to understand why we created a psychological buffer like the stereotypic "mere gook" to keep those appalling losses at bay.

Strictly speaking, stereotyping is neutral; the word denotes having beliefs about the characteristics of a group, but not necessarily all its individuals. Indeed, without stereotypes, we would struggle to deal with complex collectives. But the practice can degenerate into a prejudice that demeans and diminishes others.

According to researchers, this corruption commonly happens through the exaggeration of differences, even in the face of clear similarities. Moreover, members of the "in group" often assume that these distortions are true without testing them. And as they can be willing to attribute an individual's negative action to the entire "out group," they likewise can forget that a collective characteristic may not be true of an individual.[13]

Even among the most offensive aspects of stereotyping, some, but not

In This Was Not Our War: Bosnian Women Reclaiming the Peace, *I described Fahrija Ganić (wife of Ejup Ganić, a "Muslim extremist," according to the CIA). Fahrija fled rebel Serbs with her daughter Emina just before the total blockade of Sarajevo. Despite the trauma of life as a refugee, a few months after her return, Emina drove me into Republika Srpska to visit a Bosnian Serb, Nada Rakovic, whose flight from Croat paramilitaries I was documenting. Scenes like these, with everyday people uniting across expectations, reinforced the insanity of war.*

all, are linked to intergroup violence. Beliefs about a group's competence (or lack thereof) influence only that group's status, potentially resulting in economic—but not physical—harm. But beliefs about their beneficence (or lack thereof) predict the degree of conflict that can erupt between groups. That is, assumptions about a group's warmth, morality, malevolence, likability, and so on are the "social emotions" that determine intergroup behavior.

Perhaps the most pernicious quality of a prejudice is that it is normative—"caught not taught," as it spreads from those who hold it to become a common and acceptable belief.[14] In addition, the farther out the observer, the simpler—and more simply wrong—a stereotype may be, because it cannot be tested with immediate contact.

As we notice ourselves attributing characteristics and predicting actions, whether in close proximity or, more dangerously, from a distance, we must pause. Policymakers must resist the pressure of foregone conclusions and have no personal stake in the answers that data provide.

Such a careful perspective is notably absent in the Israeli-Palestinian conflict, where stereotypes pass from one generation to the next. Repeatedly, Palestinians and Jewish Israeli young people admit to me that they have never met someone from "the other side." Even within Jerusalem, such dramatic divides exist. Visiting the city, I found this almost incredible, until I remembered the segregation of Dallas, Texas. Growing up there in the 1950s, I never once played with a black or Hispanic child, even though there were no walls separating our neighborhoods. Similarly, most Israeli children have never played with a Palestinian, and many parents are convinced that the other parents either unquestioningly support illegal settlements or suicide bombers.

It takes more than unbiased information to educate across the lines. It takes innovative approaches to expose such entrenched beliefs. More than five hundred heartbroken families in the Parents Circle, headquartered in a suburb of Tel Aviv, are tackling misperceptions head-on. In high schools and community groups, facilitators who run their Family Forum recount their losses—members of their immediate families—then explain why they are determined not to perpetuate a cycle of revenge. Through their stories, they demonstrate to the students the power of transformation: from suspicion and vengeance to healing and reconciliation.[15] The group has radio broadcasts twice a week, across Israel and Palestine, and nineteen thousand people listen online. They conduct dialogues among Israeli and Palestinian university students in Jerusalem.

After her sister (a public health consultant educated at Harvard) was stabbed on a street in Jerusalem, Nadwa Sarandah grew more hostile toward Israelis. She relented only after a visit from Yitzhak Frankenthal, the orthodox Jewish founder of the Parents Circle, who apologized to her for Naila's murder and for the occupation's cruelty. Sarandah responded: "I thought if an orthodox Jew, an Israeli, can reach out to a Palestinian, then maybe there is hope." Building on that hope, the group established a hot line called "Hello Shalom/Hello Salaam." More than one million calls between Israelis and Palestinians have been made. In one case, a right-wing settler and a Palestinian began by exchanging abuses; they ended up exchanging phone numbers.

Given the human propensity to demonize those who have caused us pain, we must be wary of sweeping statements that justify our policies. After intelligence briefings on Bosnia in which I was warned of the "Muslim extremists" President Alija Izetbegović and wartime Vice President Ejup Ganić, I received a "Merry Christmas/Happy New Millennium" fax from Izetbegović's foreign advisor, Mirza Hajric, with a champagne bottle popping its cork. Hardly the motif of Muslim intolerance. Meanwhile, Ganić is consistently denied a US visa, despite his being known by the State Department as one of the most moderate of all the participants at the Dayton peace talks.

These group-based stereotypes were embedded in the writing of Robert Kaplan, whose *Balkan Ghosts* was so influential on Vice President Gore: "Here [in the Balkans] men have been isolated by poverty and ethnic rivalry, dooming them to hate."[16] Many Yugoslavs and Balkan advocates disapproved of Kaplan's method of collecting evidence and presenting impressions rather than analysis. The author later asserted that he had not intended to paint a full picture of the disintegrating country; instead, he had aimed only to show that Yugoslavs were still haunted by old rivalries. But as he focused on these "ghosts" at the expense of contrary examples like intermarriage, he failed to convey the mingling of heritages that was characteristic of Bosnia. Whole segments of the population—those who lived in harmony with their different brethren—were absent from his portrayal. Kaplan later recognized the problem. "If I knew what would happen, I would have been clearer in bringing out those points," he admitted. "I did add a more blunt preface to later editions, that says this is only a travel book."[17]

With so much focus on the extraordinarily bad, some people were, thankfully, reporting on the extraordinarily good. Svetlana Broz, the cardiologist and granddaughter of Josip Broz (Marshall Tito) mentioned in section 5, collected and preserved in her book *Good People in an Evil Time* hundreds of accounts of just and generous citizens throughout Bosnia who defied hatred and division.

But voices like Svetlana Broz's were muted in the halls of power, in part because they did not fit the prevailing stereotypes. Instead, the salient assertions in the United States were along the lines of those I recorded in my journal, this one from a trusted advisor to President Clinton.

He: "The only solution for Bosnia is division. Split it up between Croatia and Serbia."

SH: "No one across the Atlantic would suggest ethnic segregation in Los Angeles after the race riots—and Yugoslavs were integrated much more than Americans."

He: "You can't compare the two. The Bosnians all wear gray or black hats."

SH: "Where is that different? In the United States?"

He: "At least we don't cut each other's throats."

SH: "Let's talk about inner-city Chicago, or Watts. We have neighborhoods where neither of us would let our children go, day or night."

He: "Yes, but that's because of gangs."

SH: "The war in Bosnia was fought mostly by militarized gangs."

He: "But the higher-ups were behind them."

SH: "And people like you and me tolerate U.S. gangs."

He: "Because we don't know what to do about them."

SH: "The people in Bosnia don't know what to do about the violence in their society either."

He: "They're a violent people, divided by extremists who will never live together."

The conversation ended where it began. There was no acknowledgment of violent pressures coming from outside, or of internal resources for peace that might be mobilized and supported. The presidential advisor was blinded by poorly informed preconceptions about Balkan history, mistakes he further applied to the contemporary situation. In fact, the last time one group of Yugoslavs fought another, Germany was storming across the borders of France, committing war crimes more heinous than those of the Bosnian conflict. Moreover, World War II was only the most recent in centuries of fighting between Germany and France. But by 1993, with stabilizing structures like the Marshall Plan, NATO, and the EU, an outbreak of violence between the two countries was unthinkable. Similarly, Tito had created scores of measures to unify the republics of the South Slavs, so it should have been just as unlikely for Yugoslav republics to go to war with each other. Why did pundits not think of Serbia, Croatia, and Bosnia the way they did the French and Germans?

The British historian Noel Malcolm concluded:

> The biggest obstacle to all understanding of the conflict is the assumption that what has happened in that country is the product—natural, spontaneous and at the same time necessary—of forces lying within Bosnia's own internal history. That is the myth which was carefully propagated by those who caused the conflict, who wanted the world to believe that what they and their gunmen were doing was done not by them, but by impersonal and inevitable historical forces beyond anyone's control.[18]

Part of the myth was the formidable cunning and reach of Slobodan Milošević. But perhaps he was just a bully, who was actually stoppable. Such myths waste resources and destroy lives. They are powerful, shaping even the independent media whose charge it is to expose them. Thus, generalized assumptions are best questioned before the force of money spent and deaths tallied makes unprejudiced analysis seem heretical or—more damning—unpatriotic.

The war in Vietnam might have been shorter and less deadly had policymakers in Washington recognized the Vietnamese people as equals in ability and value. And the many bungled attempts to make peace between Israelis and Palestinians might have been fewer with earnest inquiry into each community. In short, the careful policymaker recognizes stereotypical assumptions, sets aside bias, and looks for alternatives to the "obvious" course of action.

3. Find Out-of-Power Allies

> Nearly every American I saw in Kabul was hidden behind high walls or racing through the streets in armored convoys. . . . When we retreat behind body armor and concrete barriers, it becomes impossible to understand the society we claim to defend. If we emphasize "force protection" above all else, we will never develop the cultural understanding, relationships and intelligence we need to win. —NATHANIEL FICK, "Fight Less, Win More," *Washington Post*

That sentiment, written by an American Marine in Afghanistan, is not isolated. Some units took an apposite approach. According to Captain Mario Renna, an Italian soldier in NATO's International Security Assistance Force to Afghanistan, "in my opinion things are going quite well here because our patrols, our men are spending a lot of time on the ground." An English-speaking shopkeeper echoes the sentiment: "I think security is much better when the Italian soldiers come here and do their patrols on the streets."[19]

Holed up behind piles of sand bags, we cannot find allies to advance our mission. Instead, we need to be in their homes—and not because we just kicked in their doors. Nor do we find these valuable partners in the corridors of the Pentagon or State Department. In fact, the farther decision makers are from the field, the less likely we are to recognize those who could line up behind our mission.

Despite that wisdom, in general, the hotter the conflict, the less political reporting there is from the field—and the less seriously such accounts are treated. Granted, accuracy drops as information travels over the miles. Eyewitness statements are translated and retold, details are lost; meanwhile, the situation on the ground changes. But even with those limitations, the most insightful data about the dynamics in the war zone come from those closest to the situation.

Still, military and foreign policy establishments tend to keep the ultimate management of a conflict in the hands of high-ranking officers and officials back at headquarters. Those at the top of the chain of com-

In every conflict there are groups on the margins who, if brought in, change the chemistry of the process. These allies generally produce a more sustainable peace, since they have important insights; they may become spoilers if excluded; and they can help sell the agreement back in their communities. I've worked in sixty countries to elevate women into leadership positions, but the principle of inclusion is the same for minority groups, youth, and others who have no place at the table.

mand understandably want to stay in control of what is likely to be one of the most pressing situations on their plates. Those experts may be influenced by their extensive experience in prior conflicts elsewhere, during which they may have had much more on-the-ground contact. With higher-level responsibility in a more rarified administrative position, they may be cut off from untapped resources such as women, indigenous groups, the poor, young, old, displaced, or disabled. But these portions of the population may hold the key to sustainable peace.

"Inclusive security"[20] requires that all stakeholders be fully involved in peace processes, whether before, during, or after a conflict. My experience for three decades has emphasized the importance of women, who more often than not are the primary peace promoters. Yet as a group, they have been dismissed as pitiable victims rather than acknowledged as tough survivors, leaders, or experts. Quite apart from the fairness argument (women constitute more than half a postwar population and thus should have a vital voice), the concept of inclusive security is driven by efficiency: women bring essential tools, perspectives, and spheres of influence that policymakers cannot afford to overlook.

At all levels—from grass-roots organizers to domestic and international leaders—women cross divides, heal fissures, create communities, and contribute in myriad other ways to conflict resolution. Even as they craft peace agreements, women provide the very style by which accord can be reached: they tend to be more cooperative, better equipped to stabilize regions in conflict. As a group, they have an aptitude for influencing change in the manner described above as "soft power," increasingly important in the ongoing fight against terrorism.

It is not only women's formal education and training that equips them for key roles. As they head up NGOs, popular protests, electoral referendums, data gathering, and other citizen-empowering movements, women have a wealth of grass-roots experience. That local credibility helps secure the buy in of those affected by the conflict, as the women sell the peace agreement to the community. Their influence is in part because, compared to men, they are more invested in stopping the violence, due to their roles as family caregivers. And they have a broader definition of security than men generally use, including issues such as safe food and clean water. As one woman said to me: "What does it matter to me if my daughter is killed by a bullet or starves to death?"

Although concurrent, the 1991–96 peace talks in Guatemala contain important contrasts to the Bosnian experience. Those negotiations ended thirty-six years of war that resulted in more than one hundred thousand deaths and two hundred thousand "disappearances" among a population of fewer than eleven million.[21] When dissidents overthrew a military dictator in 1944, a sequence of conflicts was set off in which leftist insurgents clashed with an army backed by the United States, which was concerned about a Communist rise to power. As military governments and corruption prevailed, rebel groups—some allied with Cuba—joined together as the Guatemalan National Revolutionary Unity.

Although the country's democratic institutions were introduced in the 1980s, the transition was rocky and marked by economic crisis and continuing corruption. But by the early 1990s, a congressionally appointed president began to support a peace process with UN involvement.

Negotiation team member Luz Mendez, part of the Guatemalan National Revolutionary Unity, was for years the only woman among thirty participants int the talks. Despite the imbalance, the presence of just one woman made a significant difference. When Mendez returned from the UN Conference on Women in Beijing, Guatemalan women's rights groups asked her to represent their interests. Embracing that responsibility, she fought to add to the peace agreement measures ensuring gender equality in a society in which women had been denied the right even to inherit property. Knowing that their daughters' economic futures were at stake, Guatemalan women were even more highly invested in the accord's implementation, helping ensure its success. Stability in this state came about through a process that brought all the stakeholders together not only across political and economic lines, but also across the gender divide.

Similarly, most women leaders in Bosnia were virtually unknown to the international community. Toward the end of the war, an American shuttle diplomacy team led by Richard Holbrooke came in and out of Yugoslavia. Even though the fighting was in Bosnia, they spent every night in Belgrade or Zagreb—not Sarajevo. During the few hours they were in Bosnia, the team had no meaningful contact with everyday citizens. When Holbrooke's team drew up the guest list for the Dayton negotiations, they failed to consult with grass-roots organizers. Instead, the United States invited to the peace table those who had waged the war. Those who had waged the peace were excluded. Based on my observations in scores of other conflicts, I believe a gender-balanced group would have devised and insisted on concrete mechanisms for the admirable but unenforceable "freedom of movement" protections.

Even in the primary vehicle for transitional justice, the International Criminal Tribunal for the Former Yugoslavia, women have been instrumental at every stage. Women's groups have located and prepared key witnesses as well as collected essential evidence. And because they saw atrocities that men did not, such as rape and mass murder, women's testimony has been critical at many trials. These contributions extend to procedural levels as well; female judges have required greater witness protection and evidentiary precision than previously found in international processes.[22]

Ignoring strong allies among more than half of the population was only one way blinders hindered our progress in Bosnia. If we had asked religious leaders for input, we would have heard opinions confirming that parts of the Dayton plan were ill advised. Cardinal Vinko Puljić, for example, spoke of the "unjust division of the country." The two-entity system adopted in Dayton was "a terrible invention" that "cannot work," he said. "Divide the country and then pretend it is one nation? This is deeply illogical."[23]

Ultimately, it was a grass-roots group on the margins of Washington's attention that brought down Milošević. His ouster was attempted by international might but accomplished by a student movement called Otpor! (resistance!). In 1999, Serbs were clashing with the Kosovar Liberation Army. When Milošević refused to sign an agreement including Kosovar autonomy, NATO threatened military action, which led to a $1 billion bombing campaign. I supported military intervention, believing it necessary to prevent another genocide. But that action, hailed by Kosovars, became the Serbian regime's justification to suppress internal opposition. And many Serbs who otherwise would have supported the West felt betrayed.

Looking back, I believe I was wrong. For a fraction of the human or monetary cost, the international community might have supported strikers, broadcasters, and underground publishers. What bombing alone could not accomplish, Otpor's nonviolent action did. Given that Milošević controlled the army, policy, and media, the students had limited tools to use against him; they resorted to whistles, tin pans, and flowers. Inspiring others to join the resistance, the students forced the leader to call an early election. Results were unfavorable, yet Milošević refused to stand aside.

Crowds poured into the streets, waving baby rattles in ridicule. The young people used satire and humor on T-shirts, graffiti, and nearly two million stickers that read "he's finished." A general strike was declared 2 October 2000, with roads blockaded, classes boycotted, and a rally of 250,000. Three days later, in the "bulldozer revolution," striking miners led heavy equipment, trucks, buses, and cars into the capital, as the police stood by.[24] Protesters stormed the Parliament building. On 7 October, Vojislav Koštunica assumed the presidency.

Because negotiated agreements struck by international hosts and warlords are not designed to reflect the demands of out-of-power allies, implementation is difficult if not impossible. Moreover, negotiations generally are framed to be about stopping war rather than building peace. Given this perspective, community leaders who are not killers are invisible to the organizers. Unsurprisingly, half of all peace agreements fail, and others must be held together at the important cost of a long-term international presence.

In addition to the foreign policy limitations inherent in blanketing theories and too-easy stereotypes, we suffer from culturally reinforced blindness to those without formal power but with enormous informal sway. The result is untapped resources.

Aiming for the absence of war is not enough; policymakers must strive for sustainable peace. But lasting stability requires broad input. A Marine in Afghanistan recognized the danger of isolation and advocated finding allies who, though unexpected, were best informed about peacebuilding opportunities. And in Guatemala, a leader of an oppressed minority pushed that country's new constitution in a progressive direction.

Likewise, the answers to some of our greatest security conundrums lie in places we have been overlooking. To find them, we need to create farther-reaching mechanisms to identify actors who can prevent or stop conflict, so that those peace builders can be supported and supportive.

4. Appreciate Domestic Dynamics

> If you want to investigate Colombia's violence, you need to go to the rural regions and jungles and see the context of poverty and lack of access to education, and a dearth of other opportunities—within which the violence, mixed with a variety of criminal activities, has proliferated. In many regions, the children have more access to guns than to a toy or a book. —MARIA CRISTINA CABALLERO, interview with the author, 2005

Colombia's impact on its neighbors, and now on the world, is intrinsically tied to spontaneous and organized violence within the state. It is impossible to respond with helpful foreign policy without a grasp of the domestic strife that forms the backdrop of the conflict. The bloody decade of 1948 to 1958, which took nearly two hundred thousand lives, was only an early twist in a spiral of hopelessness, violence, and drugs that escalated during the 1990s, becoming one of the most important pre-September 11 challenges of US foreign policy. Burdened by widespread poverty and the need for land reform, Colombia has been entrenched in violence for more than forty years. Some 88 percent of sixty thousand deaths since 1985 have been domestic civilian casualties. Yet the conflict can be called transnational, since addressing the illegal narcotic trade spawned by the war now costs other countries billions of dollars. The controversial Plan Colombia has emphasized military equipment and training rather than focusing on root causes of the problem.

Decisions to sign a trade agreement, go to war, or engage in any of countless other international actions are stronger if we enter the halls of foreign policy through the chambers of domestic policy. Yet professionals devoted to foreign affairs are more likely to be at home with the broader sweeps of current history, from which they can extrapolate relevant findings to any of a number of countries in a region. However intelligent and experienced they are, they may not perceive social mechanics and dynamics—the how and why of internal chaos measured in judicial corruption, jobs lost, homelessness, sinking property values, high inflation, and inaccessible healthcare.

But for understandable reasons, members of the international community usually do not devote themselves to on-the-ground issues. Even with their strong commitment to public service, the most senior career diplomats usually have not spent their weekends volunteering with NGOs at home or abroad. Thus, they often lack an intuitive feel for individual and popular needs—the very needs that may drive a political shift or fuel a conflict.

Instead, the diplomats have spent the majority of their professional years moving from country to country. In addition to dealing with the resulting stress on their families, they create a tight community among their expatriate colleagues: after all, they share alma maters, reading lists, and overseas assignments. Unfortunately, every year one third of these colleagues rotate out. Similarly, their interlocutors in the military or foreign ministries are constantly rotating outside their own countries. All these factors conspire to leave international players little time or incentive to drill down into complex domestic concerns of the host country.

The Foreign Service culture does not value or reward local expertise. Instead, analysts trained in political and economic "cones" who rotate through brief (three-month to two-year) assignments in a war zone are regarded as experts on the conflict, even though they may have come from a posting in another part of the world. Meanwhile, host-country "foreign service nationals," who may have worked in an embassy or NGO for decades, are often treated as second class, excluded from meetings where overarching direction is set.

The one area of international work that might base its activity on the domestic scene is intelligence operations. Spies may have an on-the-street system to gather data; however, they usually are instructed to conceal from nonintelligence colleagues their dealings with locals. Although they must feel free to withhold "sources and methods," they may use a tight interpretation of that freedom to justify not sharing their data. The result is a mystique: the rest of an overseas mission has no way to judge whether the information gathered by intelligence officers or the conclusions reached by analysts are grounded in trustworthy conversations and intercepted communications or simply based on assumptions.

The groups that are, in fact, most in touch with the domestic situation are NGOs. As a new diplomat, when I asked a group of fellow ambassadors how they were dealing with such organizations, they responded with a plan for "damage control." In other words, they saw these groups as adversaries. And so the insights of the NGO community—whether recording human rights abuses, exposing corruption, or setting up refugee camps—have been welcomed only rarely by officials, although starved budgets are now forcing diplomats to glean information and support where they formerly had not.

Political upheaval, especially, must be entered at the local level.

Civilian-based crisis management can be engaged during all phases, from prevention to postconflict stabilization. The Finnish minister of defense, admittedly representing a country with security options constrained by geography and history, called on these "enhanced peacekeeping operations" to encompass a range of efforts, from observing elections and monitoring human rights to providing humanitarian aid and policing support.[25] Along these lines, during the 1990s the European Civilian Peace Corps put together a Balkan Peace Team, the first transnational civil society endeavor to promote local efforts toward peace. Subsequently, in 1998, the German government institutionalized a Civil Peace Service (Ziviler Friedensdienst, or ZFD). Conceived of by a consortium of peace and development organizations, the ZFD deploys "peace consultants" to help local partners address medium- and low-level conflict resolution methods often overlooked by high-level diplomacy — such as establishing a dialogue between adversaries and creating civil-society structures.

In a similar vein, in 2008 the Norwegian government inspired and funded the UN's new Standby Team of Mediation Experts. On call to join peace envoys in the field, the group's six high-level specialists manage complex negotiation issues that can bring peace talks to a standstill. Coaxing the talks back into motion means enabling all sides to describe their needs and then find ways to meet them. That, in turn, requires uncovering domestic dynamics behind the stalled issues. For example, writing a constitution might depend on a grasp of tribal leadership structures. Advancing justice might benefit from knowledge of indigenous practices for reconciliation. Helping former combatants reintegrate into civilian life might require ingenuity grounded in local custom. The first Standby Team deployment exemplified this need for broad domestic understanding: at the request of the formal negotiating team, the experts were sent to Kenya during the 2008 political crisis to assist with constitutional development and security sector reform — two classic deal breakers.

The international community has a long way to go toward ensuring that civilian peacekeeping components are well planned and readily available. While operations with tens of thousands of soldiers can be organized quickly, for example during the Kosovo crisis, providing a few thousand police officers there has been nearly impossible. But unlike soldiers, police are in the community. And it is at the community level that peace must take root.

Foreign policy that takes account of domestic policy confronts the questions of whom to heed and how to respond. But making assumptions about a conflict without giving thought to local dynamics can lead to the inaccurate conclusions on which bad policy is based. Russia is a case in point. While that vast country is not experiencing widespread internal unrest, ongoing conflict in one of the republics is a telling blot. Since the beginning of the first Chechen war in 1994, when the Russian military intervened to stop secession, extrajudicial civilian executions have soared. Few suspected perpetrators have been tried, although the European Court of Human Rights has found Russia guilty of serious violations, including the use of disproportionate military force and civilian targeting. The way Russian leaders dealt with Chechnya (a harbinger of their undemocratic tendencies) and the troubling complacency among the Russian people could have been a signal to the international community, as it made decisions about relationships with the Russian state.

The beginning of the second Chechen war in 1999 provided the occasion for Vladimir Putin's rise to power. Then the deputy prime minister, Putin had been little known prior to his August appointment, but his uncompromising approach to the resurgent conflict was impressive to President Yeltsin as well as immensely popular among a people starved for law and order. Moreover, widespread domestic prejudice against people from the Caucasus fed into fears of terrorism and unrest. These factors catapulted him ahead of his opponents and into the prime minister position.

One of Putin's most outspoken critics was the journalist Anna Politkovskaia, who from the beginning of the Chechen wars ventured into the thick of the conflict. For years, she investigated and exposed human rights abuses, nearly alone in her mission. She was close to publishing yet another article detailing Russian military wrongs in Chechnya when, on 7 October 2006, she was shot at pointblank range outside her Moscow apartment.

Nearly a year later, Russian prosecutors finally made the first arrests related to her murder, accusing a Chechen-led gang and Russian security officers. Authorities refused to cite motives but alleged, nonsensically, that only those living outside Russia could have been interested in her death.[26] The reporter's friends were unconvinced. The director of Human Rights Watch believes "there can be no question but that Politkovskaia was killed in retribution for her work."[27]

In 2003, Chechnya adopted a new constitution and declared itself part of Russia, effectively cooling the conflict. But Putin's tough image at home had been established. Despite their country's slide back toward tyranny, Russians, by and large, seem willing to live with the state's control of the news media—shutting down independent stations, banning unfavorable coverage, and harassing uncooperative journalists. In mid-2007, then-President Putin enjoyed an approval rating higher than that of any other world leader, at 81 percent.[28]

For international policymakers or activists trying to effect change in Russia, it is crucial to understand that these ratings are real and that they matter. After the turmoil of the Yeltsin years, Russian citizens craved stability. Under Putin, the economy improved, along with education, social services, and security; but the population opted for these advances at the expense of intellectual freedom.

Similarly, a grass-roots view of domestic dynamics in Yugoslavia would have revealed what was and was not real about that conflict. Many foreign policy analysts failed to recognize that "ethnic hatred" was only a smokescreen for conniving politicians. The real issues were economic stress and political uncertainty caused by Tito's poor succession planning. Although alarming for all groups, this instability was most threatening to the Serbs, who feared losing the privilege they had enjoyed during Tito's long rule. They were thus highly motivated to support leaders promising to restore that system. Yet few international actors took the time to see the Yugoslav disintegration from the perspective of those living through it.

Following the war, the same limitations plagued international efforts. Within days of the new peace, the dread expressed to me by Foreign Minister Muhamed Saćirbey about a flood of international "helpers" was substantiated. A wave of mostly Western Europeans and Americans crashed onto the scene as wealthy nations attempting to be responsible global citizens sent money, goods, volunteers, coordinators, and trainers. Although flawed, these aid organizations did the best they could with policies and procedures developed over dozens of years of crisis work, but local groups could have delivered the aid while also developing leadership and widespread citizen participation. In addition, the new arrivals seemed oblivious to the messages they were sending with their high salaries, expense accounts, and new vehicles—as well as their two-class standard that rewarded heroic Bosnian professionals with less salary and less respect. Outsiders wondered, often aloud and rudely, about the ingratitude of "locals."

Even when Milošević was arrested on 20 March 2001, and eventually extradited to stand trial at The Hague, outsiders did not fully appreciate the Bosnian domestic situation. Although that legal process had long been awaited, the remote trial disempowered the local population, who otherwise might have experienced greater healing. Civilians harmed by the conflict were not in the courtroom to hear their representatives testify to the injury they all had experienced. Without a community-by-community process in which citizens could express their reservations, voice their agreement, or otherwise respond to the dis-

Listening to those at the grass-roots level, a policymaker gains a very different perspective on needs, challenges, and opportunities. Here, rural people from eastern Bosnia who have lost their homes and sources of livelihood bear out the reports of what happened during the conflict.

tant developments, much of the reconciliatory potential of the ICTY was unrealized.[29]

Every solution is a problem. Every intervention is imperfect. But costs and flaws can be mitigated. Our policies toward Colombia's massive drug trade must emerge from a familiarity with the internal social-justice issues to which it is linked. Our responses to Russia's harsh practices must be based on a grasp of the local desires that brought strongmen to power. Clearly, decisions about if, when, or how war—and peace, for that matter—should be waged should be based on domestic dynamics, since distant power brokers often miss the earliest signs of conflict, ignore the most effective peace advocates on the scene, and stunt the postconflict growth of fledgling local institutions. Even when that is complicated by ongoing violence, a surer approach would be engaging in extensive consultation with the real experts: the wide array of people on the ground.

Our foreign policy is first, and ultimately, someone else's domestic policy.

5. Find Fault

> Forty years ago, a young man awoke, and he found himself an orphan in an orphaned world. What have I learned in the last 40 years—small things. I learned the perils of language and those of silence. I learned that in extreme situations when human lives and dignity are at stake, neutrality is a sin. It helps the killers not the victims. . . . I have learned the danger of indifference, the crime of indifference. For the opposite of love, I have learned, is not hate but indifference. Jews were killed by the enemy but betrayed by their so-called allies who found political reasons to justify their indifference or passivity. —ELIE WIESEL, on receiving the Congressional Gold Medal, 19 April 1985

For two decades, the United States watched the rise of Hitler in Germany. His language became progressively extreme, his prejudice less masked. He was no wolf in sheep's clothing, pouncing in surprise attack. Instead, as Hitler ascended to power, silence among those watching allowed ordinary Germans to accept the authority of the state and cast their increasingly hate-filled actions as normal.

In an unholy alliance, those who lack the courage to stand up to evil find themselves, by omission, on the side of that evil. But cowardice is not the only barrier to action. As we mature as individuals or as a society, we learn tolerance; ironically, it is those most tolerant who may tolerate wrong.

Reluctance to find fault in others is understandable: we know that none of us gets it right all the time. Blame can seem too blunt an instrument, too unmeasured a reaction. We pride ourselves on being fair, and blame, we may mistakenly assume, is the opposite of fairness. So in our efforts to be enlightened, open, and self-critical, we are tempted to declare ourselves "neutral."

But neutrality and fairness are not interchangeable. Neutrality means not taking sides; fairness, although it includes impartiality, requires justice. The international community often stumbles over this distinction, as if afraid to take a stand. That fear at best is grounded in the intent to maintain credibility. At worst, however, neutrality is grounded in aversion to risk, a spineless or heartless nonresponse to crisis.

At other times, the international community gets it right. The apartheid system in South Africa was brought down largely because outsiders took organized action against it. That action required a stance, not just an opinion. Even before the formal apartheid system was instituted in 1948, the South African treatment of Indian citizens drew criticism from the inaugural gathering of the new United Nations. Unfortunately, through the 1950s, although the subject was again on the UN's agenda, the consensus was that apartheid was essentially a domestic concern and therefore not a proper target of international action.

The Sharpeville massacre in 1960 increased the urgency of the debate. After police opened fire on five thousand peaceful protestors, shooting many in the back as they fled and killing sixty-nine, the UN Security Council issued a demand for reform. Although that demand was ignored, momentum was building. Less than a year later, South Africa was forced to withdraw from the British Commonwealth after it became clear that other member states would not support its continued presence. The UN General Assembly, too, became involved, passing resolutions condemning apartheid policies. Motions to take stronger action often were blocked by South Africa's largest trading partners— France, Britain, and the United States. But even they ended arms trade with South Africa after a UN Security Council Resolution called for such action. By the late 1970s, the arms embargo was no longer optional; a decade later, trade sanctions were in place, and governments and corporations were divesting from the regime.

Of course the South African story of violence was not one-sided. After Sharpeville, the African National Congress (ANC) abandoned its reliance on nonviolent resistance. Its new military wing was called Umkhonto we Sizwe (MK), meaning "spear of the nation." With Nelson Mandela at its head, MK focused its early attacks on government facilities. (In 1962, Mandela was sentenced to life imprisonment for these activities.) But MK targets expanded in the next two decades to government and military-industrial properties. Once civilians at these targets began to die, Western countries joined the South African government in classifying the ANC as a terrorist organization.

Strong geopolitical forces influenced the domestic situation. The Soviets supported the ANC, and once again—to use an African expression—as the elephants fought, the grass was trampled. The US mission of fighting Communism trumped our concern for justice and human rights. With the implosion of Soviet Communism, however, the South African regime could be judged on its own merits. On 9 November 1989, East Germans climbed through openings in the Berlin Wall; On 11 February 1990, Mandela walked out of prison. Now the United States joined most of the West, pulling its support from the ruling National Party, which slowly and reluctantly began opening up the apartheid system.

After nearly five decades, international action against the oppressive South African government brought down an unjust system. The actions were not vigorous enough to achieve immediate results, but they showed that a bold and rare decision to take sides can make a difference. Fairness trumped neutrality.

In Bosnia, too, fairness meant acknowledging overwhelming (although not exclusive) guilt on one side. Like it or not, the postwar situation forced a choice: neutrality could trump fairness, or fairness could trump neutrality. After the Dayton Accords, the word on many policymakers' lips was "evenhandedness," which could have applied to either principle. Interpretation was left to the individual. Most international officials I met in Bosnia chose neutrality over fairness, and they had their reasons. For one thing, not assigning guilt where it belonged meant that action was not required. More charitably, however, getting at the truth was fraught with difficulty; and in many cases, there was no single truth to be discovered.

Were "the Serbs" to blame for war in the Balkans? Not exactly. Individual leaders who were Serbs led atrocious political and military actions, but so did some leaders who were Croat and Bosniak, or of mixed lineage. In all these cases, many regular citizens were complicit, not having the conviction or courage to stand up for what was right. Nor was the international community blameless. But acknowledgment of our own shortcomings neither mitigated Serb culpability nor absolved us from the responsibility to act. Whatever the reasons, by distributing blame evenly, we made a mockery of human rights.

With their anti-Bosniak bias, the CIA and other intelligence agencies bore heavy responsibility for US reluctance to take sides. When I complained to George Tenet, the CIA's deputy director, and later to Director John Deutsch, each insisted I was wrong. It was only after I had moved to Harvard's Kennedy School of Government that my concerns about their preconceptions were confirmed. At a small dinner in Cambridge, soon after Deutsch had left Langley and returned to MIT, a retired Clinton cabinet member asked his opinion of the Balkans. Deutsch was so plain-spoken that I wrote down his response in my journal. "The only future for Bosnia is partition," he said. "Those people will never live together."

I was taken aback. But why should I have been? Even while President Clinton was putting his weight behind integration, every CIA report I saw took the reader one more step toward segregation, if not disintegration. Perhaps it was significant that Deutsch had moved to the CIA from

UN inaction was disastrous and disgraceful. Within that system, Kofi Annan, while Under-Secretary-General for Peacekeeping Operations, tried addressing two genocides—in Rwanda and the former Yugoslavia—and failed at both.

his position as deputy secretary of defense; CIA analysis matched the military misinformation in a viral feedback loop. Decisions such as not to break up the siege of Sarajevo were being made in Washington, where they were colored by an agency's biased mind-set—counter to the State Department personnel who were putting their lives on the line.

There are no disinterested parties when it comes to justice.[30] Those who turn their backs, saying they refuse to take a stand, are, in fact, standing for impunity. The Holocaust took the lives of between eleven and seventeen million victims because a sophisticated international community would not recognize basic malevolence. In the same way, black South Africans suffered for years longer than they might have, had there been robust international intervention.

Remaining neutral in the face of evil is de facto complicity.

I am cognizant of the interrelatedness of all communities and states. I cannot sit idly in Atlanta and not be concerned about what happens in Birmingham. Injustice anywhere is a threat to justice everywhere. We are caught in an inescapable network of mutuality, tied in a single garment of destiny. Whatever affects one directly, affects all indirectly. Never again can we afford to live with the narrow, provincial "outside agitator" idea. Anyone who lives inside the United States can never be considered an outsider anywhere within its bounds. —MARTIN LUTHER KING JR., "Letter from Birmingham Jail," 16 April 1963

On the evening of 4 May 1961, an interracial group of students trained in nonviolence met at a Chinese restaurant in Washington, D.C. The next morning, these "Freedom Riders" were heading south to challenge Jim Crow laws, born in the reconstruction era and mandating "separate but equal" status for blacks and whites. On the road, the young people ate together at segregated lunch counters and used "white" and "colored" facilities interchangeably—rights affirmed in a 1960 Supreme Court decision.

They met their first angry mob in South Carolina. There and elsewhere, when white supremacists beat them, local police often refused to help. Then on Mother's Day, ten days after setting out, the Freedom Riders entered Anniston, Alabama. At the station, a waiting crowd slashed their tires. The students drove on, but as the tires flattened and the bus was forced to pull over, they were surrounded. When someone from the crowd threw a firebomb, the students tried to escape the burning bus, but the mob held the doors shut, hoping to burn them alive.

The bus's gas tank exploded, forcing the crowd back and allowing the riders to escape—only to be beaten. An undercover highway patrolman riding with them fired warning shots into the air, saving them from almost certain death. Later that day, the Freedom Riders were beaten again in Birmingham. But they accepted these ordeals as the cost of their responsibility to stop injustice wherever they found it.

Exactly four decades later, the International Commission on Intervention and State Sovereignty published a landmark report titled "The Responsibility to Protect." A response to rising intrastate violence, the concept—for some, the doctrine—set forth a moral imperative: states have responsibilities toward their populations, but the international community has the responsibility to step in when states ignore harm to, or turn against, their own citizens.

Some fretted that such a transnational responsibility would erode state sovereignty and be abused by powerful outsiders—a new imperialism. They also feared it justified military intervention in violation of long-standing international law. Others saw an inherent, prior responsibility to warn about, prevent, and respond to violence against any people, using diplomatic and other pressure. The doctrine, its framers hoped, would provide a stronger legal framework for international intervention when a state is allowing or perpetrating atrocities.

Most UN member states sided with the hopeful. By consensus, at the UN World Summit of 2005, they affirmed the new principle allowing intervention. Less than a year later, the UN Security Council deepened the commitment by passing a resolution with provisions that set forth the responsibility of not only states but the international community to protect citizens. From that day forward, the responsibility would be shared. No longer could an unscrupulous despot deny outsiders the right to step in to put a stop to unjustifiable suffering.

It is easy to forget that those in the highest decision-making positions need to be concerned about far-reaching implications of intervening on foreign soil. Representing the Clinton administration, my fellow diplomats and I had to be particularly sensitive to internal pressures on the administration: overhaul of the national welfare system, failing healthcare reform, and disastrous midterm elections were consuming the attention of the White House. Meanwhile, in addition to the ongoing Balkan war, a similar story was breaking on another continent. But Kigali had never hosted the Olympics, and its dark-skinned people were divided by confusing names like Hutu and Tutsi.

Americans were not feeling particularly sympathetic about the conflicts in Africa after October 1993, when the world watched CNN's footage of eighteen dead US Marines being dragged through the streets of Mogadishu, Somalia. Trouble in Rwanda seemed like more of the same, and a good place for Americans not to be.

The size of Maryland, that country was extremely poor, had no significant exports, and was wracked with seemingly intractable conflict. More than two decades prior to the 1994 mass killing, more than a million of the Belgian-favored and better educated Tutsis had fled to neighboring Uganda, where they lived as refugees from vengeful Hutu extremists. This was the background of violence against which the Hutu majority (90 percent of Rwanda's population) decided to rid the country of Tutsis once and for all.

For close observers, the subsequent genocide was no surprise. On 11 January 1994, UN General Roméo Dallaire sent an urgent fax to headquarters in New York, where Kofi Annan was director of the Department of Peacekeeping Operations. The fax was titled "Request for Protection for Informant." The informant, no sympathizer of the Tutsis but opposed to the killing of innocents, had been charged with organizing a plot involving forty-eight commandos and a government minister to kill opposition leaders, thus provoking a civil war. He also described how Hutus were registering Tutsis—a step toward an efficient extermination of the "cockroaches."[31]

Kofi Annan, favored by the United States to succeed Boutros Boutros-Ghali as UN Secretary General, rejected the suggestion of a raid to seize massive caches of weapons, maintaining that was beyond the scope of a peacekeeping operation.

Three months later, thirty thousand Tutsis and Hutu moderates were slaughtered over two days. Within a hundred days, those numbers grew to some eight hundred thousand, with virtually no protection from the international community. General Dallaire repeatedly and courageously put himself in harm's way, but he and his 450 troops were surrounded by carnage they were unable to stop.

The consensus of other countries seemed to be that intervention was not worth the risk. The killing was exhausting to the killers, as neighbors hacked at bodies with machetes or hoes. Victims with money paid to be killed with a bullet. Many gathered at churches for refuge, but the protection was a ruse, primarily for the purpose of collecting the victims into convenient groups. At their most "efficient" pace, Hutus were killing at nearly three times the rate achieved during the Holocaust.

In May, the UN started discussions about sending in 5,500 troops. But the Clinton administration called for a smaller force. Three weeks later, Secretary General Boutros-Ghali reported to the Security Council: "We have failed in our response to the agony of Rwanda, and thus we have acquiesced in the continued loss of human lives. . . . There can be little doubt [that the killing] constitutes genocide."[32] Clinton's ambassador to Rwanda, David Rawson, objected: "As a responsible government, you don't just go around hollering 'genocide.'"[33]

When President Clinton came to Kigali four years later, he said: "All over the world there were people like me sitting in offices, day after day after day, who did not fully appreciate the depth and the speed with which you were being engulfed by this unimaginable terror."[34] "Did not fully appreciate" or did not see it as their responsibility?

Before, during, and after the war in Bosnia, officials with enormous power were denying their responsibility for the destruction happening within their spheres of influence. The most callous shrugged their shoulders at the inevitability of war. Others wrung their hands but did not, or could not, accept their part in allowing the carnage to occur, fighting to continue, and injustice to be written into a permanent political structure.

Jealousies among key players may have diluted their sense of responsibility. Many in the US leadership seemed relieved when allies protested that Americans were playing too strong a role. US officials were concerned that this backwater maelstrom could threaten a close relationship between the West and a democratic Russia—a major foreign policy objective.

Throughout the debates over intervention, language had to be tweaked to fit the low level of response that influential people were willing to risk. To protect policymakers from being dragged into action, euphemisms were used to describe the war. "Genocide," for example, would invoke the 1948 UN Convention on the Prevention and Punishment of the Crime of Genocide, requiring international intervention.[35] But "ethnic cleansing" could be used to describe how paramilitary thugs were forcing fathers to mutilate their sons, murdering mothers in front of their children, and driving families from their homes by the hundreds of thousands.

"Cleansing." "Ethnic cleansing." The words had a salubrious timbre, a promise of a clean result. The words also implied, although no one said it, that mixed communities were ethnically dirty. Still, for whatever reason, "ethnic cleansing" was a label that policymakers could live with. International journalists, too, picked up the term as a gentle shorthand for atrocities.

Then came Dayton. In his memoir, former Assistant Secretary of State for Europe Richard Holbrooke explains: "While some people criticized us for trying to do too much at Dayton, my main regret is that we did not attempt more."[36] He devotes only one page to flaws in the agreement: creating a divided army, allowing the Serb-controlled portion of the country to be called Republika Srpska, ending the bombing too early, relying on a weak international police task force, creating a weak Office of the High Representative, and agreeing to arbitrary deadlines for international troop withdrawal. The list makes good sense, and Holbrooke shows courage in laying out the weaknesses of the peace talks he negotiated. Still, while "Milošević could dance circles around some of the world's most senior diplomats and statesmen,"[37] Holbrooke does not assume personal responsibility for the flaws he lists. More than a decade later, his report card on Bosnia again gives high marks to the Dayton Peace Agreement, instead attributing failures to Balkan political problems and lack of international follow-up.[38]

Even after the world finally insisted that the carnage had to end, it was difficult to convert words to actions. Regret may cause a perpetrator to atone for sins, but shame is another matter. Their shame over Srebrenica was so intense that UN representatives seemed to lapse into denial, failing to recognize the necessity of housing and jobs for the survivors, even as a report accepting significant responsibility was being drafted in UN headquarters in New York.

The same split could be seen on the ground. Sector commanders differed in how to interpret their mandate. During the next few years, IFOR troops assigned to different parts of the country assumed quite different levels of responsibility for the Bosnians around them.

US military commanders came into the country with an explicit directive not to lose any troops. That, and the military's desire to avoid failure, meant that preventing "mission creep" became the goal. "Security" was applied to their own forces, rather than addressing causes of destabilization such as hunger, fear, and hopelessness. Most of the ten thousand American soldiers were thus confined to their barracks, sealed off from a country desperate for help. When I visited a US-run IFOR field camp near Brčko, the officers were proud to tell me they brought in a few members of the community from time to time to talk. But in general, soldiers in battle gear ventured into the surrounding farmland for only brief reconnaissance missions. I saw no normalized interaction between the troops and the people they had been sent to protect. Interpreted narrowly, the protector had no responsibility to know the protected.

The thirteen thousand British in the northwest were much more involved in helping rebuild communities—physically reconstructing towns, getting supplies to schools, and interacting with citizens. In contrast, the French, with another ten thousand troops, oversaw the southeast sector, including Sarajevo and its airport. High-level US officials, including President Clinton, repeatedly accused them of sheltering the indicted war criminal Radovan Karadžić, foiling efforts of the war crimes tribunal to bring him to justice.

Because they had to be interpreted, mandates often became more than guidelines—they became shields behind which players could avoid responsibility. For example, the French decision not to allow others to pursue indicted war criminals in their sector was a barrier to justice. And the refusal of some international commanders to interpret their mandates as apprehending war criminals sent a message of impunity throughout Bosnia. Such decisions had real and tragic consequences for those who subsequently lost their homes, limbs, or family members at the hands of thugs emboldened by military inaction.

The Carnegie Endowment for International Peace said it well: "The real culprits in this long list of executions, assassinations, drownings, burnings, massacres and atrocities . . . are not . . . the Balkan people. . . . The

Among the ten thousand US troops who entered Bosnia, these at Camp McGovern, near the contested hot spot of Brčko, had one another's safety on their minds — and rightly so. It's not clear, however, that top ranks passed down with the same urgency goals other than "force protection."

real culprits are those who by interest or inclination, declaring that war is inevitable, end by making it so, asserting that they are powerless to prevent it."[39] That was the endowment's assessment in 1914.

As countries across the globe wrestle with the question of where their responsibility begins or ends, we find no simple answer. After a conflict, it is easy to point fingers at aggressors, but when it comes to assigning responsibility for intercession, policymakers have the same tendencies that we have in our personal lives—to point elsewhere.

Part of our reluctance to assume responsibility is because conflict situations are cloudy at best, notwithstanding public officials' attempts to lay out to the citizenry a clear case for military intervention. Arguments are almost always cast in bold terms of the acting nation's interest—even if the expressed mission is as nonsensical as going after a terrorist who is actually in another country.

But progressive foreign policy must be informed, if not motivated, by empathy. How to make people care is another question, one that Bill Clinton faced as he laid out the humanitarian case, then sent troops into Bosnia with support from less than half of the US population.[40] Perhaps our problem as Americans is that we are on the whole too comfortable. Just as African Americans are among the least prosperous but also the most generous people in our country,[41] emptying their purses into the church collection plate and donating 25 percent more of their discretionary income than wealthier whites, Rwandans were the first in the African Union to send troops to protect victims in Darfur in 2004. When asked why they stepped up so readily, Rwandan officials answered that they understood at a visceral level the desperation of being alone in the world as citizens are tortured, raped, and slaughtered.

In addition to national interest and empathy, a driving force for foreign policymaking must be a moral understanding befitting countries with twenty-first-century concepts of human rights and obligations. Post–World War II Secretary of State George Marshall stands apart as a leader able to stir the conscience of a tired United States, inspiring us to share our resources beyond wartime, to cement the peace. He understood that the truest security requires an integration of duty with privilege. Following his lead, surely we who live in comfort can spend a small portion of our treasure—and even our talent—to save a disproportionate number of others.

Those of us who decry the military buildup in the United States in particular can take comfort that the "responsibility to protect" does not necessarily require a more aggressive foreign policy. Harking back to the first lesson, an active, innovative, and early "soft power" offensive can transform the environment in which strongmen arise or hate-mongering groups grow. Extensive diplomatic efforts can often mitigate a danger, but it may be throngs with whistles and rattles who bring down a dictator. Likewise, if half of the Greens in Europe who opposed our military intervention had marched on Belgrade years earlier, perhaps two hundred would have been killed. Instead, two hundred thousand died. Only when such efforts fail can blunt, undiscriminating hard power be the best option.

Ultimately, the question of responsibility leads to the rather trivial question: Are we Americans the world's police? The serious answer is an awesome, *collective* yes. In a virtual sense, we are part of a force made up of scores of nations with the mandate to protect. We can regard this as a burden, or we can accept it as a privilege. But from either stance, the lesson of Bosnia is that we must not shirk that responsibility.

Epilogue

In the prologue to this book, I insisted that I had no intention of turning well-intentioned officials into cannon fodder for critics of US involvement in the Bosnian war. No one set out to do any harm. As we watched the conflagration, we were troubled; but we truly did not know how to respond. However imperfectly, we were doing the best we could with the leadership, information, experience, and training we had.

As these pages have described, in Bosnia we were hampered by a flaw in a foreign policy design that has shaped history across time and across conflicts. At the heart of that flaw is the insular thinking of actors who perceive the conflict from different stances—none of which bridge the policy arena and life on the ground. That gulf is due partly to the often conflicting points of view of the players, each of whom comes onto the scene with her or his own agenda, wrestling with a host of questions.

The military demand an answer: "What is the job we're being sent to do, and what is our exit strategy? What will this do to our standing back home—will we return to our families and communities heroes or villains?" Humanitarian agencies worry: "Can we work quickly, in a streamlined fashion, so that we can leave this disaster as soon as possible and go on to the next? Will our staff be safe?" Reporters must assess: "Will this conflict draw an audience and hold its attention? What will it cost to cover the conflict—in dollars, in my future access to key players, and in my career trajectory?" Meanwhile, politicians want to know: "Can I sell this action on patriotic or moral grounds to the voters? Will it highjack my political agenda or damage my reelection campaign?"

Diplomats pose the questions: "How will this situation affect our image and effectiveness on the global stage? And will our actions here jeopardize congressional funding for the State Department?" The intel-

Viktor Frankl, Nazi Holocaust survivor, turned his tragedy into help for tens of millions worldwide.

ligence community asks: "How does this crisis connect to other threats? Is this part of a global web of evildoers whom Foreign Service officers are not taking seriously enough?" And from more of a distance, ethicists wonder: "What principles are at stake here? What values are worth dying—or killing—for?"

The ensuing strain among different parts of government and civil society is worse than simple lack of integration. During the Bosnian war, the split was so severe that the chief of the CIA station at the US embassy in Croatia actually spied on his chief of mission, Ambassador Peter Galbraith, sending covert reports back to Washington.

More damning than stereotypical thinking and competing points of view, however, is the act of inaction. That was the analysis of my Viennese mentor, the great theorist and psychiatrist Viktor Frankl. I went to see him at his small apartment near our embassy and just a few blocks from where Freud had lived.

I was representing an administration that talked about justice as it allowed genocide. How could I live with the deadly stalling? I asked Frankl: "Should I resign in protest?"

Frankl leaned toward me sympathetically. "Madame Ambassador, sometimes the right thing to do is only 55 percent right and is 45 percent wrong. It's hard enough for an individual to act in those situations. For a giant like the US government, it's paralyzing."

I left our conversation still disappointed by the failure of Washington to act, but at least more understanding of the complexities blocking decisive leadership. Only when I had some distance in the ensuing years, as I worked in and wrote about Bosnia, did I realize the need to connect head and heart—to connect the policies determined in logic-driven consultations and the pathos bred in brutalizing situations.

It is for the Bosnian people, and all those affected by war, that for nine years I kept coming back to this manuscript. And it is for all of us who bear the mental, physical, and economic costs of war that I hope I have presented a compelling case. The life-or-death decisions—which wartime actions are 55 percent right?—must not be made from a single vantage point. However challenging it is to move beyond the familiar, we must examine every truism and every stereotype, find new allies and new perspectives, know when to find fault and when to embrace responsibility. Only then will we have the intellectual and emotional wherewithal to bring together the two worlds apart, making them one, more just and secure.

Notes

PROLOGUE

1. The full name is Bosnia-Herzegovina, but I will be using "Bosnia" throughout the text.

2. At my side in almost all my Balkan work was Valerie Gillen, a wise and energetic partner. She was assisted by the up-and-coming Sarah Gauger.

CONTEXT

1. Robert Kaplan, *Balkan Ghosts: A Journey through History* (New York: Vintage, 1993), xxiii.

2. Arabic for the Muslim "grand mufti."

3. Noel Malcolm, *Bosnia: A Short History* (New York: New York University Press, 1994), 166.

4. The classic work on losses in World War II is Vladimir Zerjavic, *Population Losses in Yugoslavia 1941–1945* (Zagreb: Dom i Svijet, Hrvatski Institut za Povijest, 1997).

5. The 1974 Yugoslav constitution made Kosovo and Vojvodina autonomous provinces with the same status at the republics.

6. It is estimated that between thirty thousand and forty thousand people passed through Goli Otok before it was closed in 1989, though some estimates are as high as fifty thousand. See Stephane Courtois and Nicolas Werth, *The Black Book of Communism* (Cambridge: Harvard University Press, 1999).

7. See Susan L. Woodward, *Balkan Tragedy: Chaos and Dissolution after the Cold War* (Washington: Brookings Institution, 1995), especially chapter 3.

8. Malcolm, *Bosnia*, 210.

9. For a thorough discussion of Yugoslavia's post-Tito political chaos, see V. P. Gagnon Jr., *The Myth of Ethnic War: Serbia and Croatia in the 1990s* (Ithaca: Cornell University Press, 2004).

10. For background on the role of the media during the wars of succession, see Mark Thompson, *Forging War: The Media in Serbia, Croatia, Bosnia and Hercegovina* (Luton, England: University of Luton Press, 1999).

11. Robert Niebuhr, "Death of the Yugoslav People's Army and the Wars of Succession," *Polemos* 7, nos. 1–2 (December 2004): 91–106.

12. Chuck Sudetic, "Cease-Fire Stills Gunfire in Croatia," *New York Times*, 4 January 1992.

13. For an excellent (and concise) work on the Bosnian army, see Marko Attila Hoare, *How Bosnia Armed* (London: Saqi, 2004).

14. James Gow, *The Serbian Project and Its Adversaries: A Strategy of War Crimes* (London: C. Hurst, 2002).

15. Robert J. Donia, *Sarajevo: A Biography* (Ann Arbor: University of Michigan Press, 2006), 334.

16. The agreement's official name is the General Framework Agreement for Peace (GFAP).

SECTION 1. Officialdom

1. James J. Sadkovich, *The U.S. Media and Yugoslavia, 1991–1995* (Westport, Conn.: Praeger, 1998), 112.

2. Mark Danner and David Gelber, "While America Watched: The Bosnia Tragedy," *Peter Jennings Reporting*, ABC, 30 March 1994 (transcript available at http://www.markdanner.com/articles/print/70).

3. Ibid.

4. Ibid.

5. UN General Assembly, *Report of the Secretary-General Pursuant to General Assembly Resolution 53/35: The Fall of Srebrenica*, 15 November 1999 (http://www.unhcr.org/refworld/docid/3ae6afb34.html).

6. Danner and Gelber, "While America Watched."

7. Quoted in UN General Assembly, *Report of the Secretary-General*, 18.

8. Tim Judah, *The Serbs: History, Myth and the Destruction of Yugoslavia* (New Haven: Yale University Press, 1997), 75.

9. Lewis C. Mainzer, letter to the editor, *New York Times*, April 24, 1993.

10. The full text of the memorandum can be found at the Hrvatski Informativni Centar website, http://www.hic.hr/books/greatserbia/sanu.htm.

11. Jonathan C. Randal. "Ahmici Massacre—Bosnian Turning Point," *Washington Post*, 20 June 1993.

12. Drago Štambuk, "Rocky Soil." Translated in *Perihelion* by Tom Butler (http://www.webdelsol.com/Perihelion/stambuk.htm).

13. Quoted in Russell Watson, "Ethnic Cleansing," *Newsweek*, 17 August 1992.

14. William Safire, "The U.N. Entraps Clinton," *New York Times*, 30 August 1993.

15. Christopher Ogden, *Life of the Party: The Biography of Pamela Digby Churchill Hayward Harriman* (Boston: Little, Brown, 1994), 9.

16. Ibid., 470.

17. Winston Churchill, speech to the House of Commons of the United Kingdom, 5 October 1938.

18. Roger Cohen, "2 Towns, Symbols of Serbian Killings, Snag Balkan Talks," *New York Times*, 16 November 1995.

SECTION 2. Victims or Agents?

1. Medica Zenica was set up by Monika Hauser, a German gynecologist.

2. A summary (in English) of the history of Medica Zenica can be found at http://www.medicamondiale.org/en/ueber-uns/geschichte/.

3. Alexandra Stiglmayer, ed., *Mass Rape: The War Against Women in Bosnia-Herzegovina* (Lincoln: University of Nebraska Press, 1994).

4. Roy Gutman, Foreword, in ibid., ix–xiii.

5. "Medica: Surviving the Violence," Medica Zenica and Medica Mondiale *Bulletin*, January 1996.

6. James J. Sadkovich, *The U.S. Media and Yugoslavia, 1991–1995* (Westport, Conn.: Praeger, 1998), 94.

7. Speech by Medica Zenica, founder Monika Hauser, in Bonn on 4 September 1995.

8. "Rape in Bosnia," Balkan Repository Project, 17 February 1993.

9. Quoted in Roy Gutman, "Rape Camps: Evidence Serb Leaders in Bosnia OKd Attacks," *Newsday*, 19 April 1993.

10. Human Rights Watch, "Human Rights Watch Global Report on Women's Human Rights," 1 August 1995 (http://www.hrw.org/en/reports/1995/08/01/human-rights-watch-global-report-womens-human-rights).

11. There is general agreement in the policy world that "rape and other gender-based crimes [were] . . . key catalysts for the establishment of the [International Criminal Tribunal for the Former Yugoslavia]." The documentation of the strategic use of rape "spurred widespread public outrage against the ineffectiveness of international responses. . . . Under intense public pressure to respond to the atrocities, the [UN] Security Council issued Resolution 808, expressing 'grave concern' over the 'treatment of Muslim women in the former Yugoslavia,' and declared that 'an international tribunal shall be established for the prosecution of persons responsible for serious violations of international humanitarian law committed in the territory of the former Yugoslavia since 1991'" (July Mertus with Olja Hocevar van Wely, *Women's Participation in the International Criminal Tribunal for the Former Yugoslavia (ICTY): Transitional Justice for Bosnia and Herzegovina*, Women Waging Peace Policy Commission (Washington: Hunts Alternatives Fund, 2004), 7.

12. For a complete study of the experiences of ICTY witnesses, see Eric Stover, *The Witnesses: War Crimes and the Promise of Justice in the Hague* (Philadelphia: University of Pennsylvania Press, 2005).

13. Zlatko Dizdarević, "Under the Gun in Sarajevo," *Time*, 21 February 1994, 32–33.

14. The agreement was eventually rejected by the Bosnian Serbs. See Chuck Sudetic, "Bosnians Urge Tougher Response to Serb Rejection of Accord," *New York Times*, 1 August 1994, and "Bosnian Serbs Reject Peace Plan for 3d Time, Defying Russia," *New York Times*, 2 August 1994.

15. Laura Silber and John Murray Brown, "Geneva Talks on New Map of

Bosnia," *Financial Times*, 4 July 1994; and William Drozdiak, "Big Powers Give Final Endorsement to Partition Plan for Bosnia," *Washington Post*, 6 July 1994.

SECTION 3. Deadly Stereotypes

1. Miloš Vasić. "Comment: Quiet Voices from the Balkans," *New Yorker*, 15 March 1993, 4.

2. Zlatko Dizdarević, "Under the Gun in Sarajevo," *Time*, 21 February 1994, 33, 34.

3. Elizabeth Neuffer, *The Key to My Neighbor's House: Seeking Justice in Bosnia and Rwanda* (New York: Picador, 2001), 5.

4. James J. Sadkovich, *The U.S. Media and Yugoslavia, 1991–1995* (Westport, Conn.: Praeger, 1998), 112.

5. Samuel P. Huntington, "The Clash of Civilizations?," *Foreign Affairs* 72, no. 3 (1993): 22.

6. Samuel P. Huntington, *The Clash of Civilizations and the Remaking of World Order* (New York: Touchstone, 1997).

7. Louis Sell, *Slobodan Milošević and the Destruction of Yugoslavia* (Durham: Duke University Press, 2002), 237.

8. Quoted in Peter Lippman, "Two Towns Divided: Goražde, Kopaci," *On the Record: Bosnia*, issue 17, 6 July 2000 (http://www.advocacynet.org/resource/1057).

9. *On the Record: Bosnia*, "Division and Destruction on the Drina." The Advocacy Project, 6 July 2000 (http://www.advocacynet.org/resource/1057).

10. Vaughn S. Forrest and Yossef Bodansky, "The Truth about Goražde," Task Force on Terrorism and Unconventional Warfare, House Republican Research Committee, US House of Representatives, 4 May 1994.

11. Jovan Divjak has since published a book in French. See Jovan Divjak, *Sarajevo, Mon Amour*, interviews with Florence La Bruyère (Paris: Buchet-Chastel, 2004).

12. Quoted in Noel Malcolm, *Bosnia: A Short History* (New York: New York University Press, 1994), 220.

13. Alija Izetbegović, *Islam between East and West* (Indianapolis, Ind.: American Trust, 1984).

14. For background on arms supplies to the Bosnian government, see Cees Wiebes, *Intelligence and the War in Bosnia* (New Brunswick, N.J.: Transaction Publishers, 2003), especially chapter 4.

15. See Kurt Schork, "NATO Finds 'Terrorist' Camp near Sarajevo," *Independent* (London), 17 February 1996; and John Promfret, "Bosnian Head of 'Terrorist' Camp Calls U.S. Concerns 'Very Silly,'" *Washington Post*, 15 March 1996.

16. "Gun Running," *Online NewsHour*, 24 April 1996 (http://www.pbs.org/newshour/bb/bosnia/iran_4–24.html).

1. Drago Hedl, "Milošević's Hotline," Institute for War and Peace Reporting, 20 March 2000 (http://iwpr.net/report-news/milosevics-hotline).

2. Laura Blumenfeld, "A Sense of Resignation: The Bosnia Dissenters, Three Young Men Cut Short Their Careers on Principle," *Washington Post*, 28 August 1993. The first major resignation was that of George Kenney in August 1992; he was followed by the three young analysts, including Jon Western, the following year.

3. See, for example, Patrick Cockburn, "Dole Will Push for End of US Arms Embargo," *Independent* (London), 17 December 1994.

4. For a pictorial look at the conditions in Goražde in 1992, see Joe Sacco and Christopher Hitchens, *Safe Area Goražde: The War in Eastern Bosnia 1992–1995* (Seattle: Fantagraphics, 2002).

5. For a stunning portrayal of the physical and psychological exigencies of life in Srebrenica, see Sheri Fink, *War Hospital: A True Story of Surgery and Survival* (New York: Public Affairs, 2003).

SECTION 5. The End Approaches

1. At that December meeting, CSCE was renamed the Organization on Security and Cooperation in Europe, or OSCE.

2. "While Bosnia Burns," *Christian Science Monitor*, 7 December 1994.

3. Budapest Document 1994, "Towards a Genuine Partnership in a New Era," Organization for Security and Co-operation in Europe, 5–6 December 1994, 2–3 (http://www.osce.org/documents/mcs/1994/12/4050_en.pdf).

4. "The Fog of Post–Cold War Peace," *Chicago Tribune*, 6 December 1994.

5. Quoted in Andrew N. Guthrie, "Russia and NATO's Future at the European Security Conference," *Voice of America*, 7 December 1994.

6. Kirsten Young, "UNHCR and ICRC in the Former Yugoslavia: Bosnia-Herzegovina." *International Review of the Red Cross* 83, no. 843 (September 2001): 781. There were other ways that Bosnians kept in touch with their loved ones during the war, such as the tireless shortwave radio operators. See Peter Maass, "Unlikely Ham Hero Wins the Battle of the Air Waves," *Guardian* (Manchester), 9 March 1993.

7. According to the *Sarajevo Survival Guide*: "It doesn't matter that the pipe emerges from the disaster left after the big Olympic hall has burned to ground. There is a pipe, and there is water, and there are big lines with people who do not worry anymore whether the water is clean, or not" (Sarajevo: FAMA International, 1992–93, 13). As this satirical guidebook to besieged Sarajevo explains, water access became a life-threatening problem. Bullet holes would sometimes provide surprise access to water pipes. In any case, "the best thing that can happen is a discovery of water somewhere in the neighborhood where you live." Information about this well-known book is available on FAMA International's website (http://www.famainternational.com/timeline/guide1.htm).

8. UN General Assembly, *Report of the Secretary General Pursuant to General Assembly Resolution 53/35: The Fall of Srebrenica*, 15 November 1999, 6.

9. Jan Willem Honig and Norbert Both, *Srebrenica: Record of a War Crime* (New York: Penguin, 1997), 79.

10. Ibid., 86.

11. Quoted in David Rohde, *Endgame* (New York: Farrar, Straus, and Giroux, 1997), 46.

12. Honig and Both, *Srebrenica*, 105–7.

13. Ibid., 118–27.

14. Prime Minister Lubbers, private conversation with the author, March 2001.

15. Noel Malcolm, *Bosnia: A Short History* (New York: New York University Press, 1994), 264.

16. Quote in Diego Arria, "Setting the Stage for Genocide," SENSE Tribunal, The Hague, 12 May 2005.

17. Honig and Both, *Srebrenica*, 128–33.

18. Bianca Jagger, "The Betrayal of Srebrenica," *European*, 25 September–1 October 1995.

19. Ibid.

20. Quoted in David Rohde, *Endgame: The Betrayal and Fall of Srebrenica, Europe's Worst Massacre Since World War II* (New York: Farrar, Straus and Giroux, 1997). 420.

21. Marlise Simons, "Bosnia Massacre Mars Do-Right Self-Image the Dutch Hold Dear," *New York Times*, 13 September 1998.

22. Quoted in Bianca Jagger, "The Betrayal of Srebrenica," *European*, 25 September–1 October 1995.

23. Quoted in ibid.

24. Debriefing report of Brigadier General van der Wind delivered to the Dutch government, quoted in "The Betrayal of Srebrenica: Why Did the Massacre Happen? Will It Happen Again?," hearing before the Subcommittee on International Operations and Human Rights, Committee on International Relations, United States House of Representatives, 105th Congress, 31 March 1998, 54.

25. Quoted in Jagger, "The Betrayal of Srebrenica."

26. Honig and Both, *Srebrenica*, 35.

27. David Rhode, "Evidence Indicates Bosnia Massacre," *Christian Science Monitor*, 18 August 1995.

28. Ibid.

29. Thomas Lippman, "Senior Policy Advisers Regroup on U.S. Peace Effort in Balkans," *Washington Post*, 22 August 1995.

30. Christiane Amanpour reporting for CNN News, 4 September 1995 (http://articles.cnn.com/1995-09-04/world/Bosnia_updates_august95_8-19_1_joseph-kruzel-sarajevo-peace-plan?_s=PM:WORLD).

31. UN Department of Public Information, "Former Yugoslavia–UNPROFOR: United Nations Protection Force—Profile," New York, 31 August 1996 (http://www.un.org/Depts/DPKO/Missions/unprof_p.htm).

32. Major John R. Snider, USMC, "War in Bosnia: The Evolution of the United Nations and Air Power in Peace Operations," 1997 (http://www.globalsecurity.org/military/library/report/1997/Snider.htm).

33. Quoted in Major John R. Snider, *War In Bosnia: The Evolution of the United Nations and Air Power in Peace Operations*, CSC 1997 (www.globalsecurity.org/military/library/report/1997/Snider.htm).

34. A version of this story appears in Svetlana Broz, *Good People in an Evil Time* (New York: Other Press), 399–402.

35. Richard C. Holbrooke, *To End a War* (New York: Modern Library, 1999), 232.

36. Ibid.

37. The full text of the Dayton Peace Agreement is formally known as the General Framework Agreement for Peace in Bosnia and Herzegovina can be found on the Office of the High Representative website (http://www.ohr.int/dpa/default.asp?content_id=380).

SECTION 6. After Dayton

1. Quoted in Ron Jensen, "In Sarajevo the Muses Were Not Silent: Despite Deprivations during War, Sarajevans Continue Enjoying Art," *Stars and Stripes*, 24 June 2001, 9.

2. A report by the CIA, published in March 1995, before the Srebrenica genocide, reported this. See Roger Cohen, "C.I.A. Report on Bosnia Blames Serbs for 90 Percent of the War Crimes," *New York Times*, 9 March 1995.

3. UN High Commissioner for Refugees (UNHCR) in Austria, "A Long Tradition of Assisting Refugees" (http://www.unis.unvienna.org/documents/unis/25vic/25years_vic_unhcr.pdf).

4. Reproduced in Österreichs Außenpolitik Dokumentation, N4–5, December 1993, 7.

5. "Backgrounder," IFOR Coalition Press Information Center, December 1995.

6. Quoted in the original International Criminal Tribunal for the Former Yugoslavia indictment of Radovan Karadžić and Ratko Mladić (http://www.icty.org/case/karadzic/4).

SECTION 7. Imperfect Justice

1. "Bosnia Extradites 2 to Tribunal," *New York Times*, 14 June 1996.

2. US State Department cable, 5 November 1996.

3. Tracy Wilkinson, "Wife Adds to Rumors About Bosnian War-Crimes Suspect," *Los Angeles Times*, 12 April 1998.

4. Jim Hoagland, "The Danger of Dayton," *Washington Post*, 24 March 1996. The article describes the US inability to put together the two hundred police trainers we had promised to send to Bosnia. It was a particularly discouraging example, since I'd witnessed Louis Freeh, head of the FBI, being rebuffed in his offer to supply the trainers, because the State Department official in charge was guarding his turf.

5. John White, former assistant secretary of defense, private conversation with the author at the Kennedy School of Government, Harvard University, Cambridge, Massachusetts, June 1998.

6. Philip Shenon, "From the U.S., Mixed Signals on Bosnia War Crime Issue," *New York Times*, 4 June 1996.

7. Tom Philpott, "Enforcing Peace in Bosnia," *Retired Officer's Magazine*, September 1996, 63.

8. In 1996, IFOR was replaced by the Stabilisation Force in Bosnia and Herzegovina (SFOR), which worked closely with the UN International Police Task Force (IPTF) to promote local law and order. The IPTF was purely advisory.

9. See Chris Hedges, "Karadžić and Hussein, Survivors; Bosnia and Iraq: The West Repeats Itself," *New York Times*, 3 March 1996. See also Christine Spolar, "NATO Troops Spotted Karadžić This Week; Capture Too Risky, Spokesmen Say," *Washington Post*, 29 February 1996.

10. Led by Representative Benjamin Gilman.

11. Steven Komarow, "NATO Raid Nets Bosnia Suspects," *USA Today*, 11 July 1997.

12. Elizabeth Neuffer, *The Key to My Neighbor's House: Seeking Justice in Bosnia and Rwanda* (New York: Picador, 2001), 165.

13. Ultimately, Simić turned himself in; he was transferred to the ICTY on 12 March 2001. Though he pled not guilty, at the end of a trial lasting more than two years, he was convicted of crimes against humanity (persecutions and expulsions) and serious violations of the Geneva Conventions of 1949. Without the involvement of the international troops sent to provide peace and security to Bosnia, the highest-ranking civilian official of Bosanski Šamac was sentenced to seventeen years in prison.

14. Quoted in Jerrold M. Post, *Leaders and Their Followers in a Dangerous World: The Psychology of Political Behavior* (Ithaca: Cornell University Press, 2004), 173.

15. Kurt W. Bassuener, "A Weekly Review of Current Events," *Balkan Watch*, 21 January 1998.

16. Mark Danner, "The Marketplace Massacre and Radovan Karadzic," *Frontline*, 5 February 1998

17. Karadžić would elude capture and justice for thirteen years. It wasn't until July 2008 that Serb forces—hoping, perhaps, to gain favor with the European Union for eventual membership—stepped up to their international obligations and arrested the president-turned-fugitive.

18. For his views on US policy, see Charles G. Boyd, "U.S. Stumbles in Balkans: Nation's Actions Contradict Its Policies," *Plain Dealer*, 10 August 1995.

19. "Memorandum of Bosnian Organisations to the Western Community on the Occasion of the Balkans Conference at Sarajevo on 29/30 July 1999" (http://www.peacelink.nu/Bosnia/Bosnia_memo.html).

20. Quoted in Philip Shenon, "G.I.'s in Bosnia Shun Hunt for War-Crimes Suspects," *New York Times*, 2 March 1996.

21. Quoted in the original International Criminal Tribunal for the Former Yugoslavia indictment of Radovan Karadžić and Ratko Mladić (http://www.icty.org/case/karadzic/4).

22. Quoted in "Biljana Plavsic: Serbian Iron Lady," *BBC News*, 27 February 2003.

23. Quoted in Slobodan Inic, "Biljana Plavšić: Geneticist in the Service of

a Great Crime," *Helsinki Charter*, November 1996 (http://www.bosnia.org.uk/bosrep/report_format.cfm?articleID=1856&reportid=118).

24. Quoted in ibid.

25. Quoted in Selma Lomigora, "On Biljana Plavsic's Early Release," *International Security Forum*, 25 November 2009.

26. Christiane Amanpour, "Paramilitaries," in *Crimes of War: What the Public Should Know*, ed. Roy Gutman and David Rieff (New York: Norton, 1999), 312–15.

27. Quoted in Inic, "Biljana Plavšić."

28. In 2000, Plavšić *was* indicted and became the only one of the evil trio to turn herself in. At seventy-two, she was sentenced to eleven years in prison.

SECTION 8. International Inadequacies

1. For background on the seizure, see Chris Hedges, "NATO Troops in Bosnia Silence Karadžić's Television Station," *New York Times*, 2 October 1997; Elizabeth Neuffer, *The Key to My Neighbor's House: Seeking Justice in Bosnia and Rwanda* (New York: Macmillan, 2002), 352.

2. "Interview: Jacques Klein," *Frontline*, no date (http://www.pbs.org/wgbh/pages/frontline/shows/karadzic/interviews/klein.html).

3. "Application of the Law on Missing Persons of Bosnia and Herzegovina: Guide for Families of Missing Persons," Ministry for Human Rights and Refugees, Bosnia and Herzegovina, Sarajevo, 2006 (http://www.ic-mp.org/wp-content/uploads/2007/11/vodic_web_en.pdf).

4. Cherif Bassiouni, testimony at "Genocide in Bosnia-Herzegovina," a hearing before the US Congressional Commission on Security and Cooperation in Europe, Washington, 4 April 1995.

5. Quoted in "Missing Persons Institute for Sarajevo," *BBC News*, 28 August 2000 (http://news.bbc.co.uk/2/hi/europe/900055.stm).

6. Eventually, the commission would identify nearly sixteen thousand Bosnian victims, and its Tuzla facility would become the most prolific identification facility in the world. See the ICMP website (http://www.ic-mp.org/about-icmp/).

7. Manfred Nowak, "Final Statement by Manfred Nowak, Expert, Fifty-Third Session of the Commission on Human Rights," UN Special Process on Missing Persons in the former Yugoslavia, 26 March 1997. Reproduced in Michael O'Flaherty, "Post-War Protection of Human Rights in Bosnia and Herzegovina," in *International Studies in Human Rights*, vol. 53 (Cambridge, Mass: Kluwer Law International, 1998), 318.

8. Eight years after the fighting ended, the suicide rate for the population as a whole was double its prewar level ("Suicide Rate Doubles in Post-War Bosnia," *ABC News*, 6 May 2003).

9. Quoted in Tanja Subotic, "Suicide Rate Doubles in Post-War Bosnia," *Agence France-Presse*, 6 May 2003 (http://www.balkanpeace.org/index.php?index=article&articleid=11787).

10. Quoted in ibid.

SECTION 9. Women's Initiative

1. Valerie Gillen, Debbie Cavin, and Terry Laggner-Brown were spectacularly helpful colleagues.

2. UN High Commissioner for Refugees, UNHCR *Policy on Refugee Women*, 20 August 1990, 8–9 (http://www.unhcr.org/refworld/docid/3bf1338f4.html).

3. In dizzying juxtaposition, the UN High Commissioner for Refugees, Sadako Ogata, was so pleased with the Bosnian Women's Initiative that the model was replicated in Kosovo, Rwanda, Burundi, and East Timor. Ogata bemoaned to me the fact that the budget was too small to permit further expansion.

4. A month later, I would meet with an expanded group of sixty women; some had boarded buses at 4:00 a.m. to come to the capital to learn how to start a chapter in their towns.

SECTION 10. Recreating Community

1. Quoted in Steven Erlanger, "Bosnian Elections to Go Ahead in '96, Christopher Says," *New York Times*, 3 June 1996.

2. Anthony Lewis, "Abroad at Home; Bosnia Betrayed Again," *New York Times*, 3 June 1996.

3. Quoted in Erlanger, "Bosnian Elections to Go Ahead in '96."

4. Quoted in Adam Nagourney, "Dole, at Site of Bosnia Accords, Says They Have Failed," *New York Times*, 6 September 1996.

5. Henry Kissinger, "America in the Eye of a Hurricane," *Washington Post*, 8 September 1996.

6. International Helsinki Federation for Human Rights, 14 May 1997.

7. International Crisis Group (ICG), *Is Dayton Failing?: Bosnia Four Years After the Peace Agreement*, 28 October 1999 (http://www.unhcr.org/refworld/docid/3ae6a6ea4.html).

8. Kemal Kurspahic, "Trees for Sarajevo," *American Forests*, spring 1998.

9. Christiane Amanpour, CNN *News*, 18 October 1995.

10. Alexandra Kroeger, "Victims of Bosnia's Sex Trade," BBC *News*, 22 March 2002 (http://news.bbc.co.uk/1/hi/world/europe/1807189.stm).

11. Quoted in Chris Hedges, "At Last, a Unifying Force in Bosnia: Making Money," *New York Times*, 17 October 1996.

12. Mitja Velikonja, "In Hoc Signo Vinces: Religious Symbolism in the Balkan Wars 1991–1995," conference paper presented at Nationality and Citizenship in Post-Communist Europe, Paris, 9–10 July 2001, 8 (http://www.georgefox.edu/academics/undergrad/departments/soc-swk/ree/Velikonja_In%20Hoc%20Signo%20Vinces_Oct%202001.pdf).

13. Quoted in Noreen Herzfeld, "Lessons from Srebrenica: The Dangers of Religious Nationalism," *Journal of Religion and Society*, supplement 2 (2007) (http://moses.creighton.edu/JRS/2007/2007-8.html).

14. Josip Stilinovic, "A Visit to a Vanishing Diocese," *Catholic World News*, 17 July 1996.

15. The Grand Mufti of Bosnia.

16. Michael Sells, *The Bridge Betrayed: Religion and Genocide in Bosnia* (Berkeley: University of California Press, 1998), 82.

17. Warren Christopher, "Remarks at One-year Anniversary of Formation of the Federation, and the Founding of the 'Friends of the Federation,'" Washington, 16 March 1995, State Department transcript.

18. Present-day value.

19. OEM interview with Hans Koschnick, January 1995.

20. Anthony Lewis, "Fixing Division of Mostar Critical to Bosnian Peace," *Sun Sentinel*, 18 February 1997.

21. Translated by Amila Čelebić, *Spirit of Bosnia*, 1, no. 4 (October 2006).

22. Brian Knowlton, "France Backs a US Call to Keep NATO in Bosnia," *International Herald Tribune*, 25 September 1997.

23. Elizabeth Neuffer, "Decision Time for NATO in Bosnia: Future of Peacekeeping Mission Tests Alliance's Resolve," *Boston Globe*, 3 December 1997.

24. Ibid.

25. Hillary Clinton had refined to a fine art group meetings with women all over the world. A few months earlier she had keynoted the first in a series of regional meetings called "Vital Voices: Women in Democracy," which we had launched in Vienna.

26. "Clinton Appeals for Harmony in Bosnia," BBC News, 22 December 1997 (http://news.bbc.co.uk/2/hi/41718.stm).

BRIDGING

1. Joseph S. Nye, "Propaganda Isn't the Way: Soft Power," *International Herald Tribune*, 10 January 2003 (http://belfercenter.ksg.harvard.edu/publication/1240/propaganda_isnt_the_way.html).

2. Jacob Weisberg, "Party of Defeat: AEI's Weird Celebration," *Slate*, 14 March 2007 (http://www.slate.com/id/2161800).

3. Samuel P. Huntington, *The Soldier and the State: The Theory and Politics of Civil-Military Relations* (Cambridge: Harvard University Press, 1981), vii.

4. Gilles Kepel, *Bad Moon Rising: A Chronicle of the Middle East Today*, trans. Pascale Ghazaleh (London: Saqi, 2003), 133.

5. Ibid., 74.

6. See for example a University of Pennsylvania announcement from 2009 (http://www.sas.upenn.edu/anthro/node/142799).

7. Michael R. Gordon and Jeff Zeleny, "Obama Would Engage Iran if Elected, He Says," *New York Times*, 1 November 2007.

8. Press Release, "Bernard Lewis to Receive AEI's Irving Kristol Award for 2007," American Enterprise Institute for Public Policy Research, 2007 (http://www.aei.org/press/25632).

9. Bernard Lewis, "The 2007 Irving Kristol Lecture," 7 March 2007 (http://www.aei.org/speech/25815).

10. Roger Cohen, *Hearts Gone Brutal* (New York: Random House, 1998), 188.

11. Adi Schwartz, "UN Commissioner for Winning Hearts," *Haaretz*, 1 June 2008 (http://www.haaretz.com/hasen/spages/988827.html).

12. Quoted in ibid.

13. David O. Sears, Leonie Huddy, and Robert Jervis, eds., *Oxford Handbook of Political Psychology* (Oxford: Oxford University Press, 2003).

14. John Duckitt, "Prejudice and Intergroup Hostility," in *The Oxford Handbook of Political Psychology*, ed. David O. Sears, Leonie Huddy, and Robert Jervis (Oxford: Oxford University Press, 2003), 559–600.

15. "IIE Awards Prize to Members of Parents Circle Family Forum," Institute of International Education, 20 June 2008 (http://www.theparentscircle.com/ActivitiesMain.asp?id=147&sivug_id=3).

16. Robert D. Kaplan, *Balkan Ghosts: A Journey Through History* (New York: Macmillan, 1994), li.

17. Quoted in Laura Rozen, "Robert Kaplan," *Salon*, 17 April 2001 (http://archive.salon.com/people/bc/2001/04/17/kaplan/print.html).

18. Noel Malcolm, *Bosnia: A Short History* (New York: New York University Press, 1994), xix.

19. Quoted in Alastair Leithead, "An Italian Oasis in Afghanistan," *BBC News*, 26 May 2008 (http://news.bbc.co.uk/2/hi/south_asia/7419925.stm).

20. Swanee Hunt and Cristina Posa, "Women Waging Peace: Inclusive Security," *Foreign Policy*, May–June 2001 (http://www.swaneehunt.com/articles/FP_InclusiveSecurity.pdf).

21. Amnesty International, "Guatemala: 'Disappearances'; Briefing to the UN Committee against Torture," 30 November 2000 (http://www.amnesty.org/en/library/info/AMR34/044/2000/en).

22. Julie Mertus with Olja Hocevar van Wely, "Women's Participation in the International Criminal Tribunal for the Former Yugoslavia (ICTY): Transitional Justice for Bosnia and Herzegovina," July 2004 (available at http://www.huntalternatives.org).

23. Quoted in "Bosnian Cardinal Saw Yugoslavian Split, Worked for Reconciliation," *Catholic News Service*, 1 April 2005 (http://www.catholicnews.com/jpii/cardinals/0501849.htm).

24. Marty Branagan, "The Toppling of Slobodan Milošević," *Neucleus*, no. 6 (2004): 12–13.

25. Kari Hoglund, "Finland's Contributions to Peacekeeping," Ministry for Foreign Affairs of Finland, 4 November 1998 (http://virtual.finland.fi/finfo/english/peace.html).

26. "Ten Arrested over Politkovskaya Murder," *Spiegel International*, 27 August 2007 (http://www.spiegel.de/international/world/0,1518,502286,00.html).

27. Quoted in "Russia: Courageous Journalist Mourned," Human Rights Watch press release, 9 October 2006.

28. Jorn Madslien, "Russia's Economic Might: Spooky or Soothing?" *BBC News*, 4 July 2007 (http://news.bbc.co.uk/2/hi/business/6265068.stm).

29. See Sanam Naraghi Anderlini, Camille Pampell Conaway and Lisa Kays, "Transitional Justice and Reconciliation," *Inclusive Security, Sustainable Peace: A Toolkit for Advocacy and Action: Justice, Governance, and Civil Society* (Washington: Hunt Alternatives Fund and International Alert, 2004) (http://www.huntalternatives.org/download/49_transitional_justice.pdf). The International Criminal Tribunal for the Former Yugoslavia (ICTY) and the International Criminal Tribunal for Rwanda (ICTR) were the first courts employing Chapter VII of the UN Charter since the aftermath of World War II.

30. Of course, some nations may serve a purpose by refusing to take sides. Switzerland's neutrality, for whatever economic and tactical reasons, provides a home for the Red Cross, which depends on a dogged refusal to place blame in order to maintain credibility.

31. Stephen D. Wrage, "Genocide in Rwanda: Draft Case Study for Teaching Ethics and International Affairs" (paper presented at the annual meeting of the International Studies Association, Los Angeles, 14–18 March 2000).

32. *Report of the Secretary-General on the Situation in Rwanda*, Doc. S/1994/640, 31 May 1994, para. 43 (http://daccess-dds-ny.un.org/doc/UNDOC/GEN/N94/234/12/IMG/N9423412.pdf?OpenElement).

33. Quoted in Douglas Jehl, "Officials Told to Avoid Calling Rwanda Killings 'Genocide,'" *New York Times*, 10 June 1994.

34. Quoted in Samantha Power, "Bystanders to Genocide," *Atlantic*, September 2001.

35. The Convention on the Prevention and Punishment of the Crime of Genocide obligates parties that signed the document to prevent and punish the crime of genocide. The full convention can be found at http://www.un.org/millennium/law/iv-1.htm.

36. Richard Holbrooke, *To End a War* (New York: Random House, 1999), 233.

37. Misha Glenny, *The Fall of Yugoslavia: The Third Balkan War* (London: Penguin, 1992).

38. Richard Holbrooke, "Lessons from Dayton for Iraq," *Washington Post*, 23 April 2008.

39. *Report of the International Commission to Inquire into the Causes and Conduct of the Balkan Wars*, Carnegie Endowment for International Peace, 1914, 1.

40. For a thorough discussion of the highly variable US public opinion polls on intervention in Bosnia, see Steven Kull and Clay Ramsay, "US Public Opinion on Intervention in Bosnia," in *International Public Opinion and the Bosnia Crisis*, ed. Erik Shiraev and Richard Sobel, 69–106 (Lanham, Md.: Lexington, 2003).

41. Jabari Asim, "African American Lessons in Giving," *Washington Post*, 3 July 2006.

Index

of, 10–12, 30–31, 63–65, 232;
arms embargo and, 50–52, 54;
Bosniak-Croat Federation and,
63, 192; Bosnian visit by, 193–98;
Bosnian Women's Initiative and,
160–64, 167–68; at CSCE conference, 73–75; Dayton Peace
Agreement and, 93–94, 224–25;
death of US diplomats in Sarajevo, 85–86; diplomacy initiatives of, 34, 36, 204, 232; International Commission on Missing
Persons and, 151; Operation
Deliberate Force and, 89–90;
Rwanda genocide and, 228; Srebenica massacre and, 78, 80; war
crimes investigations and, 120;
Yeltsin and, 68–70, 75
Clinton, Hillary Rodham, 195–96,
198, 249n25
Cohen, Roger, 17, 205
Colombia, drug violence in, 216, 221
Conference for Security and Cooperation in Europe (CSCE),
73–75
Contact Group, 35–36, 89
Croatia: Bosniak-Croat Federation
plan and, 56–59; Bosnian con-
flict and, xxv–xxx, 14, 55–56;
ethnic cleansing in, 8; war crimes
investigations in, 117
"Crossing Borders" tour, 155

Dallaire, Roméo, 227–28
Darfur crisis, 232
Dawkins, Steve, 118
Dayton Peace Agreement, xxvii,
xxx, 92–94; Bosniak-Croat Federation and, 191–92; implementation delays of, 194; legacy of,
229–30; limits of neutrality and,
224–25; military provisions in,
147, 149, 229–32; missing persons
initiatives of, 151–52; postwar
political restructuring and, 137–
38, 176–78, 183–85, 214; refugee
policies under, 170; war crimes

investigations and, 117–18, 120,
245n4
Deutsch, John, 224
Divjak, Jovan, 43–45, 58–59,
242n11
Diždarević, Raif, 12–16
Diždarević, Zlatko, 38
Dobrinja, attacks on, xxxiv, 3–5,
101–2
Dole, Bob, 65, 150, 177, 195, 197
domestic policy, foreign policy
integration with, 216–22
Đozić, Nurdžihana, 3–4, 157–58
Drew, Nelson, 86, 90
Durkee, Michael, 171

Eagleburger, Lawrence, 6, 11–12, 64
economic conditions, history of
Yugoslavia and, xxiv–xxv
Edgar, Carol, 155
education, Bosnian conflict and
interruption of, 59–63
Eizenstat, Stuart, 68
elections in Bosnia, 176–77
ethnic cleansing: Bosniak-Croat
Federation and threat of, 63–65;
in Croatia, 89; historical background of, 6–10; humanitarian
relief and facilitation of, 18–19;
missing persons initiatives in
wake of, 151–52; in Serbia, 137–
41; sexual assault as tool of,
25–28; transnational responsibility concerning, 229–33
ethnic identity, history in Bosnia
of, xxiii–xxx
EUCOM (United States European
Command), 48
European Action Council for Peace
in the Balkans, 120, 122
European Civilian Peace Corps, 218
European Community, 2
European Court of Human Rights,
219
European Union (EU), 14; Bosnia
and, xxx, 210; Bosniak-Croat Federation and, 192

Puljić, Cardinal Vinko, xxii, 189–90, 214
Putin, Vladimir, 219–20

Radio Hajat, 113
Rakovic, Nada, 207
Ražnatović, Željko (Arkan), 137
rape camps, 24–28, 241n11
Rather, Dan, 45
Rawson, David, 228
Redman, Chuck, 64
Rehn, Elizabeth, 152
religion, historic role in Bosnia of, xxi–xxx, 185–90, 201
Renna, Mario, 211
Republika Srpska, xxx, 58, 94, 112–16; Dayton Peace Agreement provision for, 136–41, 229; postwar rebuilding of, 142–44, 183–85; postwar suicide rates in, 154; refugee crisis in, 108; religious divisions in, 189–90
Requiem (Mozart), 173
Retired Officer Magazine, 120
Rice, Condoleezza, 200
Rohan, Albert, 22
Rohde, David, 84
Rose, Michael, 204–5
Rove, Karl, 202
Rubin, Robert, 162
Russia: African National Conference and, 223–25; Chechen conflict and, 219–20; support of Serbia by, xxx; US Bosnian policy and, xiv–xviii, 68–70, 90
Rwanda, genocide in, xvii, 224, 227–28, 232

Saćirbey, Muhamed ("Mo"), 142–43, 220–21
Safire, William, 11
Sampaio, Jorge, 205–6
Šantić, Aleksa, 192–93
Sarajevo: atrocities in, 23; bombings of, 23; devastation in, xxix, xxvii, 2–4; history of, xxi–xxiii; Islamic cultural center in, 54–54,

59; media coverage of siege in, 37–38; National Library restoration in, 178–79; postwar refugee crisis in, 110–13; reconstruction of, 142–48, 173–76, 243n7; Serbian siege of, xx, xxviii–xxx, 2–4, 12–16, 19–21, 30–34, 89–91, 97–99, 102; US diplomats in, xviii, 85–86
Sarajevo Opera Orchestra, 173
Sarajevo Philharmonic, 196
Sarajevo Survival Guide, 243n7
Sarandah, Nadwa, 208
SDA (Bosniak party), 103
Sephardic Jews, history in Bosnia of, xxiii, 71
Serbia: aggression in Bosnia by, xiv–xviii, xxv–xxx, 6–12, 43–45; Bosniak-Croat Federation and, 63–65; confiscation of humanitarian relief by, 18–19; Dayton Peace Agreement and, 94, 112–13; nationalists of, 14–15; Orthodox Church in, xxii; postwar political climate in, 111–16; rape camps established by, 24–28; refugee crisis in, 99–110; Srebenica massacre and, 77–82; war crimes investigations in, 117–26
Serbian Democratic Party, 123
Serwer, Daniel, 192
Šešelj, Vojislav, 44
Seventh Muslim Brigade, 185
Shalikashvili, John, 46, 118
Sharpeville massacre, 223–25
Shelton, Hugh, 195
Silajdžić, Haris, 17–18, 93–94, 156–57, 177–78
Siler-Albring, Ursula, 22
Simić, Blagoje, 122, 246n13
Slovenia, independence from Yugoslavia, xxv–xxvi
Smajlovic, Vedran, 173
Smith, Leighton "Snuffy," Jr., 88–89, 103, 118, 122, 125
Smith, Rupert, 89

United States: ambivalence concerning Balkans in, xiv–xviii, xxvii–xxx, 11–12, 15–17, 22–23, 40–41, 51–54, 63–65, 68–70; Austria's relations with, xiv–xviii, 22–23, 34; military reluctance of, over involvement in Bosnia, 46–48, 51–54, 89, 118, 120, 124–26, 225–33

UN Protection Force (UNPROFOR), 13–14, 88–90; in Goražde, 40; rapes committed by, 26

UN Special Rapporteur on Human Rights, 152

US Agency for International Development (USAID), 112–13

USA Today, 122

US State Department: Bosniak-Croat Federation plan and, 56–59; Bosnian camps acknowledged by, 6; Bosnian Women's Initiative and, 160–64; conflict over Balkan policy in, xviii, 11–12, 46–48, 51–52, 63–65, 68–70; elections in Bosnia and, 175–76; postwar diplomatic policies of, 107; war crimes investigations and, 122–26, 129, 245n4

Vance, Cyrus, 7
Vershbow, Sandy, 161–64
Vietnam War, 206, 210
Vlasić, Miloš, 37
Vojvodina, xxiii, 239n4
von Kohl, Christine, 104–5
von Weisecker, Richard, 76

Vranitzky, Franz, xiv, 22, 69–70, 76, 104

Vreme (magazine), 37

Waldheim, Kurt, xxvii, 7
war crimes investigations: ICTY proceedings and, 129–35; postwar politics and, 117–29
Washington Agreement, xxvii
Washington Post, 86, 120
Western, Jon, 243n2
Wiesel, Elie, 222
women: Association for the Missing formed by, 151–52; in Bosnian military, 28–29; peace efforts and importance of, 212–16; political activism of, 34–35, 136–41, 157–64, 197–99, 207–9; postwar risks for, 127–29, 153–54; rape experiences of, 26–28; role in Bosnian conflict of, 64, 71–72, 201, 214–16; in Srebenica massacre, 78, 80–82
World War II, Balkan ethnic alliances during, xxix

Yeltsin, Boris, 68–70, 75, 219
Young Muslims, 47–48
Yugoslavia: collapse of, 12–15; history of, xxii–xxx
Yugoslav People's Army (JNA), xxv–xxvi, 43–44

Zhirinovsky, Vladimir, 68
Zilk, Helmut, 52
Zimmerman, Warren, 6, 14
Zmaj od Bosne (newspaper), 113

SWANEE HUNT is the founder and chair of Women Waging Peace, a global policy-oriented initiative working to integrate women into peace processes. During her tenure as US ambassador to Austria (1993–97), she hosted negotiations and several international symposia to focus efforts on securing the peace in the neighboring Balkan states. She is a member of the US Council on Foreign Relations, director of the Women and Public Policy Program at the John F. Kennedy School of Government at Harvard University, and president of the Hunt Alternatives Fund. She has written hundreds of articles for American and international newspapers and professional journals, including *Foreign Affairs*, *Foreign Policy*, the *International Herald Tribune*, the *Chicago Tribune*, the *Boston Globe*, and the *Denver Post*. She is a syndicated columnist for the Scripps Howard news service. She is also the author of *Half-Life of a Zealot* (Duke, 2006) and *This Was Not Our War: Bosnian Women Reclaiming the Peace* (Duke, 2004).

As this book was in production, Charles made his farewell tour in Bosnia, where he led the Sarajevo Philharmonic Orchestra for the twenty-fifth time. A place in the National Theater was dedicated in appreciation of his courage and fidelity. Seven months later, he succumbed to a brain tumor. He died on September 12, 2010, eleven days after conducting his last concert to an audience of nine thousand in a Boston park.

Library of Congress Cataloging-in-Publication Data

Hunt, Swanee.
p. cm.
Includes bibliographical references and index.
ISBN 978-0-8223-4975-4 (cloth : alk. paper)
1. Yugoslav War, 1991–1995—Campaigns—Bosnia and Hercegovina—
Srebrenica. 2. Srebrenica (Bosnia and Hercegovina)—History, Military.
3. International relations. 4. United States—Foreign relations—2001–2009.
I. Title.
DR1313.H868 2011
949.703—dc22
2011015532